A Lucky Chap

Orra Loon to
Lord Lieutenant

Autobiography of Sir Maitland Mackie

Illustrations by Ruth Smythe

ARDO PUBLISHING COMPANY

Published by Ardo Publishing Company, Buchan

Printed in Scotland   ISBN: 0 9518464 2 6

Contents

To both our families

My thanks are due to all the technical people who did all the typing and typesetting which went into this volume. They include Alison Mutch, Charles Allan, and Wilma Taylor. I am also grateful to my proof readers Susan Allan and Mary Levie.

Foreword

I MUST start by apologising for the conceit of writing this book but protest that it is not all my fault. Many people, notably Dr Danny Gordon and Bill Adams have badgered me for years to do it. Nothing would have been done about it had the badgerers not been joined by my nephew Charlie Allan. He said, "You'll never get round to it yourself. I'll bring my tape recorder and you'll speak into it. I'll put it on a word processor, you'll correct it and I'll get it published." So, despite my feelings that too many people write their memoirs, that has been done and here we are, less than a year later and, as I write this, I am told publication day is only two months away.

I would like to apologise to all those whose roles I may have underplayed or even missed out, for there are many of those. As we worked on the book I kept remembering more and more but as I thought it was getting to be too long we just stopped.

I have been a Lucky Chap and have enjoyed my life enormously. I hope my luck has held to the extent that this book reflects that and I also hope you will enjoy it, for that is what a life is for.

My Context

I'M LUCKY, in this my eightieth year, to have this fine
bungalow with its spacious garden on the edge of
Banchory's golf course. I've always considered myself a
lucky chap. I was born in February 1912 so, you see, I've
been lucky enough to see a great many changes. I think I
was lucky in my choice of parents. I had super parents. My
father was a great man but my mother was probably even
greater. She reared six bairns as well as, early in her
marriage, looking after the single men who came into the
house to be fed, morning, noon and night. She also
managed to do things outside and to look after my father
who would not always be the easiest man to cater for. He
would often forget to keep her informed... "Oh, I forgot to
tell you there are four folk coming to their lunch." And "I
forgot to tell you that tonight's the Literary Society meeting
and the speakers are coming here to a bite to eat before the
meeting and of course we'll invite aabody back for their tea
after the meeting." And she put up with that for sixty-seven
years.

It was rather sad towards the end of the sixty-seven
years visiting my father and mother on a Sunday afternoon,
as was our custom. They were sitting, as was their custom,
at either side of the fire when my mother, who was getting,
what we call in Aberdeenshire, 'a bittie dottled', looked
across and said "Tell me Maitland, who was it that I

married?" That was somewhat to my father's astonishment. But he managed to pass it off and all was well again.

I thought my father was a great man but so was his father, who was known as "The Father". There's a story told of him going down to Troup's the grocer in Rhynie and saying, "Mr Troup, here's a pound. Send a pound's worth of groceries up to old Mrs MacDonald. She's newly widowed and it'll make a better Christmas for her." That was done but some time later he got a letter from this lady's brother in Aberdeen telling him not to interfere with his family, that they were perfectly capable of looking after themselves without his charity and enclosing a pound. So my grandfather took the pound down to the grocer and said, "Mr Troup, Mrs MacDonald was awfu pleased with those groceries. Would you just send her the same again?"

Mr Troup said, "Oh, Mr Mackie. She's not as badly off as that."

"Oh, no, no. But it was just that she was awfu pleased and I'd just like her to get the same again."

A few days later an even angrier letter arrived enclosing another pound. Indeed 'action' was threatened if he wouldn't desist from his charity.

My grandfather walked down to the village and told Mr Troup that Mrs MacDonald had been very pleased with the groceries and would he again send fresh supplies. "Oh, I don't know if you need to do that Mr Mackie. I think Mrs MacDonald would be reasonably comfortable."

"Well you just send it. It doesn't cost me much." Indeed it cost him nothing and he got the credit... though apparently not with the brother.

My paternal grandfather had four sons with his first wife and one daughter who died soon after birth because the doctor who had attended a case of scarlet fever before coming to Mains of Elrick and had not washed his hands before attending the confinement. My grandmother died of puerperal fever and the baby died also...of scarlet fever.

The sons all became farmers. John like my father did a lot of public work but the others farmed sensibly and didn't bother with anything outside the farming. My grandfather was one of the first to buy a binder instead of the old side-delivery reaper. He was reckoned an expert because on the way home from the mart a neighbour who had just bought a binder hailed him and said, "You're the expert. You must ken aboot a binder. What's wrang wi' it?"

My grandfather looked it over and seeing nothing amiss gave it a kick and said, "There's naething wrang wi' it." The kick dislodged a little stone that had stuck in the drive chain and off it went. That enhanced the old man's reputation even further.

I didn't know my mother's father, John Yull, because he died very early. My granny, though, was quite a character. She lived on at Little Ardo for many years until she became unfit and came to live with us. We were very fond of Granny. When my father showed her the plans for the improvement of the house at North Ythsie she couldn't understand the idea of a further door from nursery to the outside and she said, "Bit nae a door and window oot intae the furth?"

Granny Yull lived with us for quite a few years at North Ythsie of Tarves and died when I was just newly gone to Methlick school. I came down one morning and looked into the big box on the dining room table. I climbed up on a chair and looked into the box and here was my granny lying dead. That was a great shock to me. And the final shock to me was seeing her lowered into the cold earth and I cried at this unseemly way of disposing of my granny. My father determined that I wouldn't be asked to go to a funeral again for some time. So when my grandfather Mackie at Huntly died soon after I wasn't taken to the funeral and my uncles thought I should have been taken like everybody else but at the time I was glad to miss out on another funeral.

All the boys had to work hard on the farm. When my father was nineteen his father's grieve left and he desperately wanted the job though very young for it and was terrified that his father would fee another grieve home to Rhynie. His father kept him in suspense until three days before the term and then said, "Well I hinna fee-ed a grieve so you'll give the orders." That experience convinced my father that being a grieve was the best education on the farm and I think he was right. All his sons got a shot at taking responsibility early.

Although my father would have worked hard when he first went to North Ythsie I never saw him with his jacket off working. By the time I was taking an interest he had taken Little Ardo of Methlick, then Westertown of Rothienorman, Thomastown of Drumblade and then Eastertown which was later worked as part of Westertown.. He was very busy expanding and when we had a great debate at Drumblade on the motion "That the farmer should take his jacket off", I took the view that he should not and that was based on my father not taking his off after his early thirties.

Mind you I saw him with his jacket off once a month when he cut our hair to save money. Just a scissors and comb... no clippers and no brose cap to leave a tuft at the front as some of the men had their's cut.

It certainly wasn't that the old man wasn't strong enough to have worked. The men on the farm used to practise throwing the hammer and the fifty sixer, and putting in the long summer evenings. One night my father took a walk past the throwers and made a disparaging remark about the throwing of Mouser Milne the grieve who was practising for Gight games. Naturally he was challenged to do better and in fact put up a mighty throw. Later the grieve appeared at the house for a shot of the tape to measure Maitland Mackie's throw. My father handed him the tape reminding him that there were three feet missing from it. Eventually the grieve arrived back full of admiration. The throw had been 105 feet, the best there had been at North Ythsie. "But," asked my father, "did you remember the missing three feet?"

"Oh aye. It measured 102 feet and we added the

missing three feet. Oh aye. We widna swick ye." Old Maitland tried in vain to make the grieve see that he should have deducted the three feet and that the throw should have measured 99 feet only. That argument went on for years.

My father seldom reproved his family though he did once when I was allowed to stay up to a dinner party. When it was time to go to bed I asked for another sweetie. I was told that I'd had enough sweeties and that I would not get one but I took one nevertheless. For some reason that really annoyed the old man and for the first and only time I got a real thrashing. I also saw him angry in the time of the great storm of 1924. We had great difficulty getting home from school and when we did our neighbour Jack Hay from Little Ythsie came in and said that we should phone and warn our parents not to try to get home from Aberdeen because he had just made it and no one else would get through that night. Knowing that the car would have been left at T C Smith's garage we phoned to tell him not to come home and as far as we were concerned that was what happened. He appeared the next morning and John and I were fighting as usual and we got a terrible row for "fighting when your mother and me were nearly killed". But, of course, we had no idea they had been nearly killed.

It was his own fault. He was a determined chap and despite the warning which he had got he had set off for home. My mother was supposed to be watching one side and he was watching his side with the door open. Something went wrong with this plan and they landed in the ditch and the car turned over on its side. Unlike my uncle Willie who also got stuck and spent the night in the car, they decided to walk. It was a terrible blizzard and they could hardly see where they were going. They stumbled over the fence and found themselves in the middle of a field and lost. They pressed on until they came to another fence and that proved to be alongside a road. My father said to my mother, "you sit down in the road and I'll give you my coat and go for help" but my mother said, "You'll no leave me here". They struggled on, my father walking backwards and using his coat to shield my mother against the blast. In that way they walked right past Denend of Udny and then stumbled against another wall. My mother said, "If this is a byre or whatever it is we're going in here." But it was the cottage at Denend and they spent the night there, only half a mile from his brother John at Coullie. They could go no further. They got a sledge the next day to take them home. Even the sledge stuck at Tolquhon and my father walked the mile home and arrived in time to give us a row for fighting.

It was very exciting for us because we had five pairs of horse at the time and four pairs and a single were taken to rescue mother. The four pairs went first and broke and trampled the snow and mother was then led home in the cart drawn by the single horse from the fifth pair. We children each got to ride on a second horse of the various pairs

That night two people were lost in the snow and it could so easily have been four.

I was once reproved by my father for not asking questions. I had apparently not understood something but had not liked to ask and he told me in no uncertain terms that if I didn't ask questions I would never learn anything and I think he was right and have been asking questions ever since.

John Sleigh of Tolquhon was not much older than us but when he was visiting I had the temerity to join in the conversation and said, "But John..." I didn't get any further but I was silenced by my father in a very stern voice saying, "Mr Sleigh to you." He was a bit old-fashioned.

I got many lessons from my father. John and I were roguing tatties on one hot day and we got a bit tired and sat down at the edge of the field, not knowing that my father would come down before he went to Aberdeen. "Look at the men working coling hay and I bet they're not as hot as you are." He was right. When we started working it was better than lying feeling lazy and feeling the heat.

My father went on to be President of the National Farmer's Union of Scotland in 1924, at forty, one of the youngest the union had ever had. Then he became chairman of the governors of the college and took a great interest for many years. He was an even tempered man but he could get angry. He was angry when we dressed up a bolster with a pair of trousers and a jacket and let this go with a mighty yell to frighten my mother who was at the kitchen window. She did get a terrible fleg and ran outside. My father said it was a terrible thing to do to our mother in her condition... but we had no idea that she was then pregnant with what turned out to be our little sister Catherine.

His last agricultural expansion was to buy Woodlands, a four hundred acre farm at Udny at the beginning of the war. There he set up a poultry unit. He was a far seeing chap and started doing line breeding to get a hybrid with all the best qualities from several breeds and strains. He'd got so far down the road that despite the very limited facilities he had, Thornbers who had somehow got to hear of this bought his stock and carried on his work towards breeding the new hybrids. It was the same with the dairy cow. He went to a British Association meeting and came back with ideas for breeding a better cow. He phoned me up and said that he wanted to use my herd at Westertown and my cows at Thomastown as part of the programme and we would swop bulls and organise the breeding. And I said, "But Dad, you'll be forty years before you get the results of that programme." He replied that if you want to make a great big hole you've to start with the first shovelful. So we made a start.

One of my father's ambitions was that he would give each of his six children a farm and eventually he did that. John got Bent in the Howe of the Mearns, I got Westertown, Eastertown and Thomastown and George got the fine farm of Ballinshoe in the Howe of Strathmore. Even the girls got a farm. Jean got Little Ardo, Mary was helped to buy a farm in England and Catherine got

Woodlands though she lived in London and he became her tenant. He paid her a very modest rent but when it was sold she got the price.

My father depended very heavily on our grieves and we had many fine grieves. The first I remember at North Ythsie was a man called Smith. I don't remember much about his work but what I do remember was that he had an illegitimate son called Dosh who in the custom of the time was brought up by the wife along with her own. However Mrs Smith didn't like Dosh and at Christmas time I was always sorry for Dosh because he got no presents. One Christmas Dosh had hung up a stocking and wakened in the morning to find his stocking filled with ashes from the fire. At that time we were so well treated that we used to hang up a pillow-case so when my mother got to hear about Dosh's stocking she gave him some presents.

A grieve of a higher calibre was Andrew Cheyne. He was one of my father's best grieves and a man who in today's circumstances, where you get an education if you are any good at all, would have been a professor or such. He could have done anything but because he left school at thirteen the best he could do was grieve. My father was by this time growing a whole shift of potatoes. To gather the potatoes we used to get a gang of young people, unemployed fishermen from Boddam one year, for example. We put bunks at the end of the potato shed and they slept the night. Andrew Cheyne said it was the only time he got to act like a gentleman, walking up and down the drills to keep them in order. He used to be invited into the house to discuss the work for the next day or two. One time in general conversation my father said, "Did you notice that man who drowned himself at Ellon. They say he did it while of unsound mind."

"Well, I dinna believe he was of unsound mind," said the grieve. "If he had been unsound he wouldna hae made such a tidy job of folding his jacket on the bank and leavin his gold watch in it. Na, na. Them that kill themselves ken what they are daein a' right. Ye dinna get them sheetin themsels wi the tattie chapper nor droonin themsel in the ash midden." On another occasion when the men had just taken delivery of their half tonne of coal my father asked how the men had liked the coal as he had just changed coal merchants. Andrew said, "Na, they're nae pleased ava."

"Oh, what's wrong."

"Well, ae half's half steens and the ither half's a' steens."

On one occasion, as we came out from having what we called our dinner (which seems to be called lunch nowadays) he seized John and said, "John, take the first horse from the third pair and ging and shim neeps." And then when I appeared he said, "Mike, tak ye the ither horse fae the third pair and gan doon tae the hay and pull coles." Then Mary appeared. "Mary, tak yer bike and tak that drill sock thats lyin at the garage door up tae the smiddy and get it sharpened." When George emerged John, who had been much amused by everybody getting a job, asked the grieve if he didn't have a job for the four year old. Without a moments hesitation the grieve replied, "Aye, George. Gang ye roon tae the gairden and scare the fleas oot amang the carrots."

One of the best stories of grieves was the one at Balquhindachy, Jock Wilson. The farmer, a Mr Bremner who was an MA of Aberdeen University which was very unusual in a farmer, was trying to be very modern. The usual manure was bird's dirt from Chile called Guano where you could smell the nitrogen, phosphates from crushed bone and the potash came from Morocco. Then all three were mixed on the floor of the sheds and then put on the fields. On this occasion Bremner had gone all modern and bought the new finely ground compounds. Jock Wilson looked at this and could smell no guano, see no bits of bone and was quite sure the mannie had bought stuff that would do no good. However it was his job to see that it was put on and all the men were yoked with the orraman filling the happer and the men, a happer each, side by side throwing the stuff out. Just before lowsin time the orraman came to Jock Wilson with the news that the manure was nearly finished and there was not enough to do the gushet. Jock without batting an eye said, "G'wa back and tell them tae wag their airms. It'll mak nae bloody difference." I used to like telling that story to SAI and the other chemical companies.

I was born into hard times and a world peopled by tough men. When the old farmers went off to play solo they very seldom took their wives with them, the wives were supposed to stay at home. So it was when a neighbour of my grandfather, Frank Duff from Old Noth, was at Drumdelgie in Cairnie playing solo and got home about five in the morning. When he didn't see any smoke from the foreman's chimney at an hour when he should have been up giving the horses their first feed he went to the door and shouted, "Fire, fire!" and immediately the foreman came to the door in his shirt tail.

"Far, far?"

"In aabody's hoose but yours, you bugger. Get up."

Frank Duff was a volunteer before the 1914 war and when the war came he duly went off. He went to my grandfather and asked if he would look after the farm and the cattle. He said, "I've asked Tom (my grandfather's youngest son) to look after the horse. He kens about horse."

"And what about the sheep?"

"Oh, the shepherd'll manage the sheep. He kens about sheep."

My grandfather thought that the queerest set of arrangements but poor Frank seemed to think he'd be back in a week or two whereas he was away for four years and lucky to get back at all.

My father had a great grieve at Little Ardo called Geordie Gill, an immensely strong man. When they were dressing potatoes outside in the pits he could load the riddle for a long time without shifting the machine. That was a great saving in time and Geordie, without spilling a single potato, could land a whole graipful on the riddle from prodigious distances.

On one occasion he thought he had fallen behind with emptying the midden of muck. When my father went over he found that all the muck was out on the fields and spread ready to plough down. "Mercy Geordie, how did you manage that?"

"Oh, well, I just got my ain loon tae tak the single horse back and fore to the field, and the horseman had to tip his cart in the field and spread it, and I loaded it aa' mysel." He had filled ninety-six loads in the one day. That meant tearing the tramped dung from the midden and throwing it up and heaping it on the carts... when the cart was fully loaded he must have been throwing it eight feet up... an immense labour and he did it all, emptied the whole midden, in three days. He did say to my father, "I was ready for my meat when I went in at nicht."

Geordie was very fond of a dram and he left at last because he went over the top. In winter time we used to stay at Little Ardo in case bad weather stopped us getting home from school. The shepherd from Westertown was down with a flock of sheep to eat up the last of the grass, and he and Geordie had a bet of a bottle of whisky. I held the stake which was twelve shillings and sixpence. I bought the bottle of whisky and gave it to Geordie who took the cork out and handed it to the shepherd. "Well shepherd," he said, "you've won the bet you'd better have a dram."

"Na, na," said the shepherd, "You're the auldest man. You take the first swig." Geordie put the bottle to his lips and he just left enough in the bottle for the shepherd to get a dram.

At three o'clock one morning Pat Joss, who, with his brother, ran Grant's shop in Methlick, was wakened by Geordie saying he had to have a bottle of whisky for a stirk that was not well. In those days if you had a beast with pneumonia you rubbed its chest with mustard plaster and gave it whisky. Pat got up and gave Geordie the bottle of whisky which he neatly cracked open on the window ledge outside the shop and put it to his lips and let it trickle down his throat. Then he patted his chest and said, "Ye see, I'm the stirkie."

That only came to light because when my father got his half yearly account and there was an item "Medicine for stirk... 12/6." As that was the price of a bottle of whisky it wasn't hard to guess what had happened.

On one occasion my father engaged a shepherd called Big Bob who had a reputation for having an enormous appetite. So enormous in fact that he found difficulty in getting a job. But my father engaged him which was alright for him because the feeding of Big Bob was not his problem but that of the grieve's wife. She fed the single men for, I think, a shilling a meal. After Big Bob had been home for a while my father asked the grieve how his wife was getting on feeding Big Bob.

"Nae bother ava. We gie him a bowl of brose afore ilka diet and that dachels the bugger some."

Life on the farm was a very disciplined affair and everybody knew exactly what they were supposed to do. And the grieves were religious about starting the men at one minute to six and at one minute to one in the afternoon. The men lined up in the stable with the cattleman standing next to the orraman just inside the door. When the grieve came in he never looked at them but went straight to the foreman, then the second horseman, then the third. And at North Ythsie the foreman was immediately opposite the stable door and the second was on the right. He then went down to the far end to the third and back again to give the fourth horseman his orders. After my father started the shift of potatoes he needed another pair and they were kept in a little stable added on. So after that the grieve had to tell the fourth then march outside, ignoring the cattleman and the orraman and round to the little stable and then come back to tell the orraman and the cattleman what to do. By this time it would be a second or two before yokin time. There would be silence for a few seconds until the hour then the foreman would grab the collar of his horse and everybody jumped up and got their horses ready. The collars were put on and whatever was needed. Coming back, the horsemen were absolutely expert at arriving on the dot at dead-on lowsin time. The farmer once asked the foreman at Brawlandknowes, a Jake Simpson, "What way is it, Jake, that you jist aye land back wi your ploo or your last straik o' neeps comin doon richt for lowsin time?'

"Well but ye see, if ye kent that, ye'd be fit tae be foreman yersel at Brawlandknowes." A good grieve also knew how many rounds they should have been doing and quickly told them if they were falling behind.

Of my father's brothers my favourite was John who farmed at Coullie which was only six miles away and I went there quite often to play with my cousin John, the one who went to Canada and became a whisky tycoon. When I was at Thomastown as grieve to my father my uncle John would sometimes come and see me there and on one occasion he came in bye and told me about the time that they had been at Auntie Elsie's. She was the widow of John Bruce who owned the Free Press in Aberdeen and Auntie Elsie was reckoned to be the head of the family at that time. She had a family party every year. She was a Mackie, my grandfather John Mackie's sister. Anyway, at this party the men had been standing round as was the habit then after dinner - the ladies withdrew to the drawing room and the men stayed in the dining room telling stories. My Uncle John told what he thought was a good but certainly rude story and as he told me later, "And you know Mike, your father turned to me and said, 'You know John, I wouldna dirty my mouth wi a story like that'."

I thought that was the best story of them all. Yes. My father was a bit of a prude about that sort of thing. It used to astonish the rest of us when our brother George came home from the war and proceeded to tell somewhat rude stories. Oddly enough my mother, who had a bit of a Rabelaisian sense of humour, would laugh heartily but my father would just give a grim half smile.

I have inherited some of my father's prudishness about rude stories. Like most people I enjoy a clever story whether it's dirty or not, but I don't like it if they are just dirty stories. I think there really is a distinction. I remember going once to a Round Table dinner in Ellon where the chairman told a dirty story every time he spoke and everyone who got up told dirty stories and I remember feeling slightly disgusted. I said to myself that I would never go back to a Round Table if that was the way they behaved. Whether they do or not I know not for I never have. I really don't think public speaking is a suitable venue for that kind of story. On any public occasion where I was speaking I would be absolutely prudish and exclude any dirty stories.

My Uncle John from Coullie was the first of the family to be involved with the College of Agriculture. When he died my father took his place on the College and it's been a family involvement ever since. My brother John followed my father as a governor and I was vice-chairman for a long time and after I left my cousin John Mackie from Milton of Noth followed me as a governor but unfortunately there is no Mackie among the College governors now.

I was always afraid of the trend towards co-operation between the three colleges and, like Doig Scott who was chairman, I always argued against the total integration of the colleges. I think now that they have amalgamated they are too big and too much time is spent on administration and travelling up and down to meet together instead of each College being compact and getting on with its own job. We have now the dreadful prospect of the college being totally separated from the University. It happened once before when Professor Bywater tried to get the University to buy a farm and when they didn't get one immediately left for a professorship at Leeds. Fortunately at that moment great pressure was brought on the powers that be to get the college to unite with the University and a very happy marriage took place which has worked very well until recently when there appears to be a rift emerging again. That's a great pity for I am very thoroughly of the opinion that there were advantages for the College students to being part of the University and advantages for the University being part of the College.

Uncle William farmed at Skilmafilly of Auchnagatt and how's this for a coincidence? On my way back from America on the Empress of Britain I met a Canadian couple who were in the shoe business and having had a drink or two on the boat with them I said to the lady, "If you'd like to come to Scotland I'd be very glad to see you."

She said, "I'd love to come because my grandfather came from Scotland."

"Oh where from?" said I.

"Oh you wouldn't know, it's just a little farm in Aberdeenshire."

"Well, I come from Aberdeenshire and I know a lot of the farms. What was the farm called?"

"Skilmafilly."

"Oh," said I, "that's interesting for my grandfather came from Skilmafilly as well and my cousin is in it now, who was your grandfather?"

And it turned out that my grandfather and her grandfather were cousins. But she didn't come because her husband had to get back to Canada on business. However as soon as they got back to Canada they went to consult two old aunties and told them that they had met a man called Maitland Mackie who claimed to be a relation. At this the old aunties produced the good old Victorian scrapbook and there was a page with my grandfather's signature, my father's and his three brothers' signatures. They had come home to Aberdeenshire to visit their relations and had got everyone to sign their scrapbook. They photocopied the page and sent it over to me.

Uncle Willie moved South to farm in the Howe of Strathmore. He was a bit like my father who had always wanted a farm in the south. But when my father got one he put a son into it. Uncle Willie was much cleverer. When he bought Balwyllo he went to live there himself and enjoyed it very much. It was a fine farm between Montrose and Brechin and it is said that they got it cheap because the last two tenants had died of cancer. In those days cancer was almost a taboo word and people were put off buying the farm in case there was something about the place that was giving folk cancer. But uncle Willie died peacefully in his bed without any cancer. His grandson is now in the farm and any suspicions regarding the healthiness of the place have disappeared. Willie's son Leask resurrected an old custom for his own funeral. The service was held in the church and in line with tradition we all got out and were to follow the hearse to Montrose and the graveyard but to our surprise the hearse turned off the main road and we proceeded to the graveyard and waited until the hearse arrived some twenty minutes late. We learned later that they had driven to the farm and driven the hearse round the steading and round the farm to give Leask, my old scouting pal one last look at his farm. Apparently that's an old custom. No doubt it would traditionally have been a question of the staff carrying the coffin round the farm but I thought it was a nice tradition.

My uncle William married Auntie Bella when she was a Miss Knox. It is said that when he married her my grandfather said, "She'll be an expensive een that." He was suspicious because she had been to a finishing school in France, but whether my Auntie Bella had heard this or not, I don't know, but she became the most economical person you could imagine and wouldn't spend a penny. Her husband would have liked to do the house up but couldn't get his wife to put in new fireplaces or anything if it would cost anything ava. Auntie Bella wouldn't even buy much in the way of new clothes and on one occasion when the whole family were going to a family wedding my father had met Bella and said, "Now Bella. You'll just get a new hat for the wedding," and practically took her by force to Madame Lefever's and made her buy a new hat. It intrigues me, that aspect of my father's character. I don't really understand it. It doesn't really seem to fit with the rest of his makeup. The same Maitland Mackie gave his own wife a row when she came back from Aberdeen with a doll costing two shillings and sixpence for my big sister Jean, "Do you think I'm a millionaire?" he said to my mother.

My father's third brother, uncle Tom, was a devil-may-care and it's said that he was recklessly fast with his horses and after he got a car he was always being caught for speeding. He had farmed at Mains of Rhynie but like Uncle Willie he went south to a nice farm with river land at the bottom. He took Broombarns, at Forgendenny in Perthshire, without consulting any of his brothers which was strange but he made a good choice and now his eldest son farms there very well so it had been a good choice after all.

My brother John and I used to spend a holiday at Rhynie with my Uncle Tom who I much enjoyed.

Of course my grandfather married twice, the second time when he was fifty. The second marriage yielded an uncle and an aunt of my own age. They were Bruce who was a great pal of mine and Lizzie Mackie who married James Stephen of Conglass. I became very fond of James Stephen who was a real character in Aberdeenshire. He was on the College Governors Board with me. He was very useful because he chaired a little committee that looked after the farms and spent a lot of time, (probably too much time) with the staff and managers, but after he left the Board the managers realised what a useful man he had been when he visited to help them planning what the farms should be doing. He was also interested in pedigree cattle and used to call once a year on the late Jack Reid of Cromley Bank at Ellon, who at that time bred Shorthorns. It was one of the oldest Shorthorn herds in the country. But in the 1930s or a bit later the price of Shorthorns had gone down and down because they had bred them smaller and smaller and people were getting tired of the Shorthorn breed and anyway times were hard and big prices were not got unless you were at the top. So on this occasion James looked at Jack Reid's shorthorns and said in his well known clipped fashion. "Tell me Jack, why do you keep these Shorthorn cattle, you're nae getting ony mair than commercial prices for them?"

Jack's reply was, "Well, all my friends tell me they just keep cattle to make dung to grow tatties and they make a profit oot o' the tatties. Well, my cattle jist shite as much as theirs so I get as much dung as they get."

James had tremendous energy but apart from that he took a great interest in his staff and on one occasion they had a maid in the house and she said she wanted a bicycle. James, typical of him, had been keeping part of her salary back and putting it into a savings account which he had opened for her and she wanted to take the money out and buy a new bicycle. And James said, "that's just a waste of money, I'll go down to Benzies and get a second hand bicycle for you," which he did and she got a second hand bicycle. A little later when the savings had grown a bit more she became attached to a young man from Oldmeldrum and she announced that she was maybe going to be marrying this chap and would be leaving and James said, "Well now, I would like to see the young man," and somewhat reluctantly the girl had told the young man that her boss would like to meet him and he, even more reluctantly appeared one day, to be addressed by James, "I believe you want to marry Bella. Well now, how much money have you got?"

"It's nae business of yours."

"I ken that fine. Now how much money have ye got?"

So the man was forced to relate his circumstances and he was given a lot of good advice but he did marry the maid and all ended happily. That was fairly typical of the interest and indeed the practical interest that he took in his staff. His employees stayed a long time with him because they liked him.

On one occasion James had been coming through Inverurie as usual way above the speed limit on his motorbike. He was pursued by the policeman on his pushbike. When the policeman eventually arrived at Conglass he was accused of speeding.

"Oh, it couldn't have been me," said James, "Come

oot and see the motorbike."

Knowing that the cylinder would still be hot he invited the policeman to observe that the bike obviously had not been out because it was still cold. So he put his hand on the cylinder and got quite smartly burned. I guess James thought he'd got his own back, but he was charged.

Then there was the terrible occasion when James crashed his gig. Two elderly ladies had stopped at the roadside and were admiring their gleaming red Morris Minor car which was their pride and joy. Now James had kept his gig much longer than most farmers because he liked to take time to drive through the countryside and study what his neighbours were doing. On this occasion he was doing just that and had gone too near the parked car. The hub of the wheel had caught the mudguard, startling the horse, couping the gig and landing James and the shelt in the ditch. The horse jumped up and somehow managed to get its feet up on the dickie seat of of the car before it jumped down trembling.

So there was James greatly concerned for his horse rubbing her legs and saying, "It's a' richt Bess. You're a' richt." Bess was his great favourite.

But the ladies were no less concerned for the Morris Minor was their pride and joy. They were clucking round it saying, "Oh, dear! Here's another scratch." and "Oh, we'll never get another car like this."

That was too much for James who burst out, "What? Never get another car like that? Mr Morris is turning one exactly like that out every minute, but search the world over. You'll never get another mare like Bess."

And I have been lucky to have lived surrounded by many great men outside my family. Like William Duthie the Shorthorn breeder who used to sell his bulls at a special sale at Collynie. When the Shorthorn prices were at ridiculous heights his best bull stuck at three thousand, five hundred guineas and William Duthie stepped further into the ring and said to the auctioneer.

"Stop, stop. It's too much."

That had the effect of exciting the crowd and the bidding took off again and the calf sold for five thousand guineas. *The Daily Express* which was not noted for the best reporting of agricultural matters thought this worth reporting and they had a headline across the page 'the bull calves, the bull calves, the bull calves' in big letters. Punch thought that so amusing that in the next edition in the Charivari column, it repeated "the bull calves, the bull calves, the bull calves," and commented 'surely a biological miracle of this kind might have been worth repeating four times'.

Old John Sleigh of St John's Wells was a great horse breeder in his time as was his son Alec. It was said in the great days of the feein market, which was very efficient at joining man and master but could be a humiliating business for the men, John Sleigh was on the point of feein a man when he thought he saw him shuffling a bit among his feet. Like they did when they were examining horses John Sleigh said to the man, "Jist run yersel oot for fifty yards or so."

It is not related whether the man feed or not or even whether he did run himself out or not, but it is true that he asked the man to run himself out.

At another feein market this man had almost made a bargain with the farmer when the farmer said, "Ah well, I think you'll suit us just fine but I'll need to get your character, so I'll meet ye here in an hour's time."

So off the farmer went and spoke to the man's previous employers who said, yes, that he was a good man. When he appeared back at the appointed time, the farmer said, "Well, I've got your character and it's good, so we'll be glad to have ye."

But the man said, "Aye, aye, bit I've had an hour to get your character, and I'm nae coming."

It is said that William Duthie went to America and went to see the great sales in the Chicago stock yards. It was a world famous sight that, tens of thousands of cattle being sold at the time. William was staying at an hotel before meeting some people at the stock yards next morning. He got a message from the hotel porter that a car was waiting for him so he went down and the driver took him to some strange haunt, produced a revolver, took him in to this place where he was surrounded by tough looking gentlemen who had apparently discovered that he was a rich man and they would rob him. They demanded a large sum of money but Mr Duthie said that of course he carried no money with him. Ah well, but they would just take him to the bank, "and just remember that we're behind you with a revolver and you'll just sign a cheque and then hand over the money to us."

William agreed to that and proceeded to the bank and produced a cheque but instead of signing it he wrote 'man with revolver behind me', passed the cheque across and the clerk had a foot pedal that rang the alarm bells and the man with the revolver ran off.

Our village has the sort of smallness which means that everybody really knows everything about everybody. Someone was once asked if the population in the village was growing and the sad reply was 'no, every time a baby is born a man leaves for the colonies'.

A lady in Tarves asked why she didn't travel said, "I did, I'm here."

Two Aberdeenshire farmers were not feared even to tell the skipper of the boat to Orkney to do a bit extra. They'd had a very rough passage and when they landed they said to the captain, "Noo man, jist gie yer grun twa straik wi the harras and een wi the roller afore we come back."

So I was a lucky chap to be preceded by such illustrious ancestors, to have been born among such men, and into such times.

I needed all my luck at my birth though.

CHAPTER ONE

An Uncertain Start

OF THE six of us I was the only one who needed a help into the world. Old Dr Munro managed to bring in my five brothers and sisters without further assistance but I was an awkward fella and needed a pull from Dr McKerron the gynaecologist from Aberdeen. Whether as a result of that or not, my father thought my ears stuck out and he went to Aberdeen and bought a scrumcap to put on my ears to train then to lie better in to my head. I was quite sick for some time after my birth and at the scrumcap my mother was more than somewhat offended. She said, "If only that bairn will live I'll not care whether his ears are upside doon." So the scrumcap was thrown away and no one has ever objected to the set of my ears since.

   Of 1912 I don't remember much, of course. My memories start at the age of three. I was a faithful companion to my elder brother John. He was always up to some devilment or other in which I was always most willing to take part. We would make a hurlie... that was just an apple box or something like that with a couple of boards nailed along the side and then of course you had to have wheels. What we did in those days was to cut a round log with a saw, bore a hole in the middle and put that on the axle. We were cutting a round log, John had the saw and I was holding, when he let the saw slip and cut my knee which bled like mad. I needed two stitches and I bear the scar to this day. That was the end of the log for that day... though

29

we did eventually finish the hurlie.

Much later when we were making another hurlie - a much more sophisticated hurlie - which needed real wheels, John sent me to the village to Gibb's bicycle shop to buy two wheels. I asked what I was to pay for them. "You silly ass," said John, "if they cost onything ava, dinna buy them." Which seemed excellent advice though I've never been able to get away with it since. But I did get a free pair of wheels from Gibb's and the hurlie was made. This was a great hurlie with a complicated steering mechanism on the front wheels and as we lived on a hill we had the option of careering down, at great risk to life and limb, the good five hundred yards to Little Ythsie, or we could go the other way and it was just possible to coast the half mile to the main Tarves to Aberdeen road. It was a lot of fun and I can't remember any accidents. Perhaps one doesn't.

And it wasn't just hurlies that we made. One time it was a boat. There was a dam at Little Ythsie and we would sail our boat there. It floated just fine but it was a square boat and my brother John thought, "Ye canna hae a square boat." So we sawed off the corners. But when we sat in it now there was no free-board and the water was just lipping each edge.

Jack Hay, the farmer at Little Ythsie, came hot-foot up to my father and said, "If you don't want your sons drowned you'd better tell them to get a bigger boat or at least stop using that one." So we stopped.

Those were just the first of many escapades with John. Much later, when I was eight, John Sleigh, one of that great farming family, had married and came to work the neighbouring farm of Tolquhon. He had been in the airforce at the tail end of the First World War and he gave a talk, illustrated with slides, to the Tarves Literary and Debating Society. And one of the slides showed them coming down from the sky in a parachute. This excited my brother John who said when we got home, "We'll make a parachute tomorrow."

So immediately after breakfast, as soon as my mother's back was turned, we nipped the cover off the nursery table. It was the most unsuitable thing to make a parachute with because it was totally porous and all round the edge it had a shaggy fringe. But that was John's choice. From the stable we got a halter and harness and a few ropes and in no time, tying the ropes to the corners of the table - cloth and the ropes to the halter, we had a parachute. So, accompanied by some more of the kids on the farm, we went up to one of our favourite play places the Prop of Ythsie, a ninety foot high monument erected to the fourth Earl of Aberdeen 'from his grateful tenants' according to the plaque over the door.

From the top was deemed a suitable place to try out the parachute. Being the youngest and the lightest I was given the high honour of trying out the parachute and was very excited by the prospect. I was strapped into the horse's halter. Four boys took a corner of the thing each and my brother was to throw me over. As I looked down it didn't look so enticing and I started to cry. John said, "What are you greetin at Mike?"

"It disna look like what we saw."

"It's jist exactly like what you saw." However he was persuaded by my tears to try it out with a stone. I was replaced by a big stone which hurtled to earth with a great thud which persuaded John that a further period of experimentation was required before the parachute should be tried on humans. So I survived... lucky again.

The Prop of Ythsie was of course a great attraction to us kids and why no one was killed by falling off the thing I'll never know. When my own children became of an age to go I used to tell them not to go up the Prop but I suppose my father and mother had also told us not to go and we went often. We used to play our own special version of tag round the battlements. It's a square tower on the top with four embrasures, one on each side, about two and a half feet wide. We put four kids up on the top and played tag. We went round and round and if you could jump over onto the next person's battlement he was out. The winner was the one who was left. No one ever fell off.

Our neighbours, the Hays of South Ythsie, had two grandsons who were great pals of ours. And Jock Hay, who was a very adventurous young man, led us on a great expedition to the Prop to see who would hang over the edge by their hands and then get up again. Fortunately for me, Jock did it first and he got as far as hanging over the edge. But when it came to getting up again he wasn't fit. I can still remember the sickening feeling with my brother and I, one on each side, an arm each trying to pull him up. Every now and again we failed and had to let him go down again and I was quite sure that we were going to have to let him drop or go with him. Fortunately with one extra heave we got him up with his elbows on the edge and from then on it was fairly simple. So again discretion was thought to be of more use than valour and no one else tried it. I would have been twelve when I had that stroke of luck.

The Prop used to have a glass door which you pushed open when you got to the top and there was a steel door at the bottom and anybody who wanted to go up it had to come to us for the key. But that came to be a confounded nuisance and my father managed to delegate that job to one of the cattlemen. He solved the nuisance problem by losing the key so when we were young there was no key and we and others had the freedom of the prop. A stot even managed to get up the ninety-odd spiral stairs and got itself stuck at the top. Having failed to push it or pull it down a pulley was finally made and the stot lowered down the outside of the monument.

One of the games that children played there was demolition which nowadays would be called vandalism. The glass door was broken and the battlements were thrown down to see how fast they would fall.

That meant that the once proud monument erected to the British Prime Minister by his grateful tenants was in a poor as well as a dangerous state. My father thought it should be repaired and he went to Haddo House to see the factor, a Mr C G Smith who was a very careful factor from the Laird's point of view. C G Smith just looked at my father and said, "The tenants put it up, so they can keep it up." However the millionaire (or he would have been by today's standards) John Duthie-Webster, the nephew of William Duthie of Collynie, said that, if my father would do the work, he would pay. So the stones that his sons had prized off the top were replaced and the Prop got a new floor and a door and a new flagpole with a rope for raising and lowering flags on appropriate days. Unfortunately the vandalism was not done yet and somebody kept stealing the rope and whenever they wanted to raise the flag some poor devil had to shin up the pole and thread in a new rope.

One occasion upon which the flagpole had to be climbed was the wedding of our neighbour Mary Hay to Major Keith of Pitmedden. Again the rope had gone and my mother's brother John was the climber on that occasion so that we could raise the flag for Miss Hay. I thought him very brave. I was a great admirer of my uncle John Yull. He adventured all over the world including China and the United States. Each time he came home he had a new trick to teach me including how to make a paper boat and how to make a paper kettle. I can still do both of those and that comes in very handy for amusing my grandchildren and no doubt will be just as popular with the great grandchildren in their turn.

I am sorry to keep digressing but the factor had a daughter and she was courting another of our neighbours from Mill of Ythsie. On a fine harvest day Jimmy MacNaughton was off playing golf with his sweetheart on the nine hole course at Haddo House. The only man left on the farm was a young boy of sixteen or so, one Charlie Alexander who was to become the Millionaire King of the Road... Alexander's Transport. It was one of the earliest indications of what he was going to become. He looked round and saw that North Ythsie was leading, that Shethin was leading and Little Ythsie was leading home the sheaves. It was Saturday afternoon when lots of boys would have been glad to do nothing. But Charlie Alexander couldn't stand it. He yoked a single horse and cart and went out into the field, forked on a few stooks climbed on and arranged them as well as he could, off the cart, loaded on a few more stooks, got as big a load as he could still climb up on, took it home to the corn yard, forked them off onto a found for a ruck and built it as well as he could, jumping on and off. He later told my father, "I couldna stand and see aabody workin and us daein naething," and pounding his right fist into his left hand as he always did in his later days.

I didn't see him pounding on that occasion but the fist was flying after the second war and the nationalisation of Charlie's business. "If they had only made me manager I'd have made a lot of money for them. Instead, I bought it back again and made mair tae mysel."

The parachute and the Prop were early memories from the time of the Great War but there were others. You see it was still going on when I was going to school. As five and six-year olds we used to knit woolly cuffs for the men at the front. Then there was Jake Duffus, the foreman. He was a favourite of mine. When I was around and they'd be coming back from the fields he would always get me up on his second horse and I would ride home with him. I thought the world of Jake Duffus. I clearly remember the recruiting man coming round and swearing in Jake Duffus to be a volunteer and handed the King's shilling. And Jake was off the next day. Our maid was his sweetheart. And three weeks later she got a telegram that he was killed. I never got over Jake Duffus. I couldn't imagine that he was away and was killed and was dead. To this day if I'm in Edinburgh I go to the castle to the War Memorial and I look up the Gordon Highlanders... the list of all those that were killed... and just look at the name John C Duffus.

That seemed to me to be terrible. That they would give a man a week's training and take him out to France to be shot.

I don't remember much else about the war apart from the Armistice when there were great jollifications and they rang the kirk bell with such enthusiasm that it fell down. A flag-pole was erected in the middle of the square and all sorts of people made speeches and we all prayed and sang. There must have been great relief at the end of that war for it was a terrible slaughter and, as it turns out, the slaughter on both sides could have been avoided.

CHAPTER TWO

Tarves Public School

THE FIRST expansion to my world of home and farm came when I was four and was deemed ready for Tarves Public School. At first that meant Miss Bannerman. She was a holy terror. She drank a little. In fact it is said that she drank a lot. She used to put us all in a circle and make us pronounce the alphabet. The first time it came to my turn I had to pronounce "c". I knew perfectly well how but I was a bit too excited and stammered "aaaaaaa..."

"Ye ken fine it's nae, 'eh, eh'," said Miss Bannerman and I got six of the strap for not being able to pronounce "c". I think it must have been sore but not so sore as when she gave the girl Campbell a slap on the side of the face and she fell and hit her head on a stove and developed a mastoid on her ear. There was a big enquiry and a Mr Topping, one of the school inspectors, came round and investigated this dreadful occurrence. We were all asked to tell what happened. That was much more exciting than having lessons.

When brother John had been loitering on the way to school he thought he would appease the teacher by pulling some flowers for her. They were mostly kind of withered but he handed these over and Miss Bannerman said, "If you think you're going to get off wi that you're much mistaken." And he got six of the strap.

I had two special friends at Tarves school, the first was George Strachan. He was one of a big family and all of them were first in their class and George was first in my class. I was second by virtue of copying from George. The family couldn't afford to send him to secondary school so George was coached by our splendid headmaster Mr Pirie for the police examinations and went on to become high up in the Metropolitan Police in London as did so many of the boys in the Strachan family. The family had a small croft and the father was foreman of a gang on the roads.

My second friend was Tom Shepherd, whose family had the fine farm of Shethin at Tarves. They were always very generous to their children and Tom had a Shetland pony and of course we all wanted a Shetland pony too but we didn't get one. In fact Tom had two Shetland ponies and I would go there on a Sunday and we would ride together.

We had a splendid start at the country school. It was only a mile and a quarter for us and many walked a lot further than that. The cattleman had a big family and they didn't have much to live on. In common with many others, his bairns walked to school in bare feet in the summer time. But we weren't allowed to go to school barefooted so we walked in our boots to the bottom of the garden and then left them at the back of the dyke and walked to school barfit nae to be seen to be different from the other kids.

One of the ways the cattleman's wages were stretched was that the bairns would rake about the steading for eggs that the hens laid wild and on one occasion they were convinced that a hen had a nest at the bottom of a hole in the straw. They lit a match to help them see it and set fire to the straw. In no time the steading was on fire. I was sent to fetch the men who, as ill luck would have it, were in the Target Park which was the furthest away field in the whole place. I ran as fast as I could but I didn't run as fast as the man who was first back. He was Bert Low, one of the single men. He had fifty pounds saved in his kist in the chaumer so he was first back to save his kist. He needn't have run so fast though, as that was one of the bits of the farm that was saved. But you could understand his excitement, for his fifty pounds was more than two years' pay.

When I got back to the steading not long after Bert,

When I got back to the steading not long after Bert, there was a stream of rats, pouring out of the steading and up to the corn yard. I have never seen the like of them for they were almost like a moving grey carpet. I've no idea how many there would have been but more than a thousand. Of course at that time we had an awful lot of rats on farms. In fact, when I was five, the rats were such a problem in the house at North Ythsie that they were a danger to us bairns. John and I slept in one room together and the rats had eaten a hole through the ceiling from the garret. A piece of linoleum was put over the hole to keep them out, but during the night the rats had bitten a hole through the linoleum and one big rat fell down and landed on our bed. We woke to find this rat scrambling about on top of us. I didn't care for this much and my crying brought my father who skilfully pursued the rat round the room and finally killed it in the fireplace with the poker. For the rest of that night I got to sleep with my father and mother which I thought was a great reward and it even helped me to put up with the rats.

The thing got so bad that we moved to Little Ardo to my mother's family farm. We stayed there for two or three months while they tore the house to bits and improved it immensely. They put in dormer windows upstairs to make bedrooms bigger. They put out a bow window from the nursery and the other door which puzzled my mother's mother so greatly. They put in a proper bathroom because up till then we just had one water-closet in the house. Why I don't know, but that was in the topmost room in the house and the loo was the only thing in that room. Every Saturday night we had a bath there. It was one of these tin hip baths and the maids had to carry up the pailfuls of hot water and then we all bathed in our turn in the same water. We had a bath every week whether we needed it or not but, I can assure you, the boys at least were always needing it.

Anyway, the improvements got rid of the rats in the house but not in the steading. They came back almost if not just as bad as ever. One day my father and I were going out to look at something and I said to him, "I'll go out of the door that leads out to the midden with my stick

and when you make a noise some will run out of the door
and I'll try to kill as many as I can." All went according to
plan and I killed at least three rats. But then there got up a
commotion inside and I went in to find my father dancing
on his toes and gripping onto his trousers just about his
groin. I wondered what was happening. Eventually he
shook his trousers and out fell a great big dead rat. It had
run up his trouser leg. I must say if it had been me I think
I would have gone mad but my father calmly grabbed the
rat and squeezed the life out of it. I never went through
the steading at North Ythsie again without a stick and my
socks out over the bottoms of my trousers. The discovery of
Warfarin has reduced the rat menace on farms by ninety
nine per-cent and not before time.

We took a bottle of milk with us in our schoolbags and
a penny because at William Cummings the bakers you plon-
ked the penny on the counter and said, "a penny worth o'
broken biscuits," and you got a great bag of broken biscuits,
and that, with your milk, was your lunch. Later on we went
up-market and during my last years at Tarves school I got
my dinner from Aggie and Mary Simpson... two worthies in
the village. I say worthies because if you wanted to know
anything about anyone in the village you asked them.
Especially Aggie. Mary worked as a dressmaker in Duthie's,
the general merchant's shop, and Aggie had a little platform in front of an upstair window so that she could see out
and so keep track of who was going where in the square.

For a shilling a week we got a decent lunch from
Aggie Simpson. Then Captain Mort and his wife fed us for
two shillings a week. But that was after we had moved to
Methlick School. At that time you had to leave Tarves at
thirteen and if you wanted to go on you had to leave after
class five ("the qualifying class") and change schools. I was
only six years at Tarves for I skipped a year and that meant
I was only ten and a half when I went to Methlick.

Before I leave Tarves I must say a word about Mr
Pirie, who was an absolutely splendid headmaster. He was
very fond of shooting and fishing. He used to say to the
older boys, "Come with me on Saturday and I'll teach you
how to shoot." I went with him often, even after I had left

his school. He used to take me to the Dinness Woodie, which was just at the foot of our road, and he would lend me his gun and teach me how to shoot. Very much later, when I was farming on my own at Westertown, I invited Mr Pirie to come and shoot round the farm. Going through the turnips a pheasant got up quite near me and I missed it. He turned to me and said, "Now Maitland, that's not the way I taught you to shoot." I was suitably reproached.

Mr Pirie, whose first wife had died very young, remarried when he was seventy two. In due time his wife bore him a son. Everybody was delighted but when he was eighty two she then produced a daughter. My sister Jean met him soon after in the square in Oldmeldrum. She congratulated him, of course, and he said to her, "Oh, well. I know you and your family are probably pleased for me but I do know that some people in the village think it's awful an old man like me having children. But you see Jean, I just don't believe in birth control."

I must confess when I heard that story it gave me hope for the future. But all sorts of people said, "Goodness me. He'll never live to see his daughter grow up." But I told them he'd see his daughter graduate. So he did, despite her choosing the longer course of Medicine. When he was a hundred and three I was learning to fly an aeroplane and I thought I would take Mr Pirie, who had never been in an aeroplane, for a flight. I was a mere chicken of sixty at the time and I arranged for Mr Forbes, my instructor, to take my old schoolteacher up. I drove him into Aberdeen and on the way he said to his wife, "You'll need to give me a penny for the man." I assured him he wouldn't need any money but he insisted.

So Peter Forbes took him up in the aeroplane and over to the back of Bennachie where he was born and round Aberdeen. And when they landed Mr Pirie, who was always used to giving a tip for any service he got, handed over a penny. It happened to be the very same day that the old penny went out of circulation but the pilot said he would keep it as a good luck charm. Mr Pirie was a hundred and four when he died.

One of Mr Pirie's teachers at Tarves was Miss Chalmers. We had her in classes three and four and she was another holy terror. She was a very good teacher but on the slightest excuse we got the strap from Miss Chalmers. And if it was a really serious crime, like copying off your neighbour in class, you got sent through to confess your crimes and be belted by Mr Pirie. We were told to "go and see the table", referring, no doubt, to the table behind which the dominie sat. But Mr Pirie, wise old man, used to say, "Well now, you've seen the table. Away you go back and don't do it again." We would then go back blowing on our hands, and Miss Chalmers was satisfied, we were satisfied and no doubt Mr Pirie thought it was all good fun.

CHAPTER THREE

Methlick Public School

AFTER SIX years at Tarves I went to the secondary school
at Methlick. That was six miles away and we had to cycle
there every day. Because my father was a tenant at Little
Ardo in the parish of Methlick as well as at home at North
Ythsie of Tarves we had a permit from Lord Aberdeen to
take the short-cut through the Haddo House grounds.
That cut about a mile off the journey and meant that we
could go tearing down to Methlick in about twenty minutes.
But it took us about an hour and a half to get home... that
was altogether a more leisurely affair.

I think I got my first belief in the power of prayer
going home because if you prayed hard enough a lorry
would come along slow enough to let you get a hold of the
tail door and get a pull up the hills.

I was in the same class as one of the Massies of Neth-
ermill, a farm between the two villages, and Harold always
invited me to come in on the way home. I would get a
goose egg for my tea. That was a rare thing for a loon who
used to try to race his brothers and sisters in the morning to
be first down to breakfast and thereby earn the reward of
the top of his father's egg. He alone got an egg. The rest
of us had to be content with porridge except on Sundays
when we all got scrambled eggs. Those were the days when
a good farmer's wife could keep the house on the money
she made from her hens and her pig... so there was always
an egg but my mother didn't like to overdo it.

Harold wasn't at the top of the class by any manner of means but then the head master, Mr MacDonald, was promoted and left to go to Culter. At his final prize-giving he wanted everybody to get a prize of some sort and to the surprise of his classmates, when the prize list was read out, Harold's name was called out. He got the prize for "the best man with a spade." I thought that was a very kindly act from Mr MacDonald who was a very hard taskmaster usually. I ran into him many years later when I was Convenor of the Education Committee of the old Aberdeen County Council. MacDonald was retired but was chairman of one of the sub-committees. By then he was far from being a hard man and it always amused me when we were interviewing people for jobs, that his first question was always, "And have you applied for your expenses"... he who would never have got any expenses himself and who would never have asked for any.

At Methlick school I really got a very good education. Miss Sheriffs taught science and maths and she was very good at both. I too was quite good at both and, though she didn't have favourites, she was kind to me. I always got an extra sum or two to do for homework. She encouraged me and when I got a proof right I always got a pat on the back. But you also got a thrashing if you didn't do well, not so much for your homework as for evil deeds. We didn't have much money but it only cost tuppence to buy five Woodbines and so the boys had been taking turn about of spending tuppence. Miss Sheriffs heard about it and the whole class... not the girls but all the boys... got the strap for starting that evil habit so early. I don't know if it was that that gave me such a liking for fags but I smoked an awful lot after that and Miss Sheriffs' thrashing didna do me much good. She didna know who smoked so she thrashed us all. My mother must have suspected me of smoking for she once said she smelt smoke on my breath. She can't have been too worried for she accepted my explanation that somebody had blown smoke in my face.

Anyway I became an inveterate smoker puffing away fifty a day though, like Marc Twain, I gave up many times, until I was in hospital having two fingers removed because they were showing a progressive curling up. That's a condition which is hereditary in males in the Mackie family called 'Dupytren's Contracture'. They'd been straightened a few times but they kept curling up so I thought I'd better have them off. I woke up having had my two pinkies removed and with my hands heavily bandaged. However the tips of my other fingers were sticking out and I managed to extract a cigarette from the packet by my bedside. I managed to get a match out too but in lighting the cigarette the cotton wool of one of my bandages caught fire and I tried to dab it out with the other hand but that caught fire too. This was a little alarming and so I thrust both hands under the sheets and dabbed the clothes down with my chin and the fire went out. I was very unpopular and no one gave me any sympathy for having burned all three tips of my fingers. So I decided to give up. The surgeon would allow me one. The sister would allow me one. My wife might light two for me and another visitor might have one with me, but five a day wasn't enough.

I didn't succeed in giving up then but much later, when I was seventy, I was again in hospital for ten days with no cigarettes. When I went home I'd had a week with no cigarettes so I said I'll do another week. Then I did another week and I haven't had another cigarette since... and I don't feel any better.

So Miss Sheriffs' justice didn't seem to have the desired effect or at least took a long time to work. But then we were used to that sort of justice for we had a super maid at North Ythsie who acted as a nursemaid. Now John was always up to devilment and getting a thrashing for it. On one occasion Mary Mutch came into the nursery and imagined she had caught John again and gave him a good box round the ears. But I stood up for my brother and said, "It wasna John. It was me."

"Ah well", said Mary Mutch "It'll dae him for next time."

My mother was determined that her two oldest sons should learn to play the piano and have a little culture. Now there was, as well as Mary Mutch, a mother's help in the house at North Ythsie called Mary Morrison and she was given the job of piano teacher. About a month later she came to my mother and said, "Oh, it's really hopeless. I can't get the boys to practise and they're not really interested."

My mother said, "Well now, if you were to play something to them and explain to them what it was about they might become interested that way."

She came back the next week and said, "No, it's hopeless. I played the Robin's Return to John and said, 'Now here comes the robin. Look he's up on the branch. Do you see him?' and he just said 'No. If I saw it I would sheet it'."

I have told you that my father was a right-thinking man but he seems to have had a somewhat lax attitude to the law as it related to his sons' driving. Certainly my old diaries show that from the age of eleven onwards I was at the wheel. It records, "Drove to church," or a disappointed, "John drove to church." Latterly we used to take shot about. Although the policeman complained from time to time it didn't seem to worry my father, who was very glad sometimes to have the services of his sons as drivers. On one occasion I was sent in, aged fourteen, with my sister Jean to collect an Australian off the train at Aberdeen. We had a big Minerva car at the time and I said, "Oh Dad. We've just newly had a row from the policeman. I canna possibly go to Aberdeen."

"No, no. You'll be alright. Just sit on a cushion and I'll give you my hat." So the hat was stuffed with some papers and I set off proudly. I stopped at the station and Jean went in to meet the guest. The train was a little late and by the time that she came out it was dark. But because all the street lights were on I didn't notice and set off proudly for home. Going up Guild Street I passed a taxi with a flourish and turned up Bridge Street. There the taxi-driver drove up along side me, leaned out and said, "Put up your lights, sonny," with great emphasis on the sonny. I was very glad to do so as there was a policeman at the top of Bridge Street. Some time later we had a visit from some South Africans and while Dad was showing the men round the farm he asked me to take the ladies over to Haddo House to see the fine Adam mansion and the beautiful grounds, lakes and what-not. Again I protested, "Oh Dad. The bobby'll come to hear of it and I'll get another row."

"No, no," said this saintly man. "The bobby'll be having a nap on Sunday afternoon. Away you go." So away I went and I was just about a couple of hundred yards from being into the private grounds of Haddo House when here was the bobby out for a Sunday stroll with his wife. All I could do was to wave, knowing that there would be consequences to follow. Next day the policeman came down and had words with my father. Then he said, "Well now. I've given you a row. Let me see your son and I'll give him a bigger row." So I don't think I drove for a week or two after that.

Times change and though I'd have been glad to send my children off on errands with the car I was more careful than my father and waited until they were nearly old enough to be legal.

Although we were very excited to drive the car we were equally excited to drive Mrs Hay from South Ythsie to church in her gig. It was made ready for her every Sunday by her strapper and she used to like to have one of us loons to drive her to church, stable the horse and then have it ready to drive her home again after the service. Kate Hay from South Ythsie was a very lively dame with quite a tongue. One of her scathing remarks was directed at another neighbour, my friend Tom Shepherd. He had failed to get a job when he left school. Kate had said to my mother. "I hear Tom Shepherd is going abroad, as if going abroad was a job in itself."

MacDonald taught English, history and singing at Methlick school. He was a Highlander and liked to teach us Highland songs. I was never very musical. When we were singing he used to come round the class and listen to us individually and on one occasion he stopped at me and listened. "Mackie you're singing like a rat in a barrel. Go through to room five and do extra maths." So I was excused from the singing from then on. MacDonald was pretty hard on you if you didn't do well. When John was at school MacDonald taught him Latin (Ogilvie's Latin Grammar). MacDonald was very fond of that. John wasn't too good at the Latin. However once, when we were going to school from Little Ardo, as we did to avoid the five mile daily cycle in winter, there was a great Latin scholar staying with the widows who lived in the front of the farmhouse there. John came home with this exercise to translate into Latin. He was making pretty heavy weather of the whole thing when this Latin scholar took it in hand and wrote the whole exercise out. MacDonald must have been astonished at the good Latin and then suddenly remembered who was staying at Little Ardo. He put two great big pencil marks through it and wrote "Rubbish, and show this to Dr Kellas." So he wasn't to be cheated.

Those two widows had been ladies of the Manse and it is said that there was quite a lot of spirit about them. Indeed one of them was second generation divine for she was the daughter of the minister of Auchterless, Dr Gray, and he seems to have been a little above the ordinary too. He was a great favourite with the Duff children at Hatton Castle and it was his custom to play childish games with them. He called unannounced one day and asked the maid where the children were. He was directed upstairs. At the door he got down on his hands and knees, pulled his frock coat over his head and entered the room roaring like a lion. What he didn't know was that Lady Duff was having an afternoon tea party and when he stood up, not only were the children there but so were those polite ladies there for their afternoon tea. Lady Duff appeared quite unruffled, "And this is our minister, Dr Gray."

CHAPTER FOUR

The Grammar School

ANYWAY, I did my three years of Latin. I think I was the last to do the old Intermediate Examinations. I left Methlick School at 13, and went to the Grammar School in Aberdeen. You could attend by paying a very small fee and it was reckoned to be a very good school. So I went there during the week and my father took me home after he'd been to mart on Friday. I was very much the country boy then, still wearing shorts and boots. But I had a pair of plus fours in train, made by my father's tailor... Christy & Gregor, in the corner of Rosemount Viaduct and Union Terrace, which later became the office for the theatre.

Once when I was in Christie and Gregor's with my father that greatest of Aberdeenshire farmers, Major James Keith came in. Now, in those days, anybody who was anybody wore a coat made from cloth from the Crombie woollen mills at Dyce. James Keith had such a coat and had brought it to be "turned". That meant remade so as to hide the worn cuffs, lapels and perhaps button holes. The assistant took it through the back and emerged shortly saying, "Yes, Major Keith, we can turn your coat, but I should tell you that it has been turned already." I thought that a great credit to the great Crombie cloth and I told that story many years later to Mr Ross who was managing director of Crombie's by that time. He was then on his way to America on one of his selling trips and when he came back he told me, "Your story's been worth many lengths of cloth to me.

You'll just come in and choose a length of cloth for yourself." When I duly went in he was busy but handed me
over to one of his minions and told him to give Mr Mackie
the best length of cloth I would select. By that time the
heavy Crombie cloths were being replaced by lighter material for we had heating in the cars and even central heating
in the hotels if not in the houses and I was shopping among
those lighter cloths when Mr Ross came in and was horrified. "Oh gracious, you're not going to give Mr Mackie any
of that rubbish," and led me back to the heavier cloths. I
went off with a greenish thing that I used for shooting and
any other outdoor pursuit where I could be fairly sure it
would be cold.

But I was very proud of getting out of shorts and
going off to the Grammar School with my first pair of plus
fours. I knew I should have shoes also as I'd got thirty
shillings from my mother to buy a pair for my first day. But
I got off the bus and went to school in my plus fours and
my old tackety boots. And all the Aberdeen boys, led by
one called Bookless, who was quite an amusing boy in the
same class, ridiculed me in my boots. Everywhere I went
that day everyone called at me, "boots, boots, boots". I used
to keep a diary, and for that week it just said "boots". I went
and bought a pair of shoes right away but I wouldn't put
them on for two weeks just to spite them.

The Grammar School was quite fun. I had very good
lodgings in 246 Rosemount Place with a Mrs Stewart whose
husband had been the doctor at Hatton of Fintry. She'd
bought this big house with her sister and both of them
taught and they managed to keep their own families (she
had three girls and a boy) and also keep three lodgers and
do us all very well. Incidentally, her son went to University
and became a doctor and got, at first shot, his father's old
practice at Hatton of Fintry as the people remembered what
a good chap his father had been. It was a very happy
household and that was a good thing during the week
though I was always glad to get home at the weekend.
When I went to the University I had very good digs which I
shared with Alec Giles from Gateside of Tarves for thirty
shillings a week for bed and board... the lot. It was excel-

49

lent food. So excellent, in fact, that we had a terrible job dividing it. We evolved the system of taking week about of one dividing and the other choosing. The division was always very fair indeed.

I remember one Friday, when he came to collect me at the Grammar School, my father said, "We'll just go in past Duncan's Mart. Pat McGranaghan (one of the Irish dealers) has some cattle there and I tried to buy them but he wouldn't deal at my price. Now he'll be anxious to get hame and if he's still got the cattle I'll be able to buy them." So we went to Duncan's Mart in King Street where my father and Pat had a great bargaining session. Eventually my father gave in and bought the cattle and unknown to my father Pat McGranaghan handed me ten pounds and said, "Dinna let your father see that or he'll think he's bought the cattle ower dear. This is just for you." It was a fortune for a schoolboy. We all had a bank account... I remember taking out money to buy a steam engine for our Meccano set which gave us great fun so it was useful having some money in the bank... but we were encouraged to put it in and never to take it out.

I was fortunate to have a very good teacher of Maths at the Grammar School, Pa Gray, and a very good teacher of English, Mr Walker, who had been shell-shocked during the war and sometimes got terribly excited. If there was any misbehaviour he would bring out the tawse and on one occasion when wrong had been done he thrashed the whole class because he wasn't sure who had done it. By the time he had finished giving us six each he was peching as though he had run a marathon. But the best thrasher in the school was the science master, a Mr Goodall. He was a great big tall man. He was said to be in love with the rector's secretary (and who could have blamed him, I think we all were). If you misbehaved with him he would call you out and give you the strap but there was no anger in it for him and he made quite a performance of it. So much so that we took turns of misbehaving so that we would be called out to get the strap. He made you hold your hand up in the exact right place so that he could give you the full force. It would be, "Up a bit, down a bit, a wee bit to the left," till it was just right for chastising. But he didn't mind if you took a bit of time to tie a handkerchief round your wrist so that it was only the hand that got hurt. And he didn't mind if you performed a bit between each of the six blows. You would make him stop to let you blow on your hands and the more time you wasted the more popular you were with the rest of the class.

I got all the highers I tried except French because we had an awful bad teacher called Suivi. I annoyed the poor man so much that it is said that I would have passed the exam had it not been for the very poor estimate mark he had given me. But I was not surprised. How he stood us I never knew. Bookless and I, particularly, used to torment him. We were reading in French but we never got to the end of the book because each time when he was about to start we would say, "Oh no sir, we hadn't got to this page yet," so he turned back to a bit we'd already done. When we did written exercises we would do them wrong deliberately. And when we were reading another French book we got hold of a translation into English and so we were very good at that. But Suivi wasn't as good at giving us the strap. It didn't hurt us but it hurt him, poor chap. I wouldn't have been in his shoes for all the tea in China. He just couldn't control the class. So I failed Lower French with that man. It was the only exam I ever failed. But luckily I sat the preliminary University exams at the same time and succeeded in getting a higher French in those.

My second science teacher at the Grammar was an excellent teacher, a Mr Lynch, and he actually got me through the first year at the University. There we had to do Botany, Zoology, Chemistry and Natural Philosophy (as physics is called at Aberdeen University). In Physics we had a hopeless lecturer who talked miles above our heads. I got to the stage of not even taking notes because they didn't make any sense to me when I got home. And then I was expelled from the class for throwing a handful of lead shot at the blackboard. Unfortunately he turned round quickly and caught me. I was told to come back when I was ready to apologise so I waited until the very last day. You had to have a thirty-seven per-cent attendance to get a "sign up" and be allowed to sit your exams. So I waited until the very last day and then went and apologised and was received back into the class.

I hadn't missed much for no-one had understood a word he'd been saying, but, knowing that I would have to do something about passing this exam, I went back to the Grammar School and asked Mr Lynch to help me. He said, "forget about all that stuff you've had lectures on for they will never ask you about that." He had the wit (which I lacked) to get hold of some of the past exam papers and he said, "If you work away at these and swot up what you did in your last year with me you'll be all right." He gave me various exercises and I duly passed the exam which was remarkable for only twenty-five percent passed that year. Seventy-five per cent failed and it's no wonder for their teacher was a famous scholar who went on to do research at Cambridge, but he was an infamous lecturer.

I would have liked to play games at the Grammar School but I was also a very keen Boy Scout. There was a half day for sports on a Wednesday. It was taken by a Mr Macgregor who I gather was a very good games master but of course he wanted you to be available to play in matches on the Saturday and that clashed with my Scouts. I used to be asked to turn out for the house rugby teams on a Saturday but didn't. Macgregor didn't like that much and said, "Mackie you either be a Boy Scout or you play Rugby." So I said, "Oh well, I'll be a Boy Scout."

On following Wednesdays a few of us decided to play truant from the sport and do more exciting things. The best was to go down and row on the Dee if it was a decent day. We hired a boat from Ogilvie's boat yard and did a bit of rowing. Then some of us formed a riding club and we used to hire horses from a Mr Trail at Hazlehead and it put the fear of death into the poor people who had gone for a gentle walk in the park when three or four rascals came galloping round the policies. We became quite famous for there was a letter in the *Evening Express* complaining about us. We replied to the effect that it was very good for us and for the horses and that we weren't doing any harm.

CHAPTER FIVE

Scouts and Scouting

DR STEPHEN from Methlick, had become impressed with
Baden-Powell's idea of Scouting and had started a troop of
Scouts in Methlick. That was somewhat in opposition to the
Boys' Brigade which was run by the Minister. The net
result was that the Boys' Brigade faded out and the Scouts
carried on and became a very well known troop in Aberdeenshire. Encouraged by my friends at Methlick school, I
joined the Scouts. I think I was a little young. I was only
ten and a half at my first camp at Brucklay Castle when I
was to be invested as a Boy Scout and had to take the promise. I was overwhelmed by the occasion when, in front of
the whole troop and one or two parents, I had to promise
with my hand up and my three fingers up to do my duty to
God and the King, to help other people at all times and to
obey the Scout law. At the enormity of that I started to cry.
I was soon comforted by old James Duncan from the garage
at Methlick, who told me that that wasn't a thing for a Scout
to be doing. So I stopped crying and I became, I think, a
good Scout thereafter. A bit of realisation of the enormity
of the promise I think was due to Dr Stephen's teaching
beforehand because he did impress upon every recruit that
they were expected to do their duty. But the let-out was
that you had to do your best and as some people's best was
better than others, there were some Scouts better than
others.

I think I was a good Scout and I enjoyed every minute of it for a long time. Dr Stephen ran very good camps and very good weekend affairs in the Belmuir at Methlick, which was a wood before it was all cut down. Dr Stephen was very good at outdoor activities so we had many weekend camps by ourselves or under his supervision and there was the yearly camp which was really enjoyed by all the Scouts who went. We were reasonably ambitious although to begin with there was a habit of going to Brucklay Castle, less than ten miles away near New Deer. It was a very good venue for us because we had the run of the estate. On other weekends we camped even nearer home, at Haddo House where the Aberdeens were good at letting you more or less please yourselves.

We did all kinds of things in those weekends. You could snare a rabbit, skin and cook it over an open fire. I became quite good at that but I'd been good at it before I joined the Scouts because we did a bit of that at home. I don't think the Scouts ever poached his pheasants but I'd done a bit of that and as I used, years later, to say to Lord Aberdeen, "I think I know your estate just about as well as you do yourself having cycled through it on the way to Methlick school and having camped so often and having enjoyed the freedom of the estate." It was good fun.

At the annual camps we used to do a project of some sort and one of the best projects we did, and which was admired by all, was to build a bridge in the style of the Forth Bridge. It must have been quite well done because everybody who came to see it realised that it was a copy of the Forth Bridge. It was real cantilever stuff and it worked. It was done over a burn at Brucklay Castle so it was even useful. We re-did it once at a jamboree when it wasn't built over a burn but it still was recognisable as being a bridge. Unfortunately the bridges had to be taken down. You see the timber we got from Haddo House was all sorts of shapes and sizes but it was used again and again as practice for Boy Scouts and the thing was that it was all tied together by special knots so all the ropes could be kept again to be used over and over.

The Scouting movement in Britain was very lucky to have Lord Rowallen as Chief Scout for many years and followed by Lord Maclean who was equally enthusiastic. On one occasion we had a big do at Haddo House when all the five districts, into which Aberdeenshire Scouting was divided, came to a weekend camp. Lord Rowallan was to come on the Sunday and present Queens Scout badges to five boys, all from the Stoneywood troop. To make it a memorable occasion every district had to do an outdoor project. I well remember Deeside's project because they built a great big crane and they built it over the well in the monument park at Haddo House to pull up ten gallon cans and swing them over and then the boys would take the ten gallon cans back to their camp. This was really quite a magnificent crane with a great big boom made out of what was virtually a whole fir tree. The project had been supervised by Brigadier Stirling who was the Commissioner of Scouts for Deeside and lived in Aboyne.

He was very proud of this crane and when I, who was in charge of this particular camp, came round the Brigadier asked, "Would you like to test the crane?" So I was put down into the well instead of a can of water and lifted up and swung round. But as it swung round the rope carrying the big boom broke (it had been a pretty ropey rope) and the boom fell on my head and for the first time in my life I really saw stars and was knocked out for a second or two. There was great consternation and panic and somebody sent for a doctor, forgetting that we had Dr Pat McBoyle from Huntly in the camp. Anyway, after a couple of stitches in the head I was back to work.

I did forty three years of Scouting until I gave up in 1965. I finally decided that, as there was a reorganisation going on in the Boy Scouts, somebody new had better take it on. So I resigned as County Commissioner, the head Scout in Aberdeenshire. We had a very good team for a long time. Hunter Will, schoolmaster in Aberdeen, had been a great friend of Dr Stephen and he was involved with the country Scouts although he lived in the town and he was a very meticulous man and very good at keeping the records and administration. He made a very good County Commissioner. I think I had a bit more imagination and I was very good at the arranging of camps and the exciting bits of Scouting which was what it was mostly all about. I was ably supported by chaps like Gordon Ingram from Kemnay. If Methlick wasn't winning the County Flag then Kemnay would be. And in Methlick we had Jimmy Duncan, from the garage and Leslie Shearer, the farmer of Oldtown Leys, and various other supporters... a splendid team who really worked very well together.

When I went to the University I kept going as an Assistant Scout Master at Methlick. But, when I graduated and went to Thomastown, except for going back to help Dr Stephen at summer camps, I had little connection with the movement. I missed my Scouting though and when I moved to Westertown in 1935 I started a troop in Daviot. I ran the Daviot troop off and on by myself during the war. Just after the war I had arranged a very nice programme of what we called wide games, an outside game for a fine summer night. I had gone to a great deal of trouble with written instructions for three patrols. We had three patrols of seven at the time and I went up to the Scout hut which we had built in the little wood we had bought at Daviot. It was really nicely arranged, well equipped and ideal for the job. On this particular night, to my disgust I only had six boys when I really needed the whole troop for this wonderful wide game. I felt really cross and wondered why I should waste my time on the boys who hadn't turned up. However I discovered that there was a school football match on and there was really a good excuse, so I set the six boys who had turned up to do something else. I was standing feeling a little sorry for myself, in spite of the excuse, when up walked a very smart young soldier and I suddenly recognised one of my old patrol leaders, Albert Mitchell. "Hello Albert," said I, glad to see him. "What are you doing here?"

"Oh," he says, "I just had 48 hours leave and I thought I would come up and tell you how much I learned from you as a Scout and that it's been a great help to me in the army."

So my evening was made after all.

One of the exciting things about the Scouts was the jamborees. When I was only twelve, my cousin Leask

Mackie from Skilmafilly of Auchnagatt and I went to the Wembley exhibition. That was 1924 and we were camping at Wembley for a great jamboree. We made a great fuss about doing all the right things and we all marched past King George V who was sitting with Baden-Powell. After the march past we danced eightsome and sixteensome reels and the Prince of Wales was dancing in the next set to me so I can claim to have danced with the Prince of Wales. At night, in what was supposed to be a great honour, our troop was asked to take part in guarding the Prince who later became Edward VIII. He was patron of the Boy Scouts so he would camp with the boys. When we went to guard his camp (for four hours during the night) we were somewhat amused to find an enormous double marquee and inside furniture, wooden floor, beds, the lot. However we stood outside for four hours and marched round and round and no harm was done. But it didn't look much like camping to us. Still, he was camping with the boys.

There would have been five thousand Scouts or thereby at that jamboree. They came from all over Great Britain and there were Scouts from abroad as well although Scouting wasn't so well developed abroad at that time. You see it only started in 1907 and it took on like wildfire here because Baden-Powell wrote exciting things for the boys to do in what was known as the Fortnightly Parts. The days when the Fortnightly Parts came out the boys were dying to get them to see what Baden-Powell was advising them to do next. He told them to get out and snare rabbits and how to skin and cook them, and a hundred other outdoor pursuits. In one of the Fortnightly Parts there would be a bit about first aid and Baden-Powell's advice, "If you don't understand this go and ask your doctor." So they got their doctors involved and that is how Dr Stephen became involved. But that happened all over the country and suddenly the boys realised that they needed some adults to tell them how to organise and to carry out Baden-Powell's instructions and so Scouting spread.

There is an interesting story about how it spread to America. In 1907 Baden-Powell held a pioneering camp in Brownsea Island with seven boys chosen at random from public and private schools. It was a great success and news of that spread and King Edward told Baden-Powell that he should resign from the army and give his full time to Boy Scouts. In 1908 an American businessman came over for a meeting in London and got caught in one of London's pea soup fogs and had no idea where he was. He was trying to get back to the Park Lane Hotel and he was standing under a gas lamp which was giving some sort of vague light and wondering what to do when a little Cockney boy said, "Aye sir, can I help you?"

This man, Boyce was his name, said, "Could you take me back to the Park Lane Hotel?"

"I can do that." So in the dark and gloom and thickest fog he wondered whether he was being led in the wrong way and was going to be robbed, but eventually the bright lights of the Park Lane Hotel could be seen through the gloom. The man was feeling in his pocket for half a crown to give to the boy when the boy said, "Oh, no sir. That's my good turn for the day," and ran off. So we don't know to this day who the boy was but Boyce went into the hotel and told the porter that an extraordinary thing had happened; a boy refusing half a crown. When he said that the boy had said it was his good turn the porter was able to tell him that that must be one of Baden-Powell boys, "They all have to do a good turn every day."

"Who is Baden-Powell?"

"Oh, he has opened an office in Buckingham Gate, you should go down and meet him." So Boyce went down and met the great man and was very impressed. He went back to America and started Scouts there. And that's how America got Boy Scouts only one year after Great Britain.

During the Wembley Jamboree our leaders thought we should see a bit of London so we were taken on a bit of a tour of the capital. We had tea in Lyon's Corner House but there was no room for the whole group to go in one block so we took two here and two there wherever there was a place. So my cousin Leask and I had a job ordering what we wanted but eventually we got tea with sandwiches and then some cakes. That was fine but when it came to paying the bill the Cockney waitress had no idea what these two

Buchan boys were saying in the doric about what they had had to eat. Nor did she understand when we asked for 'the bill'. "Oh, do you mean the check?" We didna know we were going to get a cheque but eventually we got her to understand that we had had sandwiches and then my cousin Leask said, "and twa funcies." This completely staggered the girl, she didn't know what "twa funcies" were; two fruit cakes or something of that order. Eventually we got our bill and we paid but we were not the only two with difficulty of ordering and getting the accounts settled. Three Scout Masters had to go and order and pay for the boys because the waitresses had no idea of what they were saying.

The progression in the Scout movement is that you start by taking the famous promise, and then you're a Tenderfoot. Then you set about acquiring various badges for doing things. After you get a certain number of badges you become a Second-Class Scout. One of my first was the cooking badge which was represented on your sleeve by a brander and there was a camping badge and a reader's badge which was very easy for me as I was very fond of reading.

The Scouts are organised in troops which were divided into patrols of seven boys with a Patrol Leader and a Second. It was a great honour to be advanced to a Second and then to be a Patrol Leader and you were all involved in the game of each one helping the other. The Second Class chaps helping the Tenderfoots to get that and the First Class helping the Second Class to become First Class. Ultimately you could become a King's Scout if you did various other things like camping alone for three weekends and doing a fourteen mile hike. There weren't any King's Scouts in our troop but Alec Giles and I decided to do the King's Scout hike, and not for just fourteen miles. My father happened to be going to Kirriemuir to look at a farm down there and he took us with him. From there we walked home via Braemar. We even climbed the hills which took our fancy on the way and the whole thing was quite an experience. But it was about a hundred miles and I decided that I would never walk again, though we did enjoy it until the very last day.

We were walking home from Ballater when the rain came on and we decided that we wouldn't camp the night. We'd just walk on rather than set up camp in the wet. But when we got to Culter we were exhausted and soaking so in the dark we crept into a field which we thought would be suitable. But when we felt around it turned out to be a field of cabbages so we moved onto the next field which thankfully turned out to be grass. There by the light of a torch with the battery going done we set up camp and fell asleep. At six o'clock in the morning an angry voice brought us out of our tent. What the hell were we doing here and who gave us permission to camp? Usually by mentioning my father's name I could get out of such scrapes but this man didn't care about my father and still wondered what the devil we were doing in his field and whatever we were doing to stop it and get out. So we had to pack up and walk home. But when we got to Aberdeen we decided with the last of our money we would take the Kerr's bus back to Tarves.

Some of this training was very good experience. It gave me a love for the hills and the open air and when I got a motor bike when I was sixteen I used to set off and climb a hill or two for the weekend. Sometimes I went alone and sometimes with Alec Giles who was a great pal. He didn't have a motorbike but there was always the pillion seat. But if you take a chap on the pillion seat and the camping gear for two the motorbike becomes a little overcrowded. However it was a lot of fun and I can recommend the Scouts.

Along with running the troop at Daviot, I became the Training Commissioner for Aberdeenshire so we had boys, particularly the Leaders and Seconds, come to the camp at Daviot for various training weekends. I always had to think of something exciting to do so that they would want to come. We'd had various County Commissioners from Lord Glentanner, Sir Ian Forbes-Leith and then Dr Stephen. He died in Kennoway's Restaurant when we were giving him his presentation to commemorate his many years of Scouting. He was giving his reply when he dropped down dead. That was rather alarming for his friends and for his poor wife. He'd been a bachelor, largely because he'd been a sufferer from tuberculosis and thought that he shouldn't marry. However he'd got cured and had married the matron of the maternity hospital which they ran at Haddo House during the war and where he had to visit in a professional capacity.

On Dr Stephen's death, Hunter Will, an Aberdeen school teacher, succeeded him, and when he died I became the County Commissioner. I gave up altogether in 1965 after about six years in the job and forty-three years of Scouting.

Looking back I still think the Boy Scouts is a wonderful movement. Of course I didn't join at the age of ten and a half to become a wonderful citizen. I joined to have fun and good Scout Masters realised that. If you had a good leader you had a lot of fun. And in the meantime they had got you interested in making things with ropes, camping, map-reading and in enjoying the countryside. I did all those things and I think it made a better man of me. All the time I was still impressed, as I think most of the other boys were, with the promise we had made at the age of eleven or ten... to do our best. And without wishing to seem too much of a prig, I think many boys learned to do their best through having to do their best in their Scouting days. I still cannot persist in a lie told for fun in the face of the challenge, "Scout's honour?"

You had to do your best in attendance, punctuality, in helping the rest of the troop to make progress, and being proud of your patrol and proud of your troop. It was great to be able to put up another badge on your sleeve.

There was always a great competition each year to see which troop would win the county flag. Methlick usually won that and I remember very keenly the year when I was Patrol Leader and we lost. We were camping at Denmore near Aberdeen. On the Sunday when we were packing up ready for final inspection at three o'clock it was pouring rain so I kept the boys inside packing their own belongings until the last minute. Then, in the last twenty minutes and with great efficiency, we took down our tent, rolling it, not packing it as it was wet, and tidying the site just in time for three o'clock.

I lost points because I didn't start soon enough. I was fifteen then and it was an enormous disappointment to me. However when I went back to Scouting and was the Scout Master at Daviot it was a great delight when Daviot won the county flag twice.

CHAPTER SIX

Aberdeen University

I LEFT the Grammar School. My father was very keen that all six of us go to the University. Of course, agriculture students had to start with a year's practical work on the farm. Now by this time my brother John had been taken away from school to be grieve at Little Ardo in Methlick and I was sent to do my year's practical with him.

My father had gone against his own rules and taken John away from school before he had a chance to get to a University. The grieve at Little Ardo had gone drunk and disorderly and had left without notice. So my father asked William Cumming, then grieve at Westertown of Rothienorman, if he knew where he would get a replacement. He said, "You've a grand grieve in Aberdeen. Tak him awa fae the school and mak him grieve at Little Ardo."

It was a great mistake. The old man regretted it and so did my brother John. Anyway he was my grieve when I went to do my year's practical. John expected me to be in the stable at six o'clock every morning to get my orders with the rest of the men. It was easy for John to tell me what to do for every day in the winter time, "Mike, ging and pu neeps." I must confess I didn't care much for puin neeps but I became an absolute expert at it and could keep up with anybody. Ah well, about half past nine the cattleman would have finished doing his cattle in the byre and came out to do an hour and a half's pulling turnips with me. On one occasion when he joined me, as was the tradition, I left my drill and took my place a step behind him... as the loon I was properly behind the cattleman. So by way of making conversation I said, "Caal on the han's this mornin Geordie."

"Well dinna hudd them sae lang," came the somewhat ungracious reply. It really was a bit unfair for I was easily keeping up with him so I couldn't have been holding them any longer than Geordie was.

But much earlier when I was a smaller boy we'd had a lot of turnips left in the field on the first of April. Now, my father had been persuaded by the famous lecturer in Aberdeen, William Findlay, that if you didn't get the oat crop in by the first of April you would lose a bushel per acre per day so there was a terrible hash on to get the fields cleared and the clean land oats in. I was coming after the second cattleman. I've forgotten his name but I'll never forget his kindness. I was having a hellova job keeping up with the men. And he kept glancing back and whenever he saw me falling a bit behind he lent over into my drill and pulled two or three of my turnips so I was able to keep up. And I've never forgotten his kindness, for he stopped me being ashamed. Nice man. But then we had a lot of nice men.

We were well looked after at Little Ardo by Mrs Emslie who was the orraman's wife and they lived in the back of the house. Anyway John, having given orders to the men at six, left to go to his classes at the University at nine o'clock by motorbike. Sometimes he would come home for lunch and one time I remember there was a whole tin of pears along with the enormous dish of semolina. I took my share and ate it with plenty semolina. Then I looked at the dish and said to myself, "Oh John will never miss one more pear." Then, the devil prompting, I decided he would never ken if I had two more. After I had eaten that I decided that John was just bound to ken, so I ate the lot and John never knew that there had been pears. I hope he won't be too angry when he reads this.

I don't know if the year's practical did me any good or not but I worked hard at the game and in due course I went to the University. I think, at seventeen, I was still too young for the University even after the year's practical.

Certainly I didn't enjoy the first year much. It didn't seem to be much connected with agriculture. The atomic theory didn't seem to me to be much to do with farming and the chemistry didn't have much relevance either so far as I could see. I did like Zoology and I think it was because we had a wonderful lecturer, Professor J Arthur Thomson. He could take a joke and make one. One of his lecturing ploys was to have a lot of specimens on the desk in front of him and he would call you down to give your opinions on them or show your ignorance. On one occasion it was bugs of various kinds and we managed to get a very lifelike toy beetle in amongst them. The professor lifted one up and said it was a May-bug and another was a Wood-bug and then "Aha! And this one is a Humbug." I was in his class when Arthur Thomson was knighted and there was a full house to greet Sir Arthur. He expressed surprise at the big turnout and said, "Is something wrong?" There was some laughter and off he went with the lecture as usual. We became more and more restive but he was only teasing us. After a few minutes he said, "that is the end of the lecture for today," and left to applause.

But Botany was terrible, for it was at eight o'clock in the morning. I used to come in by motorbike and if you were late they locked the door and if you didn't get enough attendances you didn't get the "sign-up" which you needed to be allowed to sit the exams. So that class was very unpopular. The poor lecturer didn't like agricultural students and we didn't like him so this led to lots of silly situations. On one occasion when we were being told about sports... plants which behave abnormally... Scampie Duncan and I carefully prepared a daffodil with two heads all ingeniously glued together and we asked Professor Craib if this would be a sport.

He thought it most interesting and started to examine the daffodils closely. Too closely in fact for unfortunately the glue came unstuck when we were still there. That made us even less popular.

Anyway, I thought I had done well enough in the Botany exam at the end of the year but Professor Craib failed me in the practical test. That would have been very awkward as in those days you weren't allowed to proceed to the second year until you had passed all four first year subjects. So I made history because my uncle John who was the chairman of the College of Agriculture, went to the top at the University and the College agreed that this was unfair and so I was allowed to proceed to the second year and to do the resit along with the second year's exams.

One of the demonstrators at the Botany Department came round to my digs one day and said, "I think an attempt will be made to fail you unless you make an awful good job of your practical this time." He'd brought with him a lot of the slides from the department. He said, "It's very likely that the exam will be on some of these slides so if you can get hold of a microscope and be sure you know all about these slides." And the night before the exam he came round to my digs again and he said, "I thought you would just like to know that the professor sent me down to the Dee to bring back samples of this and that and you just might be asked about them."

So if ever I made a hundred per-cent in an exam that was it. However I sat the exam and was certain I had done well. But the professor came round to tell those who would be required for an oral (being doubtful) and to my astonishment he said to me, "You'll come at three o'clock."

That meant I had to sit for another hour wondering whether I had passed or not. At three o'clock other people went in and had their oral and came out. At four o'clock the Professor came out and said, "You can go." And even then I didn't know whether I had passed or not. But I had passed and I don't know if victory went to him or to me but he did make me sweat a bit.

Having passed the first year's stupid course for agriculture students I started to enjoy the University. I was in digs with a medical student and I had another medical student round the corner. I went with them occasionally 'down the drain'. That was their picturesque name for the place in the pathology department where they kept the human bodies for dissection.

That contact with the medics made me think I would like to switch to medicine and become a surgeon and

67

spelled this out to my father. He said, "Well now, there are three more behind you coming to the University and I don't think we can afford to keep you studying for five years. You've got a job waiting for you and I think you should finish what you've started. In any case I think you'll like being a farmer." So I said, "OK". By the time I had done my three years I was enjoying the University more and more and I came again to my father and said that if I did one more year I could get an MA and that that would be a great advantage. My father could see no advantage so I got the same reply as before.

I was lucky to be at the College when the great man W J Profeit was teaching the principles of agriculture and the funny thing about Profeit was that he was very, very deaf but he could hear on the telephone and he could hear in my father's car. The vibrations of the car seemed to do something to his ears so he could hear fine there. He was a great lecturer. Just after the First World War, Lloyd George had the idea that the returning heroes should be blessed with three acres and a cow. Now, on this occasion my father had a big demonstration of something or another at Westertown and a great gathering of people. There's a nice bit of land between Westertown and Eastertown and they were standing in a field of grass looking round and all the assembled party decided, "I'll have my three acres and keep my cow in this field." Everybody had claimed three acres until the field had gone. But Profeit had not yet spoken and my father said to him, "Profeit, are you not going to have three acres and a cow?"

And Profeit said, "I'll have my three acres here too but I'll keep a bull."

Another great man during my time at the College was William Findlay, who taught us all about grass seed mixtures. He had completely altered the business of sowing grass seeds. Where at one time they would have sown as much as a bushel of grass seed per acre, a lot of it home grown and not very good, rye grass and cocksfoot and what not, he produced the 'College Mixture' which was twelve pounds of rye grass, four pounds of cocksfoot, two kinds of red clovers and half a pounds of wild white clover for which he was a great proponent. My father was one of the first to take up the wild white clover and he had a little bit on the very top of the hill at Westertown and Mr Cumming, the manager, put a white stone at its edge. They placed another stone at its edge each year to show how far the clover had moved. That was one of the best demonstations of how the clover would spread. Of course, the funny thing was that the wild white clover did too much for the fields and when we sowed oats, there was so much nitrogen in the ground that the following oat crop went flat. Findlay never pronounced until he had done things in triplicate, three years in succession. He was a very careful man. He was driving in the car with my father past Douglas Fowlie's sheep early in June and my father looked at the sheep and said to Findlay "Douglas Fowlie has got his ewes clipped." Mr Findlay didn't say anything until he came to the end of the field then he turned to my father and said, "Well, this side anyway."

Findlay was so popular that when he retired the present and former students gathered in the students' union to give him a present of a television set and a cheque. The presentation was made by Dr Caie, of the Department of Agriculture, who was a very clever chap and had written some rather good Scottish poetry. In making the presentation he said, "We know he's retired but we know he'll never stop working and that he's doing all sorts of experiments still. But Old Father Time will come along with his scythe and he'll be forced to retire from work in this world, although mind you I can see him walking round the celestial pastures looking carefully to see how he could grow more angels to the acre." In reply Findlay forgot to say thank you to begin with but gave us a long lecture on the proper grass seed which we had all heard interminably in his classes for many years. There was a bit of shuffling of feet and some coughing until even Findlay began to realise that he did not have the full attention of his audience. He said, "Oh well, I ought to say thank you, very nice of you although it is true that I have continued to work. I've always had an interest in wild oats and now since I have retired I have been sowing them." Roars of laughter from the gathered students and ex-students which Findlay did not understand having a very sparse sense of humour. He then proceeded to say, "I have found it much more interesting than I thought, I've even got results back from Bulgaria." More, even happier laughter.

I would have liked to stay on at the University but accepted my father's decision with no regrets. I've never had time for regrets. I became a BSc with no tremendous sense of achievement and looked forward to my first real job, as grieve at my father's outfarm of Thomastown, just outside Huntly.

CHAPTER SEVEN

Grieve at Thomastown

THERE WAS no question in those days of a sabbatical year after you had finished at the University. No nonsense about going off to see the world for a while. I took my parents to my graduation in the car I had just bought for three pounds. It was a 1924 Morris Oxford with a Hotchkiss engine which, had I kept it till today, would have given me a good return on my three pounds. After the ceremony they took me to lunch at the Palace Hotel. In those days you could leave your car where you liked so I parked the old heap at the door. After the meal I was dispatched to Westertown of Rothienorman where William Cumming, who was now my father's manager, was waiting for me. He was to be my mentor while I learned to be a grieve.

Mr Cumming gave me a tour of Westertown before high tea and then it was away to my first real job. We set off to drive the fifteen miles, he in his Bayliss-Thomas car (one of very few made in Britain and sold to my father for his manager by Neil Ross of Ellon) and me in my three pound Morris Oxford. We went up to the farm where a bed was prepared for me in the box room off the front room. Incidentally my first bed was a chaff bed. The chaff was renewed at the visit of the steam mill. The first night of the new chaff I was awakened by a mouse which had been sewn in as well. I had a tremendous job getting the mouse down to one corner where, like my father with the rat, I squeezed it to death. I suppose it must have rotted quietly away.

We then went in to the dairy where I was initiated in to the mysteries of what had to be done at four o'clock the next morning. There were all sorts of things that are quite out of date now... there were various milk cans with brass nameplates on them... Lockharts the woodmerchants in Huntly and the Stewarts, they were the lawyers... they each had their own special can. We had just started bottling but we had no machine for that. A girl washed up to the elbows and then dipped two bottles into a pail of milk until it gurgled to the top and then put the bottles into another pail to wash the surface milk off, placed a disc into the top and that was it. Bottles weren't very popular but the Stewarts of Cocklarachy, one of our rivals, had started them so we had to put some in bottles too.

Most of the milk was sold by roundsmen with horsedrawn carts out of fifteen gallon cans with a tap at the back. And then there were various thicknesses of cream to be prepared so all that had to be noted on the backs of postcards. And that has been a habit of mine all my life to carry postcards and write my notes on them. Any speech I have made has always been off little notes on the backs of postcards.

Ah well, it was after ten o'clock on my graduation day, I went in to the house and Mr Cumming went back to Westertown. I had bought a new alarm and I set it for half past three and went to bed. But I couldn't get to sleep for thinking about all the things I had to do the next morning. Eventually I got to sleep and woke at six o'clock and I think I would have shot myself but I didn't have a gun. I dressed and went out and there to my surprise and delight, sitting in the close, was Mr Cumming's Bayliss–Thomas... into the dairy I went, apologising profusely, but all the work was done. Mr Cumming said, 'You've just time to go round to the stable and yoke the men".

"What'll I tell them to do?"

"Just tell them 'aa you Billies gang tae the neeps'." (It was hoeing time so that did fine).

Then my saviour said, "We'll go and have wir breakfast." So we went in.

I said, "Mr Cumming, what made you think of coming up this morning?"

Although nearly everybody called me Mike he always called me "Metland". He said, "Well Metland. On the way home I just thocht 'now he'll lie there and he winna fa asleep. He'll be thinkin aboot aa he has tae dae and he'll never hear that alarm clock so I'll just go up for his first mornin.'" And although I thought a lot of Mr Cumming before I thought even more of him after that.

He was a splendid teacher. One of the best remarks he ever made to me was in my first harvest. It was a very bad harvest of pouring rains. It had dried up on this particular morning but when I went to see if the stooks were dry enough to lead I was satisfied that they were not. We had turned the stooks and turned the stooks and pulled them over so their bottoms could get the benefit of any drying wind and then set them up again until we were heartily scunnered. So when Mr Cumming arrived the men were scraping dubs from the close which was a constant worry in those days before cement and tarmac closes. "Now, that's tidy-like," said Mr Cumming, "But what about the stuffy?" I assured him that I had just been up to the field and that it wouldn't lead.

"Well now, what like a plan would it be if we went up and had another look?" So we went up and had another look. He thrust an expert hand into every sheaf in many of the stooks and finally said, "You'll get one sheaf in the south-west side of every stook." I thought in horror of taking one sheaf and having all the stooks fall down and having to build them up again with an odd number of sheaves in each heap but I did as I was told and yoked the men to take one sheaf per stook.

By this time I built the rucks despite being rather young for the job. The trick in building was to keep the heart of the ruck up so that the water would run off it and I became good at it. So I had to wait in the cornyard for the first load. Mr Cumming who was waiting with me said, "You see Metland, you'll never tak the rent oot o' the close."

Mr Cumming was a great man and a very loyal

vant to my father and he told me many fine stories. Like when he was grieve to Sandy Wishart who had many farms in Aberdeenshire. He was very young to be a grieve but he was not green. He was having a thrash and Mr Wishart had sold the corn to the local oatmeal miller. The miller had been told to send up his sacks. He came up with them himself and he handed over to Mr Cumming a one pound weight and said, "You understand that you roll up a sack and put it on the other side of the steelyard to make up for the sack that the grain is in to make sure the miller gets fair weight. Ah well, just to make sure that we've got fair weight roll this weight in the bag."

"Oh, that's the way you do it is it?" said Mr Cumming.

So, the next day the first load went off from the steam-mill down to the miller. In the shortest possible time the miller was back up. "Laddie, did ye mind about pittin' the poun weight into the bag?"

"Aye."

"And did ye dae it."

"Well, no. Mr Wishart was inbye last night and I asked him if it would be all right and he said 'no.'" That was a great shock to the miller who thought he might have lost a good customer and lost him for good.

William Cumming was a very honest man. Later, when he came to buy cattle for my father, the dealers used to give him luck-pennies in the hope that he would give them higher prices. If he thought he had beaten them down as far as he could he used to ask a luck-penny. Then, when he saw my father, he would hand over every penny of the luck money. Not many managers would have done that.

Later on when I became engaged to be married I was going to do up the house at Thomastown. We needed a bathroom for one thing as all we had was a single holer in a little shed in the corner of the garden. Fortunately the or-raman got to empty the pail. Mr Cumming decided he would retire then and he said to my father, "It's a waste of money doing up the house at Thomastown. I've bought a house in Oldmeldrum and Mike'll just come and farm at

Westertown instead of me.

My father said, "Well you'll just sell the house and we'll buy another farm for you." So they bought Drum farm at Newburgh for Mr Cumming which he farmed well until he was well over eighty. When he moved to Newburgh his wife thought it was time he learned to play bridge. He could of course play whist as all country folk could but bridge was to be a refinement. So my wife and I went down to help with the learning. But the game of bridge had to be abandoned because at every possible moment Mr Cumming would say "And how's that cow doing in the third stall... and has that drain that we mended ever burst again?"

Eventually Mrs Cumming gave up and said, "You two talk about the farm and we'll talk about something else."

He was a marvellous man who loved the land and I was very grateful for all the advice I got from Mr Cumming. He was something of a genius but he was not infallible. I was most amused to find him one day working hard to bend a staple in such a way that it could be used to take the valve out of a pneumatic tyre. I took a certain smug pride in the novelty of explaining something to him; that if you turned the valve-cap upside down you had a custom made tool for the job.

At Thomastown when I started there were seventy cows and two cattlemen looked after them and their follow- ers, that was a lot because most cattlemen thought they had a job looking after maybe thirty to thirty-five cows without the followers. They were all hand-milked when I started which meant we had to have seven milkers. The cattlemen milked, my housekeeper was a very good milker, the fore- man's wife and the orraman's wife and the cattlemen's wives also milked. I was a reserve milker.

My father thought I was grossly overpaid at eighty pounds a year and when you consider that the foreman, who was a first class single man, had twenty pounds for his first six months, maybe I was. For I was 'all found'. I had a house, a housekeeper, my food and I got something to- wards the running of my car. We gave the foreman a rise to twenty two pounds for his second half year and he was very pleased to stay for that because wages were falling at the time.

I was very proud, all the same, that I never had a married man on less than £52 pounds a year. That seems like a wage you couldn't live on but the married men did have their perquisites which at that time were four pints of milk a day, three bolls and a firlot of meal every six months, (a boll is 140 lbs and a firlot is half a boll) half a tonne of coal for a year. The men were fee-ed for a year from May and the single men left at both terms unless they were 'speered' to stay on. It was a bad, bad system.

Much later my father had seven married men at North Ythsie and they were all being asked to stay and one of the men hadn't been available and it was a week before my father got time to go over to the double cottar house where the two cattlemen lived. When he got there he found that one was digging his garden and the other was leaning disconsolately across his dyke not knowing whether he would be there to reap the fruits of this year's gardening. My father said, "Aye Geordie. It's wearin the way of the term..."

Like a shot Geordie said, "Oh, I think I will." And then he grabbed the spade and got on with his garden.

It was a terrible system especially when wages were falling. My father had an excellent orraman called Crawford, a veteran of the first world war, who kept a wonderful diary of his experiences which he once showed me. Anyway, my father thought he was being generous taking the wages down only one pound when everyone else was coming down two pounds. Crawford would not stay. "I'll bide for what I have but nae for less." Eventually he left and had to settle for four pounds less but he was a proud man and he had made his point.

Among my first projects at Thomastown was the building of two cottages at the farm and in that I was following in my father's footsteps. After the first war he had built four cottages at North Ythsie. He got a subsidy from the government of £100, the timber from the laird and did the work himself. When the laird came to see the new cottar houses my father said to him, "Lord Aberdeen, who do you think owns these houses? I have done a hundred pounds worth of work on them, you have put up a hundred pounds worth including the ground and the timber and we've had a hundred pounds worth of subsidy from the government.'

"Well," said Lord Aberdeen, "we can score the government out for a start."

So I felt I was walking in a family tradition with my two new cottages at Thomastown. They were a great boon because they meant I had another two wives to help with the milking or for other work in the dairy. I later built a third cottage as a hostel for single men because we were expanding. We doubled the byre. I thought the laird should pay for that but he said, "No. This was not let as a dairy farm. If you want an extra byre you can build it yourself." So we did and there was no government taking a third share then either. We were eventually milking eighty or ninety cows but by that time we had installed a milking machine. In that I cannot claim to have been a pioneer for I went to Bob Anderson of Acharney at Forgue to see his Alfa-Laval and bought one for Thomastown in 1933. That was how innovations spread in those days. One farmer went to see a working innovation and then copied. Farmers as a breed are very cooperative about that sort of thing but I may have gone further than most with Tom Robertson of Pirriesmill. He was one of my rivals in the retail trade at Thomastown. I had moved to Westertown by the time he phoned to ask if he could see my milking machine. I said that he was very welcome and that he could just go down to Thomastown and have a look whenever he wanted to. Oh, but no. He wanted to come and see the setup at Westertown. Well I told him that again that would be all right. "But would you come and get me?" So I went up to Pirriesmill for him, a trip of some twenty miles, showed him round, gave him his lunch and drove him home. I don't remember him saying, "Thank-you".

The expansion of the milk retailing business was interesting because Thomastown was the first of my father's farms to have milking cows on it. He had taken the farm from the Drumuir estate in 1915. By the time I got there in

1932 they were already retailing about a hundred gallons of milk a day in Huntly. We had a roundsman called Cantlay when I arrived and he took these fifteen gallon cans on the back of his cart. In filling the housewives jugs he must have been an expert at selling them a bit of froth on the top or putting his thumb in the top of the jug, for he managed to return the cash for very nearly the whole amount of milk he set off with. Milk was sold at thrupence a pint and when he had a square-up he had almost two shillings for every gallon that left the place. Unfortunately Cantlay had a row with the grieve and I never got near to the two shillings a gallon again. If I got one and ten pence that was about the best I could do. Not only that, I had to employ two men to do Cantlay's work for no other one man could do it.

However, as soon as we could, we stopped the cans and went on to bottles and that made it easier to be sure that we got paid for the milk that went out. Most people paid weekly. The men took a bit longer to go round on a Friday and a Saturday and that was when most people paid. But some of the so-called rich people thought they couldn't be bothered paying such small bills weekly and they had to get accounts. One of them, a well known family in Huntly, had been quite a few months and they hadn't paid and I had the temerity to send them a begging letter. Immediately I had a very angry man on the telephone. Any more nonsense like that and he would tell my father that I didn't realise that he always paid his milk "in the end of the day". I had to say that I really couldn't wait for the end of the day so would he please pay my account and also write my father who would be most amused. So I got my cheque and we kept his business because we gave the best service. When I went to Thomastown there were thirteen firms retailing milk into Huntly. By the time I left there were only two. Now there is only one and that is my son.

Those were the bad times of the thirties. And among the six farms that my father by this time had, the one which consistently made the best profit was Thomastown. It was the worst farm by a long way but it had this retail milk business. There weren't many pounds about but we were getting as near to the housewife's pound as possible. In those days, when the milk boards were just being started, anybody who was far from the market got ridiculously little for their milk. One man I spoke to in Huntly when I was canvassing for something many years later told me that he remembered having to sell his milk for four pence a gallon. Well, we were getting six times that. The milk boards were formed to give the farmers who were far from the market some protection.

Anyway my father could see that dairying was the steadiest business we were in and he eventually replaced all his livestock with the dairy cow. First, it spread to Westertown. Then to Eastertown next door. Then to the home farm of North Ythsie and then to Little Ardo. Even Bent of Laurencekirk, where my brother John was farming one of the finest farm in the Mearns, got a dairy. He was persuaded to put in a milking parlour. It was almost like keeping hens down there... it was considered infra-dig to have to keep cows for a living but my father never thought it was infra-dig as long as there was a bit of profit to it. And the Bent soon had hens as well.

Although we were not the first to sell attested milk our Thomastown herd was the first to be completely tuberculin tested. It was announced that we were only the second to have a whole herd attested the first being Her Majesty the Queen. My father said it was quite right that we should take second place to Her Majesty who had four cows at Balmoral whereas we had seventy.

As the business developed at Thomastown we started to retail milk at Keith and that was a chancy business as it was a stormy area and we often had a terrible job in winter getting the milk up to Keith. But even with that we still had a surplus so we used to send milk by train to Aberdeen to a man who retailed it for us. When it became a little difficult to control this man I bought a small business at the foot of Albert Street called Peters' Dairy from old Mr Peters whose two sons were retailing about fifty gallons of milk from horse carts. The sons refused to work for me but there were plenty of men about in 1935.

I took the milk to the station on a little cart on the back of my car and became very good at reversing. It used to be considered very expert to be able to reverse a tractor and cart and I became very quick at getting my trailer in about to the station. I was doing that one day when a man who had been watching me came over and said, "Would you teach me how to do that. I have a caravan and I can never back the caravan into anywhere." So I gave him a lesson but whether he was then able to reverse the caravan I never found out.

The Aberdeen business started to use up more milk than Thomastown could produce so we started to produce milk at Westertown. The retail business then grew fairly quickly. We were soon bottling four hundred gallons of milk a day on the farm and this was uneconomic. What was needed was a bottling plant in Aberdeen.

Now James Keith was in fact the first to sell tuberculin tested milk from his "Aberdeen Dairies" and he was also selling about four hundred gallons a day. His premises in Leadside Road were just what we needed for our bottling plant. So I told my father to tell his friend James Keith that if he ever wanted to sell Leadside Road that we would buy it. And one day about the beginning of the war my father got a message to me that Major Keith was tired of the milk business and would sell. So I went down to Pitmedden House to see Major Keith. He was having one of the days-in-bed he had between running his Aberdeenshire and his Norfolk farms. After a little chit-chat I said, "I hear you're willing to sell your dairy in Aberdeen. How much would you like for it?" He immediately quoted me a price which was very reasonable but, in the good old-fashioned Aberdeenshire way, I offered him a thousand pounds less.

Now, Major Keith was a somewhat fiery man and he took offence. He sat up in bed and said, "You're just a damned fool. You don't know when you've got a bargain. I'll just advertise it for sale to the highest bidder."

"Well just you do that Major Keith," said I, somewhat raised myself, "I was only doing what you'd have done yourself as a young man." With that I left in high dudgeon.

Going down the stairs I realised what a fool I'd been. I quickly phoned my father and told him to for goodness sake phone Major Keith and apologise and offer to give him his price. Ten minutes later my father phoned back and said, that he'd been too late. Keith had phoned him first, apologised and offered him the dairy at my price. So I saved a thousand pounds.

My father was a very tolerant and understanding man. That is well illustrated by the time when I had been courting in Aberdeen, had fallen asleep at the wheel of my three pound Morris Oxford and knocked down a lamp-post at two o'clock in the morning. This was only a few yards from the police station. Almost immediately I was surrounded by people some in their pyjamas or night gowns anxious to see the crash. There was a horrible sound of gas escaping and this chap was agitating that there was going to be an explosion. "Well," I said, "If you think there is going to be an explosion go into your house and bring me the cork from your cough mixture bottle - I hear you have a cough." He dutifully produced a cork and with that I was able to stop the leak. Another man kept repeating the number of the car as though I was about to escape. As the stub of the lamp-post had torn the sump of the car right off there was little chance of that.

I then went along to the police station to report what had happened. The policeman kindly said, "At least yer nae drunk." And he was right. He asked how I would get home. I said, "Oh, I'll go back to the station and get the milk train to Huntly."

"Oh well," says he, "you'd better tak my bike. Jist leave it at the station and I'll pick it up." I thought that a very kindly gesture.

So I duly caught the train and got back to Thomastown just before five when I was due to be bottling milk. To my horror my father's car was there in the close. He had come to see me and had gone to bed when it was obvious that I wasn't going to be home early. So when I got in from bottling the milk to get my breakfast he was up and dressed. He never said a word of reproof.

I did get a new sump for the Morris Oxford though that cost far more than the three pounds I had paid for her.

CHAPTER EIGHT

Marriage to Miss Ross

I SHOULD also tell you what a lucky chap I was to fall in love with the local school teacher at Drumblade, and maybe luckier still to get her to marry me. She was a Miss Isobel Ross and everyone called her Miss Ross, as they did in those days. There was a lot of competition for Miss Ross and indeed first in that competition was a minister called Horace, to whom she was engaged. I discovered that she was not desperately enamoured with Horace and felt the way was clear to pursue my case. This led to a great scene at the Palais de Dance in Diamond Street, Aberdeen. I was dancing with Miss Ross, when Horace turned up demanding, in a bucolic manner, that she leave at once. Horace and I were almost coming to blows when the good Miss Ross pulled off her engagement ring and flung it from the balcony down on to the dance floor. That did the trick because Horace, being a good Aberdonian, quickly disappeared down to the dance floor to recover his ring and we never saw him again. Somebody had found the ring and given it back to him, and he then disappeared.

My courtship caused some astonishment in the Parish of Drumblade because I succeeded in being accepted by her landlord, who was a retired Chief of Police and tended to scare the young men off. They used to say if you go near Miss Ross he'll take the gun to you. But he never took the gun to me. In fact he gave me my first Rolex watch one Christmas and we became great friends. So he kept the competition away and I got a free hand with Isobel.

One of the curious traditions of the countryside is that the bridegroom has to have his feet washed by his friends prior to his wedding. You might think that that was a good thing to do but feet washing normally meant blackening the feet and doing dreadful things to his feet and indeed to the rest of his body. The event was preceded by a great deal of drink taken and usually involved a good deal of high jinks. The potential groom was expected to put up a fight to add to the fun but on the whole most of the young men agreed that if you were to be properly married you should have your feet washed. So, as my wedding to Miss Ross approached, the lads laid plans to blacken me. Somehow they found out that I was to visit my future mother-in-law at Milltimber where she lived with her second husband and they came and caught me there. Mrs Summer's house being a small bungalow, they decided to take me to Culter to the house of Dr Macleod whose wife was a cousin of my father's. Unfortunately when they were carrying me in to Dr Macleod's house I was struggling so hard and I hit my head on the gate-post and was knocked out briefly. On my wedding day my face was still showing the bruises of that accident so I spent the day trying to ensure that the left side of my face wasn't in any of the photographs.

Despite my injuries I was pleased to have my feet washed and I would have felt there was something wrong if they hadn't been. But everyone didn't feel that way. My brother, now Lord John-Mackie, was very much against having his feet washed and let that be known in no uncertain terms. The young bloods from the Howe of the Mearns, where he was farming, could not get hold of him and asked me to trap my brother. That I agreed to do and invited him to our milk bottling plant in Aberdeen to talk business. We had not been met long when the lads from the Mearns arrived and John knew immediately what was up and he was not amused. In a fury he ran into the dairy and got behind a stack of milk bottles and kept us at bay for a long time by hurling these bottles at us. However I eventually got him round the neck and in a dreadful and bitter melee the deed was done. My father, wise man that he was, had slipped quietly across the road and bought a bottle of whisky and produced this in the hope that we would all have a drink and make up. John did calm down enough to have a drink but then went home in a bad humour which lasted for some time. I am not certain that he ever fully forgave us. He was a more serious man than the rest of us and, no doubt quite rightly, thought it was a barbarous way to behave. But it was one of our traditions and we would have thought we had failed in our duty to my brother had he been allowed to get married without a feet washing.

I can remember two other special feet washings in our family. The first was my uncle Bruce Mackie of Milton of Noth who, because he was of my grandfather's second marriage, was ages with me. He was marrying Barry Stephen of Conglass. We had some difficulty in catching Bruce because he heard we were coming and only on the third day did we succeed in getting hold of him... two days before his wedding. It was an uproarious occasion in which we finished up dashing after each other in the house at Milton of Noth until the maid arrived home and she swept us all out of the house. So there we were, standing outside the house with the lights from two cars shining to give us light and drinking the health of the bridegroom. He was meantime washing the black lead off his feet and elsewhere in the bathroom which was directly above the front door. He, looking out, saw the opportunity to get a little bit of his own back and threw out some scalding hot water onto the assembled rioters. That started the melee all over again.

One of the most uproarious of the crowd was the bride's brother James Stephen. Eventually to cool him down he had to be carried through the garden and behind the garden wall to the horse trough. He was immersed totally in that with his face held down until he gurgled a bit and that seemed to stop his exuberance. Eventually about four in the morning, we set off for home. I was driven by the auctioneer from Huntly, Sandy Yule, and Alan Turnbull of Smithston was also a passenger. When we got to the end of Alan's farm road we stopped to let him off. Then he announced, "Mike, I have a half bottle of whisky left... we'd better just finish it." In for a penny in for a pound, we duly finished the half bottle with a nice set of these little collapsable tumblers and then Alan Turnbull went staggering off down his own road.

Sandy Yule and I set off for home. Not liking the way that Sandy was swinging from one side of the road to the other, I said "Sandy, I think I should drive."

He said, "No, bi moy, I've seen you driving sober." Eventually we got to Thomastown where I was due to start bottling the milk at five and found the cattleman just taking in the cows at about half past four. We looked in the car and found there was just one dram left in one of the bottles so the cattleman got the dram and I bet you it is the one and only time he ever had a dram while taking in the cows at half past four in the morning.

Another memorable footwashing occurred a generation later. My eldest son and namesake met his pals at Meldrum House Hotel in their smart newly done up lounge bar for pre-feetwashing drinks. There was the usual crowd of about twenty all-male friends, cousins, a brother, a brother in law and so on. In those days they didn't have kitties for drinks so it was an enormous round and they were all hurrying the drinks along to make sure that they all got their round in. As closing time approached the party got wilder and wilder. They were dancing on top of the tables and then turning the tables upside down and dancing on top of the glasses thereunderneath. Then one of the my cousins from Milton of Noth had brought sheep dip which was intended for the feetwashing and it came flying across the bar, ruining the new suit of one of the spectators who had gathered to see the Mackies at play. Some of the timider participants then beat a retreat through a window followed by some of the less timid ones who took the curtains with them.

I was at home at this stage and received an urgent call from my friend the proprietor Robin Duff. He had sent for the police and would I like to come and see what my family had done. I was just leaving when the first of the revellers arrived at Westertown and I gave them a piece of my mind before I left. The bar was in an undescribable shambles. Sheep dip up the walls, curtains hanging off, broken glass everywhere. I was staggered. The damage was put at £500 pounds and I eventually paid out a cheque for £172. Fraser Durno, our neighbour at Jackston, arrived shame-facedly the next day with the offer of a cheque and my nephew Charles Allan wrote with a separate offer from Glasgow, but I paid it and forgot about it. The wedding was held in Norway and the culprits had the cheek to send a telegram to Robin Duff which read, "Skol. You should see the bars in Bergen."

The feetwashing then was carried out at Westertown where they were not very popular either. They started throwing water through the house and I remember a pail of water coming shealing down the stairs. The next morning I had to go to Aberdeen and I went in to see that happy groom and I got his feet out over the bed and his head in his hands and he said, "Oh me, never again." I told this to my brother, George, now Lord Mackie of Benshie, and he said about this remark, "Mercy Mike. Wouldn't it be nice to be saying that for the first time." I hadn't realised the irony then that while I didn't have a hangover as such my head had been just as sore after my own feet-washing.

On our honeymoon we went to Taymouth Castle which was then a hotel but later became a miner's rest home. We were there for five days. We spent a night somewhere on the way down and a night somewhere else. I was twenty-three when I got married and I now think it was a good thing to be married young and have the children when you're young and I never regretted marrying young. People said I was too young but I thought not. It was a splendid decision and we had six children.

For some reason they seemed to come in pairs. The oldest two were, Mary and then Maitland (his sister called Maitland "Boy", a nickname that stuck well into his middle age). Those two were great pals. They were playing in the room during the war and their mother heard them saying "You're a bugger Mr Hitler." and the other one then said, "You're a bugger Mr Mussolini." Isobel intervened and told them not to say that because that was a bad word. "But they are bad men." came the surprised retort. It was the start of logical thinking.

After those we had twins that died.
Then there were Elrick and Patty.
And we finished with two darling little girls; Isobel and Ruth.

We sent our two eldest children to school in Aberdeen. My son went to the Grammar School and stayed in the boarding house all week and my daughter went to St Margaret's as a boarder at Culter House. The first four started at private schools but I took Patty, the fourth one, away because I was told that the headmistress of St Margaret's had said of her, "If her father expects her to get her highers he'll have to think again." We took our second son Elrick away from the Grammar School when we heard that he was being bullied, so after that we had our four youngest children at the local school at Inverurie. As a result of better teaching at Inverurie and from coaching by her aunt Jean at Little Ardo, Patty got her highers no bother. Elrick also did well at Inverurie school and got his highers and went to University because, like my father, I wanted all my children to get further education, but like his uncle George before him he enjoyed a year at University and forgot about the work. So Elrick got married and emigrated to Australia. My eldest daughter did an MA with a struggle. For some reason she twice failed Political Economy. One of the reasons she failed the second time was that someone had given her a benzadrine tablet so that she could work through the night to prepare for the exam. I met her for lunch after the exam and she showed me the paper and she told me how she had answered the questions and I told her that she had done very well but you've answered all the wrong questions. I knew she had failed. But the next time she passed with ease. While Mary was struggling out of the University her cousin Charles Allan was trying to get into the University but was short of higher biology and needed four attempts to pass that. It was then that he made the famous remark in our family, "The world's ill-divided Mary. Here's you canna get oot o' the University and I canna get in." But Charles did eventually get in and did very well in Political Economy, funnily enough, Mary got out at the third attempt and became a very good teacher.

The two youngest also went to Inverurie and both did well, largely because Inverurie was a very good school at that time under the very well known and excellent headmaster. Dr Dickson spent all his waking hours thinking about and working for the school. You would get him in his office at half past ten at night still going over his papers. He used to read all the examination papers from class three upwards after the teachers had marked them. If they had done well he would write at the top "please see me" and if it was a bad mark he wrote at the top "see me."

As a result of this not very scientific trial of private schools versus public education I remain convinced that what matters in a school is the headmaster, the way he runs the school and the quality of the teachers.

I also became convinced that the ideologies of teaching didn't matter a lot. We had many outstanding teachers in Aberdeenshire but two in particular can be used to illustrate that point. The authorities were always changing their minds about things, bringing out a new report, changing the guidelines and on this occasion it was announced that the eleven-plus examination was a bad thing and that we shouldn't stream pupils in the secondary but should all do the same courses in the first year. We called all our headmasters of our secondary schools and explained that to them. Dr Dickson of Inverurie said, "I will not do that. I will not put back my ablest students. I'll give them separate attention."

On the other hand the headmaster of Bucksburn school, Henry Scobie, said, "Yes, I will do that. In fact, it's such a good idea that I'll give them a common course for the first two years."

The results were that both sets of pupils did extremely well and that confirmed my view that ideology is not important. It's the personalities.

Suddenly, without warning Isobel had a heart attack and died on the 30th November 1960. She was then fifty and I was just four years younger. That was a disaster. I grat a bit and I was not able at the funeral to greet all the people. We asked if we could hold it in Inverurie because the little church at Daviot would not be big enough and indeed we almost filled the church at Inverurie. There is a tradition that the chief mourner shakes hands with everyone after the funeral. I was to stand at the church door and shake hands with everyone. But after the first few people had passed by with everybody trying to say some words of comfort I said to my son, "Take me out of this." So we left.

But I was able to meet folk at the graveside, but there were fewer people at the graveside and I was kind of steadied by that time. When Jack Henderson's wife, a Stephen from Conglass, died, I went to her Highland funeral. It looked rather sad as his Glengarrie was put on top of her coffin and he stood up at the graveside and made a speech, thanking everyone for coming and saying how much he thought of his wife. At Miss Ross's funeral I could no more have made a speech than fly in the air.

When she was dying I wakened my son Boy, because the doctor thought if we got oxygen, we could perhaps save her and Boy went down to the smiddy, where we had a big oxy-acetylene burner and he carried the oxygen single handed up to the bedroom and we had lots of oxygen. It was quite a feat but it was a hopeless case. It was too late anyway, but it was a valiant try.

It was devastating for the younger children, who could not understand what had happened. But it didn't take me long to get back into gear. As soon as the funeral was over I realised that you can't step off the bus, that the world goes on. First I had to reply to something like 300 letters. She had been a very important lady in her own right. She had sung at Women's Institutes and Women's Guilds and ran the Cubs, trained a local choir to sing and won community competitions. She had been persuaded with a friend to go to Gilwell Park in London to take the Wood Badge and become an Akela (Cub mistress). So I thought the only thing I could do was go with her and help with scrubbing pots and so on, because I had been before and knew how things were done. So I finished up along with her with a Wood Badge for Cubs and indeed I later went back and did the Wood Badge for Rovers as well. But I wasn't so good at that. The first time I went to Gilwell Park was the first time I had ever been in an aeroplane.

But I got a terrible row, because aircraft were not so common in those days and I had not phoned home to say that I had arrived safely. My excuse was that I was busy, because being a new boy at Gilwell Park I was immediately put into a patrol and put into action and there were not so many phones around in those days. At any rate Isobel immediately thought that as I hadn't phoned the plane had crashed and had phoned my father to ask if I had been in touch with him. I then got a telegram to which I responded by phoning home immediately and all was well, but it did teach me a lesson to tell your wife where you are.

Anyway the marriage to Isobel led the great Mr Cumming to retire so that, rather than waste money doing up the house at Thomastown, I could move to Westertown, which, with Eastertown, quadrupled the acreage of which I had charge.

CHAPTER NINE

Farmer at Westertown

I STARTED farming at Thomastown in 1932 which didn't
seem like a good time to start, but on the other hand the
hard times taught me the value of things, how to be quite
economical and to make things pay. It was the retail milk
trade which kept us going more than anything else.

There wasn't a lot of money about. I sold my first
grain crop for sixteen shillings (little more than five pounds
a tonne) and that was a good price at the time. We were
growing black oats which you don't hear much about now.
It was grown mostly because it had a little more oil in the
oat and was liked by Irish horsey people. You got a shilling
more a quarter for it and when oats fell as far as a twelve
shillings a quarter (a quarter = three hundredweights) I
never sold anything at under sixteen shillings and got
seventeen shillings for black oats. Mind you, in those days
you thought you had a very good crop when you grew ten
quarters to the acre. Now you would be very displeased if
you did not get two and a half tonnes of oats. I also grew a
little barley and was very pleased when I got five quarters of
that. Nowadays we expect to grow more than three times as
much. And that difference wasn't just a question of manure. We were already putting on more than most people.
We used to say that some of our neighbours got their
manure through the post, which meant that they didn't use
very much.

Marriage and the move to Westertown meant that in

1935 I gave up being grieve myself and employed grieves
from then on. My first was a splendid workman called
Geordie Thompson. I came along one day and found that
Geordie had not made a good job of putting out the fertil-
iser. It was meant to be 5 hundredweights to the acre.
Some had got 10 hundredweights and some very little. I
was remonstrating with the good Geordie Thompson and
said, "It's awfa simple Geordie you just measure the length
of the field and divide that into 4840 and you will find how
many paces it is to be an acre and you put out the five bags
and you set the machine and if you have used too much you
shut the machine a bit and the next acre will be nearer the
thing and you will soon get up to it."

He said, "If I have to dae a' that you can pit oot the
bloody manure yersel."

I said, "Now come, come. Dinna be like that. We'll
just go and measure the park." So we measured the length
of one side of the park, divided it into 4840, and got the
number of yards for an acre. He suddenly perked up and
said, "God aye, I mine that figure. I learned that at school
but I niver thocht it wid be ony use to me." Next time I was
back at Thomastown (by this time I was living at Westertown) Geordie had every field measured every length and
breadth and knew how many yards it was to the acre. He
was very chuffed with himself having now found a use for
4840 square yards to an acre.

Milk was making two shillings a gallon when I started
in 1932. But then wages were very little in the 1930s and
kept being squeezed down. I never had a married man
who had less than £1 a week plus perks but quite a few
farmers waited until right at the end of the feeing time,
when men were desperate to get a job, and could get them
for as little as forty pounds a year plus the perks. Not
many had to take as little as that, but there were a great
many below fifty.

One of the biggest changes that has taken place was,
of course, the change in rotation. Rotation was sacrosanct
in Aberdeenshire. Either a six or seven course rotation,
which meant three to four years of grass, then oats and
then, if it was a seven, you had maybe yavel oats, which

93

meant you had oats two years in succession. Then turnips, back into oats, finally back to grass and on again. A seven course rotation was the commonest one. There's a nice story about the Crightons, Arthur and John, who were well known for their connection with Rowett Research Institute and College of Agriculture. Their parents had been fifty years married so the two boys would give their parents an evening 'do' to celebrate. They had a nice party and then old Mr Crighton and the man who had been best man at their wedding sat down to have a drink after the jollifica- tions. The best man said, "Tell me. Why did you wait fifty- one years before you celebrated your golden wedding?"

"Na, na. It's jist fifty years. I have my marriage cer- tificate and that says it's just fifty years."

"Ah well then, your marriage certificate is wrang because the year you were married we ploughed the stable parkie oot o' ley and it's in neeps this year and seven sevens are forty-nine and two is fifty-one and that's the length of time you've been married."

On investigation it was discovered that his copy of the marriage certificate was wrong and another certificate was got from the proper registry office in Edinburgh which proved that he had been married for fifty-one years. The reason for the mistake was that, in common with many people at that time, to be really economical, he was married on the last day of the year because New Year's Day was holiday anyway. So as little time as possible was wasted with the honeymoon. When he registered the wedding some time later the registrar was accustomed to the new date and he put the new date on the certificate which Mr Crighton got and took home with him. When he was posting his book up to Edinburgh he noticed the mistake and corrected it. So it just proved that rotation was far more accurate than the registrar in Edinburgh.

My father's friend Sandy Wishart was an interesting man who had more than twenty farms in Aberdeenshire but he had none in England, until one year when he went down to Oxfordshire to buy a bull and ended up buying not just that farm but a small estate of six farms as well. He found that he could look after his farms in Oxfordshire by taking one day in every two weeks, Wednesday night he took the night train, spent Thursday doing his business in Oxfordshire and took the night train back and was back in Aberdeen by the Friday morning. Then it was up to his butcher's shop, F W Wishart's, then to the mart. So Oxfordshire only took him one day away from his business in the North East. I used to sell him cows if they failed the tuberculin test. On one occasion I had a bit of a tubercular breakdown and had six cows to sell to Sandy. "I'll be ower to see them the morn's morning."

"Oh what time will you be?"

"Six o'clock."

So I got up, muddied my boots to make it look as though I had been up for a long time, and was ready for Sandy Wishart when he arrived. I learned that trick from the Sleighs of Tolquhon. John Sleigh and Alex Sleigh had the two Tolquhons at Tarves and their father who was a very early riser used to like to go and see them first thing. Luckily he always told his wife first and she phoned to warn them that their father was on his way. So the boys jumped out of bed and went out and made sure their boots were dirty with fresh mud by the time their father arrived. So my boots were dirtied when Sandy arrived. He looked at the cows and did as he always did, wrote down on a piece of paper how much he would pay for the cows, and I wrote down on a piece of paper how much I wanted for them. We then showed one another our pieces of paper and there was one pound of difference so I said we'll just split the difference and Sandy agreed. I then said, "You must have been on the go early this morning Mr Wishart. Would you like to come in and have some breakfast?"

"No, no. I have had my breakfast. I have been at Balquhindachy, Waterage Muir and Pitinnan afore I came to you." That was a journey of some fifty miles and three farm visits before six o'clock, and breakfast already taken.

So he must have been on the go at four in the morning. Of course, he would have needed to be because in those days there were no phones in his farms. His grieves had to manage on their own and go to the post office if they had an emergency and needed to get in touch. Otherwise it was all done by personal contact - he even went round his twenty-odd farms with the wages and on pay days it would often be late before he got round to the last of them. His son Gordon when he took over was much the same and I remember once coming down from Thomastown to Westertown by car and here's a flock of sheep on the road. To my surprise they were shepherded by Gordon Wishart. I had time to stop and news a while. Gordon Wishart said to me, "You don't know of a good dog do you?"

And I remember saying to him, "What you need is a shepherd not a dog."

In 1935 the big change was just coming... mechanisation. And in that area I scored a few of the firsts that I have had in agriculture. I was first to have no horses at all. My neighbours thought that I had gone completely mad and sometimes when they were looking at my efforts to get turnips out of a wet and muddy field with a tractor stuck and another tractor trying to pull it out, it looked like they were right. But I never regretted not keeping even one pair. In the old days the horsemen took it in turns to be toonser, which meant the man who looked after the farm at the weekend. The only difference for the man who was toonser on the Sunday was that he did not tie his laces. He went about with his feet in his tackety boots but he did not tie his pints. If you went down to one pair of horse, because tractormen did not think their horses needed any attention, the poor horseman had to look after his horses every weekend. For that and other reasons I got rid of the last pair of horses.

Just that year or the next, my neighbour retired and had a roup. You're supposed to go to your neighbour's roup and buy something. By this time I was busy with a shop and business in Aberdeen and I looked in at the roup just at end of our road, determined to buy something. Of course they were selling off all the rubbish to begin with and after I had bought a few boxes of bolts and nails they came to the harness. And I thought I would need to buy something. So I bought a whole set of harness and paid a good price for it. As I left I arranged with McIntosh of Forgue, that he would take the harness if I gave him two pounds. Immediately the story was all round the parish that Mike had come to his senses after all and was buying another pair and going back into horses. I never did, but it was quite funny how quickly the story spread.

The truth of matter is, with a pair of horses you could plough at most an acre a day. Very roughly it was an acre per foot of instrument whether you were rolling or harrowing or whatever. It was the pace of the man. Even when we got the big short board ploughs for the horses and could then plough much deeper and also taking on ten inches instead of the small cocked up furs as they used to do, the tractor was much quicker. Time was important because you could not really work your horses overtime. They would go done. In fact the hours were so arranged to start at six in the morning and stop at eleven till one. That gave a two hour break in the middle of the day, but that was not for the men. That was for the horses so that they could get another feed and a rest. The tractor did not care whether it was rested or not. Our father had always impressed on us boys that it was so important to get your crops in on time. "Now you must get your crop in by the first of April." That was because Mr William Findlay, the great man at the college at the time, had done experiments which had proved that you lost a bushel an acre every day after April 1. So speed was very important and tractors could work day and night, no matter what the weather. I think that was a great advantage of tractors - they made it easier to get your work done on time.

The tractors could handle decent double furrow ploughs which ploughed wider and deeper. With those we could easily do four or five acres in a day and then work overtime. Then, when it came to harrowing and rolling, we put three rollers together for instance and you could go much faster than with horses. It was the same with harrows. We got a harrow width of eighteen feet or more. It was just amazing how easily the work was done after we got mechanised. My brother John was one of first to mechanise in Howe o' the Mearns. We experimented a lot in making our own tipping carts and how to hook up the old farm machinery. When sowing turnips I put two horse machines together so that we could sow four rows of turnips in one go. There was a lot of head-shaking about that though our men thought it was marvellous. And the turnips grew just the same.

One thing that people thought would never be achieved was to get a man to put up straight drills with a tractor but, in fact, we got very expert at it and soon proved we could put as straight a drill with the tractor as with horses.

Of course the tractors were crude affairs compared with today's computerised models. Really all they could do at first was pull - and push at a pinch. Our first were Fordsons which were much the most popular. Some people, like the Hays at Little Ythsie, had Austins but they were not very good. Within a very short time we were getting a whole range of American tractors. John Deeres, Allis-Chalmers and my brother John, again one of the first, got an Allis-Chalmers Caterpillar tractor. Then of course the great revolution came when Harry Ferguson invented the hydraulic lift on the back of the tractor. If anyone deserves a monument in agriculture it's Harry Ferguson. There should be a great big monument on top of the biggest hill for the invention of the hydraulic lift which revolutionised a great many of the machines that you now hook on the back of the tractor. Wonderful.

Harry's hydraulic lift meant that, instead of trailing a plough or machine, you hooked it on to the three-point linkage and with a little lever you could raise and lower the thing into or out of work. Later on you could put a thing on to the front of the tractor and lift big weights, bags and what-not; a fore loader, which was also a great saving on the humping of bags around.

When you come to the end of the drill when ploughing a field you have to come out and leave a fleed or end-rig and if you wanted to be neat you had to lift the plough at just the right time. With horses it was easy. You just put your weight down on the shafts and the plough came out. When we started ploughing with tractors, the ends were a bit uneven with a trailing plough just because of the difficulty of getting it released at the right time. With the three point linkage and a handle at your side the ends became much simpler.

With the trailing plough you certainly need a wider fleed or end-rig. But often that was no great disadvantage because if you wanted to make a good job you were better to leave a fairly wide end-rig and then plough that separately, depending on the size of the field.

Talking about firsts, I think I was the first in Aberdeenshire to buy a combine harvester when they came in. A Massey-Harris it was. Again my neighbours thought I was mad and Alec Stewart of Gunhill even wrote a song about it. In fact he wrote a song about all the stupid things that went on at Westertown.

The only bit I remember was the bit about the combine harvester which said;

He his a great big combine
That barks and birrs and sheets
It cost aboot a thoosan poun
Aa jist up the lum.
"Nae much", as you may say
But it micht hae been as weel
In his waistcoat pooch
In case o' a rainy day.

In two years Alec Stewart had a combine of his own.

One of the biggest changes I made was just after the war in 1945. I got permission to build a new steading. I built it for ninety-six cows all in loose courts; six courts with sixteen cows each. There were four courts on one side, two on the other and the milking parlour in between. They were so arranged that at milking time all the cows from one court were emptied into the milking parlour and everyone else moved one round and when we had finished milking all would be back in their own court. It seemed a great arrangement at the time but it was really rather silly. The same building now houses about two hundred cows, but it was a great thing at the time and people came from miles to see a man who was keeping cows loose instead of tying them by the necks for seven months of the year. I must say it was a great success. The cows were much healthier, milked well and looked well.

We used a lot of straw though. But that was a good thing because we made a lot of muck and that went back on to the land. Again after we got fore loaders we did not have to tear the muck out with a graip. In fact again I had one of the first things instead of a graip. Well really it was a graip, but it was attached to a motor with a steel wire and the man stuck this great bit graip into the muck pulled a string and the motor started the winch which pulled a great load of muck out in one fell swoop. If you were clever you guided the graip onto a ramp and up into a cart. The snag was that the mechanical graip was even harder work for the man than a manual graip. But you could do an awful lot more in a day.

We got half a barrowful at a time, depending on the angle you put the graip into the muck. But soon we got fore loaders on the tractors which was a lot easier on the men.

The old petrol engine which powered the graip was still around when my son took charge. In fact he made it into a tow rope for skiing on the hill. The first time he tried it out it was a great success, except that the tow rope was going up the the hill at about sixty mile per hour, which we thought to be a little dangerous. After some adjusting to the gearing it worked well as a ski tow for many years.

People used to say that farming would never be the same without the horses. I personally had no regrets about that at all. It was a nice sight, no doubt, for a townsman to see a pair of horses ploughing on a nice day, but that is a piece of sentiment which did not really mean anything at all to me. Though, oddly enough, I used to like ploughing when I was at Thomastown. There is something especially satisfying about ploughing. It is the elemental job about farming - like digging the garden. When they brought in the short board plough, which you didn't have to hold so steady as the long board plough, you didn't have to hop about with one foot in the furrow and one on the grass which a man used to have to do, I used to enjoy it. It was like rowin a barrow really to plough with the new short board plough. I used a Sellar short board first, but all the plough manufacturers were soon into that.

There is something fascinating about ploughing but I have only competed once in a ploughing match. It was good fun. My uncle, Bruce Mackie of Milton of Noth, and I entered a competition which was to be held on a farm on the other side of the hill from Thomastown. I had just got a new Ferguson single furrow plough. Bruce had a new tractor, so we entered with his tractor and my plough. It was the first to be hooked on at the back of the tractor. Although it took only one furrow it ploughed at least a foot wide and just as deep as you wanted to put it in. So we entered two entries and were allocated two pieces of ground, both together as it turned out. So Bruce ploughed his bit and then I ploughed my bit. We finished both before anyone else had finished one, so at least we got the prize for being the first off the field. There must have been forty pairs of horses there that day but only seven tractors as they were still relatively new. There would have been maybe three hundred spectators.

The other five tractormen had adjusted their trailing ploughs to be as narrow as they could and set the plough up to try and copy the horse ploughing. We, of course, using the single furrow, turned a great furrow completely over, buried all the rubbish. And there was no air space as there is when you do this narrow ploughing. That was really like setting two squares against each other with a space at the bottom which was often very difficult to close in even when working in the springtime. On the other hand our ploughing was turned over. We both had girlfriends - Barry Stephen from Conglass and Isobel Ross the teacher from Drumblade, our future wives. Anyway, they came to see us but were horrified with the remarks they heard when anybody passed like, "Good God! They should be put aff the field", and "that's nae plooin" and remarks using words that they didn't even know they knew. Anyway they left the field in disgust at the efforts of their two young men.

And when it came to the prize-giving we were 6th and 7th. I don't remember who was 6th and who was 7th, but one of us got a pair of socks and the other a pair of braces for being first off the field. However, notwithstanding all the criticism, I went back in the spring and saw the ground sown with an oat crop and I went back again at harvest time and the two bits that Bruce Mackie and I had ploughed just stood out with a crop that was easily the best in the field. I think that convinced a lot of people that there was something in this new method of ploughing.

Another of my firsts was my hen battery. It was counted a wonder of the world. I think we had two thousand hens in it. It had automatic scrapers to take away the hen droppings and fancy lighting to cheat the poor birds. They went in at eighteen weeks and got four to five hours lighting and then the lighting was increased to make them think that Spring was coming with its longer days. When they started laying they got maybe twelve hours of light and when they started to go off the lay, we increased the light again by twenty minutes every day to make them think there was another Spring coming and the poor brutes started laying again like mad. With the outside hens, we might get, if very lucky, ten dozen eggs per hen. In the battery, we were soon getting two hundred, then two hundred and forty and then nearly three hundred. I don't know what the new hybrids are doing, but more than double what we used to get outside.

That was just after the war and yet it was all automatic. The feeders went up and down the middle for seven hours in the day. The original method of watering was not very successful, though. So I put in a fancy thing - a tube with a little hole opposite each opening for the hens where there was always a drop of water. It was just surface tension that kept the drop of water there until a hen picked it off and then another drop appeared. So they always got fresh water.

Of course, I didn't invent the battery system. I got this one more or less off-the-peg after seeing it in operation in Kent.

I had thought I was doing very well with hens before because we thought we had done the right thing to have the hens moving over the field in little arcs with thirty hens in each arc. And they were light enough that a man could move them forward, so that they got a fresh patch of grass every day. If there was bad weather there was a little covered bit at the end of the arc with a nest box. The most that a man could look after was a thousand hens. Although it was good for the grass, manuring it in a regular way, it was not very economical of labour though I suppose today we would be able to sell the eggs as 'organic' or something stupid like that. I doubt if the people who get nostalgic about keeping free-range hens have ever seen a hen looking miserable on a wet and windy day as compared with hens in batteries. If you go in there it is really a chorus of delighted hens with food and water and comfortable surroundings and I must confess that I am in total disagreement with people who say that we must stop keeping hens in batteries and get them outside to range free. If the hens had a choice I know what they would choose. If you take the hens out of their cage in the battery and put them on the floor they will jump in quickly. They know where their food and drink is. We even gave them music-while-you-lay.

Anyway that was another first which was very successful and of course we sold all the eggs in our shops in Aberdeen and on the milk rounds.

I think I was also the first to have cows on slatted floors. As we increased the number of cows, sixteen per court was ridiculous. So we put in the first slats along the front of the feeding troughs. That greatly reduced the amount of straw used. Eventually there were slats all over and now of course the cows are in cubicles. That's the same building which was designed for ninety-six cows, and it now holds about two hundred. But we now had a new problem - slurry and how to get rid of it. I put in collection tanks. Then I went to Switzerland to see how they pumped their stuff and sprayed it on the hillside. It was easy to see that it did a lot of good. So from Rightrain, who had organised this trip to Switzerland, I bought a pump and a sprayer. That was considered a thing of great interest and we had a demonstration to show how the pump showered the shit all round it. Two men were a little too inquisitive and they went too near the pump at this demonstration and the valve beside the pump broke and they got a nice shower. So they didn't think much of my system, but I did.

Our first combine was a very cumbersome affair. It had a fourteen foot cut and it was all right when it was going but that wasn't always and it wasn't nearly as good as the machines today when it came to picking up flattened crops. To help that I had a seat put on the front. A man sat there when it was badly laid stuff and raked it off the cutting knives onto the platform. Thank goodness and no doubt largely by good luck we never had the nasty accident that seemed to be waiting to happen, but the seat and the man made the lifting of the platform an even weightier job. And remember there were no hydraulic lifts then. The driver just had a wheel with which he pulled the table up and down. Having driven this thing for many hours I can tell you that was sore work. Mind you the regular driver who took a pride in his machine insisted that it was "nae bother ava."

Hundreds of people came to see this machine working in 1944, the first owned in Aberdeenshire. I had seen a demonstration of one at the Rowett in 1943 and I managed to get one for the next harvest. The original combine needed a man standing on it to bag off the grain which he then slid down a chute and they were left lying in the field and had to be picked up later. I remember one night when unusually there was no dew and I was able to work all night with the lights I had rigged up. I thought it was nice every time I pulled the string and a hundred weight and a half bag slid onto the ground and I thought, "That's thirty shillings."

We did use the combine on the braes but it was dangerous.

It's interesting that I used to get something of a reputation for being an innovator and starting new things. But I was never an innovator... I was a copier. We learned more, I think, by going on trips to England and seeing what they were up to there, and indeed my visit to Switzerland and also my trip to America. So I think it's important for farmers not to stay at home all the time. You have got to go and see what your neighbours are doing. But your neighbours are often thirled to the practices of their own district so you are better to get out and see what your neighbours from afar are up to. Certainly I have learned a lot by visits to the south and elsewhere.

I think that I was one of the first to have a pension scheme for the farm workers. And I was certainly one of the first to have a recreation hall for the men. After we had built the courts, we had replaced three byres with stalls for the cows, so I turned one of the byres into a recreation hall. We had a great opening night to which my father came and Joe Duncan, a great man, who first became famous as the founding secretary of the Farm Servants' Union. He never made a great success of the Union in the North because the men were loath to join, but he made a great success of everything else he tried. Although he left school at thirteen he rose to become an examiner for doctorates at Cambridge University and was a first rate Governor of the College of Agriculture in Aberdeen. He had many other achievements and was a great friend of our family. In fact the socialist streak in the family came from Joe Duncan and from my brother-in-law John R Allan, who was also a devotee of Joe Duncan's.

My father also spoke at the opening of this hall. He said, "No doubt it is a good thing but you see where Andrew Barber is sitting? (Andrew Barber was one of my cattlemen.) When the byre had stalls, just about where he is sitting there was a cow that gave two thousand gallons of milk and I doubt if this hall will be as profitable as that cow."

Joe opened it and I had particularly asked him to advise against any vandalism of the halls because there had been one at Tillycorthie which had only lasted one season as the men destroyed it. So Joe emphasised that they were lucky to have this hall and he hoped that they would look after it. And indeed they have. We have appointed a committee, the hall still exists and is still a very useful part of the organisation.

When I went to the farm there were thirteen men including outside men, cattlemen, and the people working in the dairy at a time when more and more people were getting rid of men. I never got rid of a man when we got a new labour-saving device. I doubled the production one way or another. Like when we went out of hens in the moving arc system. In batteries a man could look after several thousand and as batteries got better I just employed two men and doubled the number. In fact we went up to twelve or fifteen thousand hens. We tended to do that with other things too. As we got better at the milk job, so we employed more people because the dairy was taking it up. By the time I retired we had about forty-five men and now my son has expanded that business and there are now over two hundred people on pay day.

I was also the first in Aberdeenshire to make silage. As a young man I had to pull turnips on frosty mornings and was never very fond of the crop. It was very labour intensive. You never seemed to be finished, from putting in the crop and then hoeing them, shimming them and then second hoeing them and then pulling them and then you got them into the sheds and occasionally you had to hash them. They just annoyed me. So much so that, after I started making silage, we stopped the turnip crop altogether. It is interesting that that has gone full circle now because everything is mechanised and it is not such a labour intensive job. You put in several rows at a time. You can do single seeding so they hardly need to be hoed. You put on a spray to keep the weeds down before they're in and a spray after they emerge. Then the turnip harvesters are now excellent. They load the turnips into a cart and there's automatic hashing. So the turnip is back in favour.

When the college started giving advice, they had analysed the turnip and said that the turnip is just ninety percent water. This was related to my Grandfather, who had a great belief in the turnip, and he said, "Ah weel, it must be awfa gweed water."

My staff pension scheme was done through the Commercial Union when it was still the Northern Assurance Company. We had a great meeting with the men in the recreation hall and it was explained that the employers would pay so much and they would pay so much, (very little in fact) and at the end of the day they would get a pension. Really I forget how much it was going to be but it looked a

106

lot at the time. It wouldn't be very much today. But those who retired later got a small pension, and any addition to the rather miserable national pension was more than acceptable. There are quite a few farming companies that now have pension schemes but mine was certainly, if not the first, at least one of the first. Of course, had it not been for the success of the National Insurance Scheme, there would have been many more private schemes in farming.

One or two of the men said they would not join, but in the end they all joined. Funny - the reaction. We had a pension scheme in the Milk Board as well and the secretary of the Board, a lady, refused to join until months later it was pointed to her how much she would lose as she began to reach retiring age. So she paid all the back contributions up and is still enjoying her pension.

I think we have always been fairly good with employees. I think proof of that is the numbers of years they have stayed with us. We had a lot of men who had retired and got their gold watch having done twenty years or thirty years with us. I did have a few grieves at Westertown before Bill Cruden, but he stayed a long time and left only after my son took over. He was a very faithful and loyal servant. Very cautious like a lot of the farm men. I remember one day I had been round the hill with the gun and came down with a couple of hares. Bill Cruden was in the close as I came down. I said, "Would you like a hare, Bill?"

"Oh I wouldna care," says he, which meant that he would be very pleased if he got a hare.

Andrew Barber, one of the cattlemen at Westertown, stayed a long time with me and he had an enormous family. I think fifteen or sixteen. His wife always gave birth at two or three in the morning so there would be a rattle of stones at my window and we would get up and this would be Andrew, "Would you send for the doctor and the nurse". So I would duly phone for the doctor and the nurse and they would duly appear and Andrew would announce later that he had another son or another daughter. Three or four months after the last one was born, there was rattle of stones at the window and this was Andrew Barber. "Would you send for the doctor and the nurse."

I said, "Andrew that is impossible. It's only a few months since you had your last one."

"Aye, Aye. But it's that bugger Beldie noo." This was his eldest daughter who had started a little early and had had a liaison with a soldier who had been helping with the harvest. A casual affair, but it had resulted in another child in the family. The child was just brought up as one of them and all was well. It didn't phase them at all. Because they were so numerous I moved them into the big flat at the back of the farm-house at Eastertown which had a great big kitchen. I remember going in and they had bought two old school desks at a roup and there were ten of them sitting at these two desks waiting for their meal. Andrew wasn't very well paid, though he was well paid compared with many. But he was great worker, work all day and poach all night, but always ready for his work in the morning. It is very difficult in the milk job. But New Year was always an employer's nightmare as to who would turn up at four or five in the morning. One New Year's morning, when we had three byres at Westertown, I went in at half past four. To my great delight I had two milkman but Andrew Barber was missing. I was half way through milking his cows, when Andrew appeared with a couple of cockerels, one in each hand, swinging them with delight. "I've got my New Year's denner."

I said, "Far did you get that."

"I'm nae telling you but, if Gordon Wishart coonts his chuckens he'll find twa missing."

I was quite friendly with my neighbour Gordon Wishart and I told him some time later. He said, "Oh aye, but my ain men would have had ane or twa themselves."

Of course there were always bothies on the farm, but as the dairy business expanded and I needed more room, so I converted the cart shed and the loft above it into a hostel with a flat for a housekeeper. There we could accommodate six men, which relieved the employment situation.

During the fifties and sixties I tried to do my bit as a good citizen by taking various doubtful characters who were on probation or just out of prison and so on to give them a chance of a job with a home in the hostel. That was a most disappointing exercise. They usually just stole again so I decided I wouldn't do it again. However about 1966 I was prevailed upon by a lawyer friend to try once more. His probation officer persuaded me to keep a secret of his misdemeanours so that Jim would have a chance. In fact he proved to be a good worker and he courted Bill Cruden's daughter and the grieve and his wife were well pleased with the lad.

We seemed to have a success on our hands. But one day a student who was doing his year's practical with us and living in the hostel came and said, "Jim's away."

I said, "What do you mean 'Jim's away'?"

"Well, Jim's away with your Land-Rover, twa radios, thirteen pounds in cash, a suit ... "

We eventually got the Land-Rover back from Devon where it had been abandoned empty of diesel and oil, but I had to re-imburse the men for all that he had stolen. Unfortunately I couldn't re-imburse the poor Crudens. The daughter was very upset of course and the parents understandably blamed me for not warning them that this lad who was making moves on their daughter was a criminal. They accepted my explanation that I had been bullied into secrecy by the probation officer but it was a nasty incident and I never took any such person again in to the hostel. Jim was put away for seven years for that.

We used to have a hare shoot at New Year. To organise this I always got a professional gamekeeper from Insch, a man called Riddell. He was a somewhat irreverent man who would have lost many top posts because he didn't care who he swore at. But he was a very good gamekeeper. On this occasion I invited the minister the Reverend Douglas Trotter. He never really shot but I lent him a gun and he was lined up with the twenty of my friends and neighbours who were going to sweep the farm and dispose of many of the hares.

I had told Mr Trotter the rudiments of safety but as we were coming over the hill he got sadly out of line and was in danger of being shot. Suddenly there was a stream of oaths and abuse to the effect that if that *very stupid* man would keep in line the other *stupid* men in the shoot would know not to shoot him. At lunch time we always had a bowl of broth and a dram. I took the opportunity then to introduce the gamekeeper to the Reverend Trotter. I told Roarin Robbie, as Riddell was called, that this was my minister. Robbie recognised Douglas as the person whom he had sworn at but was none phased by that. "And why the effing hell did ye hae tell me the bugger was a minister?" he said.

With Isobel on our wedding day

CHAPTER TEN

War Breaks Out

BY THE end of the nineteen thirties my life had really
taken much of its shape. I was married and had two children. The farming business was expanding with Eastertown, Westertown and Thomastown, a total of over a thousand acres. And the policy which my father had started and
I was developing, of getting as near to the consumer as
possible, was well in hand with our retail milk business and
the bottling plant and shop in Aberdeen. We had come
through the bad economic times in a strong position and
were soon to enter a boom in agriculture that lasted, really I
suppose right up till the 1960s. The cause was war and the
effect was a shortage of everything that we produced.

I was mostly taken up with my business and was not
then at all active in politics but those were exciting times. I
thought all along that war with Germany was inevitable but
we crowded round the radio to listen as the thing developed and as our Prime Minister, Neville Chamberlain,
shuttled back and forth to Berlin being made a fool of, as it
turned out, by Mr Hitler. I remember well listening to his
speech as he returned from Munich with the deal he had
made giving Hitler all he was at that stage asking for in
Europe in exchange for 'Peace in Our Time'. Many people
believed that there would indeed be peace in our time but I
thought Chamberlain was a bit of an ass and there would
only be peace in the times of those who didn't live very
long. A couple of days after the great Munich agreement I

was speaking to our Member of Parliament, Bob Boothby, about another matter and he confirmed my view. And sure enough we were soon at war.

My brother George, who was making uncertain progress through the University, immediately joined the airforce. But I was pretty busy at home so I was only in the Home Guard which was formed after Dunkirk on the inspiration of Anthony Eden. I had a lot of fun training to defend Oldmeldrum, not that it needed defending, as it turned out.

I did in fact later try to join the airforce or the army but by that time I was on the Executive Committee which had the job of telling other farmers what they should grow and how they could serve the war effort. As I was also in the Home Guard it was reckoned that I was needed at home. I was a bit disappointed at the time but later I felt more at ease with the situation following an incident with the minister at Tarves, the Reverend James Murray. He was called up as a chaplain and we had teased him that he would need to come back with a VC. He had not been away long when he wrote home saying, "On the matter of the VC. I have decided against it. I have been reading the rules and this particular medal must be won while under enemy fire and I feel there is something distastful about that." So I guess I was a lucky chap once again.

There was no nonsense about white feathers being given in this war to shame the able-bodied men who stayed at home and I didn't feel bad about it. I was very busy with the Executive Committee, the Home Guard, my three farms, the Scouts and a lot of other community work so I never felt that I wasn't doing my bit. Somebody had to stay at home.

At first in Oldmeldrum the war didn't seem to make much difference except that supplies of everything became scarce and we could sell all we could produce. But it was suddenly brought home to me by a visit down south. I was in York buying a buncher for a thrashing mill and seeing I was so near I went on to London to see my sister Mary. She was getting her ration of two eggs a week and by the time she collected them they were often bad so she was very glad of the half dozen her mother would send her down from the farm. I remember thinking how lucky we were to be living in Oldmeldrum. We went to the theatre and an air-raid took place. A sign went up saying that those who wanted to leave might do so quietly and that the production would resume in ten minutes. Hardly anyone left the theatre and in ten minutes after listening to the bangs and shakes another sign appeared announcing the all-clear. A great sigh of relief went up and the production resumed.

It was a sad sight going back home in the tube to see all the people with their bedding down on the platform with only a small area of the platform left to walk on. I realised then how little disrupted we were in Aberdeen-shire. Aberdeen did get a fair blitz one night. It was inter-esting that the brick houses fell down whereas the granite houses next door had only a few broken windows. Unfor-tunately a bomb did crash into a room at the barracks and killed a lot of soldiers as they slept.

I was sitting at lunch one day with Arthur Wannop, the chief adviser at the College, who had come to see me about something or other. He was telling me how glad his wife was when he had to go out into the country instead of sitting in his office at forty-one and a half Union Street, when there was the most tremendous 'rat-tat-tat' and we rushed outside to see a Spitfire chasing a German bomber. I rushed in for my rifle and fired off the five rounds that I was allowed. The spitfire broke off and landed on a neigh-bouring farm. He'd got a bullet through his radiator so his cooling liquid had sprayed up onto his windscreen so that he couldn't see. He had no alternative but land just when he had had that bomber at his mercy. So there was a great enquiry and I was almost going to be court-martialed when it was discovered that the bullet-hole was the size of a point seven something and not a three-o-three. I was a relieved man and no mistake, but it all added to the excitement. The bomber pilot had dropped his incendiary bombs in a field at the back of our house and it was funny to see the cows all standing round these little fires wondering where they had come from. He jettisoned his big bombs up at the top of the hill, where he did kill a rabbit. It left a lot of holes for all my neighbours to come and see over the next few days. That was our only experience of the war and I claimed to have been the only member of the Home Guard who had been in action against the enemy.

It was really rather amusing when the call went out for all the able-bodied men to register for the Home Guard. Everybody who had a gun had to bring it. I had a twelve bore and a point two two rifle which wouldn't have been much good against enemy tanks, but the silliest thing was that not long after we got organised we were sent two parcels of long pikes. They were eight feet of galvanised piping with a first world war bayonet welded onto the end. That was to be our weaponry. I was so taken aback that, in my capacity as sergeant and in consultation with Postie Low who was the lieutenant, I decided that those would be so useless against the enemy tanks that we wouldn't even unpack them. We eventually got rifles - six old Ross rifles which had been a great thing in the Boer War. They had been replaced by the Lee-Enfield in the First World War but we were to stop the Pansers with them in the second war. We found them very accurate but they were liable to jam if you got the least bit of sand in them.

Another disheartening thing was that we were only issued with five rounds. I was quite keen on shooting and when we were taken out to a rifle range in the quarry above Oldmeldrum, I was selected to take the first shot. I got a bull's-eye and was very disappointed when old Captain Manson of Kilblean, who was our commanding officer, said, "That's enough Mackie. I can see you can shoot. Save your ammunition." If I'd known that was to be the way of it I'd have aimed off a bit.

I was a good friend of Captain Manson outside the Home Guard so I was 'Mike' to him but if ever I did anything wrong I became 'Mackie'. On one occasion I was sent down to Whiterashes where there was a rather lonely section of seven or eight men who met on their own. It was their job to guard Whiterashes. They had not had the kind of fun and games that we had had. I had been on a course on grenades and I was to show them our selection of grenades. I had a table with a thirty-six anti-tank grenade, a hand grenade and a sticky bomb with which we were expected to run out and bash them down on the tracks of a tank which would be blown up - presumably along with the Home Guard.

So I was explaining the workings of the hand grenade, how you could pull the pin and let the handle off gently and unscrew the base and take out the fuse or put in a fuse being careful that the pin was still in the top, I showed them about the four second fuse and the seven second fuse. And I showed them how to unscrew the base plug and take out the charge. If you wanted to make sure the spring was working you held it against your belt, pulled the pin, lifted out the handle, and the spring and plunger fell against your belt not on the floor. Then somebody asked to be shown again how to put in a fuse. So I put in a fuse and had started to screw in the base plug when somebody hadn't been obeying my instruction and had taken off the handle and the spring and plunger fell on the floor. I forgot that I had put in a fuse into the bomb I had in my hand. "You see you do it this way. You pull the pin out and pull the handle off with it against your belt," said I, looking angrily at the man who had offended. Then I could see that I had the full attention of the men and I looked down and there was smoke coming from this little bomb. Then, wondering if it was a four second fuse or a seven second fuse, I shouted, "Down on your bellies," and rolled it to the far end of the hall. I was tipping up the table to advance on the grenade when there was an almighty bang and I looked round to see how many people I had killed. All that had happened was that the percussion cap had blown off. It had just been on one thread and instead of the whole grenade exploding it just blew out the plug.

Order was restored and I went on with the lecture. Anyway I wasn't long home when the phone rang. "This is Major Manson, Mackie."

"Yes, sir."

"Mackie, what have you been up to? I've just had a most agitated sergeant on the phone from Whiterashes saying, 'Don't send that bloody madman down here again'."

A lot of people wondered what we could have done with the poor equipment we had. But even at the beginning, had we been asked to delay a German advance, I've no doubt that most of us would have been killed but we would have made it very awkward for the Germans because we got up to all sorts of tricks. We had barrels of petrol dug into the banks at the sides of the roads and planned to set these off so as to trap enemy patrols. We also had all sorts of wonderful Molotov cocktails that we could throw, and because we knew the area and had a number of people who could shoot accurately I think we could have delayed them... maybe enough to let the regulars get organised. But, whether that's true or not, a lot of us rather enjoyed the Home Guard. It was something new for us who had never been in the services.

As well as the course on grenades I went on a course on house-to-house fighting and another on intelligence. Alistair Forbes of Slains Park was on that one. We got the impression that as Home Guard officers we had to know more than the regulars on the course. Whereas they were experts on one or two things we had to be experts in everything. It was really rather fun. We weren't very impressed with the regular soldiers on the course but we were so impressed with the captain who was in charge that we invited him to have dinner with us at the end of the course. It was to be at the Caledonian Hotel, but at the last minute we got a message saying that the captain had been called away so Alistair Forbes and I had a wonderful meal just by ourselves, celebrating our emergence as intelligence officers of the Home Guard.

Towards the end of the war we were asked to mount guards on the high points in our area. This we did on the top of the Barra hill and on the golf course above Oldmeldrum. And remember, these were all chaps who were doing a hard day's work on top of their soldiering. We'd had two and a half hours of drill and practice when I picked six young men to go up and guard the golf course. They were supposed to patrol two hours on and two hours off and report any strange men. About five o'clock in the morning I received a phone call.

117

"Mackie." It was Major Manson as he now was and I knew I was in trouble because he didn't call me Mike.

"Yes, sir."

"A plane has come down in Meldrum Woods and everybody's there except your guards."

I went to see them and found my patrol still asleep. I asked the corporal what had happened and why he and his men were asleep in the hut. He said they had patrolled until four o'clock and then decided that, as there didn't seem to be anybody about, they would just get a bit of extra kip before starting their jobs at seven or whenever.

I managed to calm Major Manson and no action was taken.

Towards the end of our period in the Home Guard we became well equipped with all sorts of out-of-date weapons. One of the pieces we had was a radio which could send and receive over an area of about ten miles and I was trained in the use of this. There was a great plan for all the Home Guards in the county to attack the RAF headquarters at Pennan. Alec Sleigh of Mains of Tolquhon, who was by this time a Captain in the Home Guard while I was a humble Lieutenant, was put in charge of the big exercise. Alec had studied the ordinance survey map and decided that we would attack by going up the glen made famous later by Watt Taylor's reseeding project. It was a good enough plan because we were out of sight and I was carrying this forty pound radio thing on my back. When we got to the point where, according to the map, we were on the edge of the valley about forty yards from the RAF, Alec positioned two machine guns, one on the left and one on the right. The plan was that the rest of us would charge and take the RAF headquarters even before they realised they were under attack. So we crept to the top of the hill and to the chagrin of poor Alec Sleigh it wasn't forty yards to the headquarters, it was five hundred yards away through the deepest heather. So four hundred of us, commanded by our gallant captain, charged while the two machine guns fired off blank cartridges. I had my forty pound radio on my back and all the boys were in full kit carrying rifles. When we had covered two hundred yards I had a look back and there were twenty or thirty scattered up to a hundred yards behind. Alec was in front and I was trying to keep up because I was fit at the time. When we arrived at the headquarters Alec and I and about ten men who had managed to keep up with us were met by the squadron leader of the RAF base who announced, "Well, it was a gallant effort but you're all dead. Come in and have a beer."

So we went in and had two beers and all ended happily.

I wrote a song about our antics in the Home Guard. It was to the tune McGinty's Meal and Ale and was called the Udny Home Guard. I was the most unmusical of our somewhat unmusical family but I could get by if Isobel accompanied me on the piano. However, at the premier performance of this song at the Udny Home Guard's dinner in 1940, there was no one to accompany me so I performed bravely by myself. When it was the Oldmeldrum Home Guard's turn to play host my neighbour Alec Sleigh stood up and asked if I would be so kind as to give us a repeat of the splendid *recitation* I had done at the Udny dinner. Despite my singing being so unrecognisable the song was renamed the Oldmeldrum Home Guard and became quite well known.

With L to R: Isobel, Maitland, Mary, Elrick, Patricia, Isobel and Ruth

CHAPTER ELEVEN

The American Tour

ANOTHER INSTANCE of being a Lucky Chap was that I was invited to go to the USA in 1949 to do a lecture tour to tell the Americans that, although that we had a socialist government, we weren't communists and it was still worth being friends with Great Britain. They had, of course, stopped Lease-lend by that time and we were desperate for all the trade we could get.

The British Information Service, which is run by the Foreign Office, asked me to go. Why I was chosen I have no idea, but I thought it would be rather fun and agreed. Immediately my dear wife asked if she could go too. So I asked the organisers. Oh well, they didn't think so. "You are only getting ten dollars spare money a day as dollars are very scarce and we could not afford to give her any."

I said, "Oh, but she'll stay with friends. That will not be a problem in America."

"Oh well, but the biggest problem is that you have no hope of getting a berth for her on the Queen Mary which we have arranged for you to go across on."

"You just leave the berth to me."

As it happened, I knew that our potato merchant, Mr Miller, was friendly with one of the directors of Cunard. So he was approached immediately. He would certainly try. In due course he phoned and said it would be no problem. There would be a berth for both of us in the Queen Mary. So there was great excitement and great packing and arrangements to send the kids down to stay with their Grannie and Granpa while we were away for the three months.

Two days before we were due to leave, I received a telephone message at nine in the morning to say, "We're terribly sorry, but we have checked up with the Cunard people and there is no berth arranged for your wife and I'm sorry but you'll have to tell her she can't get on." As you can imagine all hell was let loose and great weeping and wailing and gnashing of teeth. However our postman came about an hour later (he usually came in for a cup of coffee) and with him he brought a letter from Cunard addressed to my wife. "Dear Mrs Mackie, I enclose your tickets for the Queen Mary for such and such a date and if there's anything we can do for you as you go through London, please do not hesitate to call. We will have you met at the boat and see that you get to your berth all right..." and so on and then, "PS a bed has been arranged for your husband in your cabin." So that put me in my proper place.

Anyway we both got on board the Queen Mary and that was an experience in itself. It was a truly enormous boat. When we got through the customs at Southampton and got through to the quay, I looked... but where was the boat? Then I looked along a bit and there was a great long gangway leading up and I realised that what I thought was a blank wall was in fact the side of the Queen Mary.

I must say we enjoyed the voyage, although at the time when she went at full speed, which I gather is about twenty four knots, there was quite a tremor and shake in the boat. And on the last day we ran into a storm and there were ropes across the lounges to let you hang on to as you crossed. We went in to dinner that night I think there were four people in addition to ourselves. All the rest were sea sick. That was out of about two thousand people on board. Though, of course, they would not all have been first class. You would not expect me to travel in anything other than first class, especially when somebody else was paying. It was a splendid trip, but the boat was so big that you met nice people in the bar which I frequented, and I was always saying, "Well, we'll see you later", but there were so many people on board you hardly ever saw them again. The food and the attention we got were very special. There were just about as many crew as there were passengers. A wonderful boat, and it was great sailing up the Hudson river and past the Statue of Liberty. From the top deck we were almost looking down on the old girl - the great Statue of Liberty. I subsequently saw the Statue from a small boat and it is then pretty majestic. It was fascinating to see this enormous ship so skilfully reversed into its berth in New York.

Our first job was to go to the office in New York to be told what to say to the Americans and what not to say, although I had already been briefed in London by an expert in American affairs. I thought that to be all most amusing. The one bit of advice that I did remember and I found to be true, was to be careful what I said about Roosevelt, who was our hero. About fifty per-cent of American people would spit on his grave even to this day. The other fifty thought, like us, that he was marvellous. So that was good advice; to watch what you said about good old Roosevelt.

The office of the British Information Services in New York was in the RCA building, which is high, we were on the sixtieth storey. I was standing in an office waiting for somebody to come and see me about tickets or something and I suddenly said to the girl, "Am I imagining things or is this dashed place moving?"

"Oh, yes. In a high wind it moves about four feet each way. Lots of people feel seasick."

"Well the sooner you give me my tickets and let me get out of this the better I'll be pleased. I'm not accustomed to buildings swaying in the wind."

I was lucky we weren't at the Empire State Building. It's over a hundred stories. We went there on a still day but at the top it actually sways in a high wind eight feet each way. That's pretty marvellous that the blooming thing still stands. Even in London at that time there were not many high rise buildings. Coming in to New York the skyline with all the big buildings is really a world sight and I was most impressed, although I confess that I would not like to live there. You just look out and see another sea of sixty to a hundred storey buildings. Every one competing with one another to build another storey to have the highest one.

Anyway arrangements were made and I think in the three months I saw more of America than most Americans up to then did in their lifetime, although they now travel about a bit more. We went from New York up to Vermont, to Washington and to Maine, across to Chicago, down to Demoines in Iowa, then to Kentucky and back to Chicago to catch a train to Denver, the mile high city. From Denver we went to Los Angeles, a dreadful place. I'd heard that the farmers around Los Angeles were very advanced in the production of eggs in batteries and, although I was hard worked every day of the week, most Sundays I was free if I wasn't travelling. I didn't have much to do on my first Sunday in Los Angeles so I asked if I could see a hen battery, "Oh, yes. There was one just on the outskirts of the city." So in the morning I got out of the hotel and took a taxi to this place. I'd been given the address on the outskirts of the city but I had no idea that that could be so far. We travelled sixty miles in this taxi to the outskirts of the city. I don't remember what it cost but I remember thinking what a dreadful city when from the hotel to the outskirts was sixty-odd miles.

I was impressed with the batteries, though, because the climate was such that they didn't need any housing except for a shelter to keep the sun, and what little rain they get, off the birds. There were rows and rows and rows of birds only three tiers high but most impressive. There was automatic egg collection and then a lovely packing system. I was interested that they produced all white eggs. They told me that, in parts of America, you couldn't sell a brown egg if you tried, while in other parts you couldn't sell a white egg. In the West they mostly liked white eggs and this company produced white eggs from a bird that looked like a White Leghorn.

They were very healthy being outside and lasted a long time. They were getting more eggs per hen than we were at that time although I think we probably have beat them, subsequently, with the production of the hybrids.

Incidentally, I thought the British Information Services didn't do me terribly well in the way of any relaxation during the three months. For example I could have got off the train when I was going from Denver to Iowa at Williams and got a connection up to see the Grand Canyon and still kept to my programme on Monday morning, but they didn't think of that. And similarly, when I was in Detroit, they could have arranged for me to go and see the Niagara Falls but didn't. I didn't see the Niagara falls until I was back in America some years later.

But on the whole it was a wonderfully arranged trip. In every town I was met by what they called a Consul. They were often American lawyers acting as the British Consul in their town. They arranged a programme for me to meet the chambers of commerce, rotary clubs and all sorts of clubs which I would address. Sometimes I would do a breakfast meeting, which I thought was a dreadfully uncivilised thing. I can't remember where the first break-fast one was but it astonished me when the consul said, "and I've arranged a breakfast meeting for you at half past seven tomorrow morning." I had to go down and talk serious business at half past seven in the morning. But it seemed to suit the busy American business man who is in his office before nine o'clock to have breakfast at seven and a fifteen minute talk at half past and then away to the office. In general I discovered that the businessman was at his work much earlier than our equivalent here. On the other hand I think they stopped a bit earlier and they work hard and play hard. They are out and away to the country club or the night-spot. I got the impression that they didn't entertain much in their homes. We had enormous hospital-ity from a great many people, lawyers, doctors and business people, but nearly always they would take you to the club and I must say that some of the clubs were magnificent.

A great many things amazed me on my first trip to America. One was the variety of clubs and I remember, for instance, in Fort Collins, which is just outside Denver, there was a university there and I was addressing the students but I was entertained to lunch by the Lions Club. They were a most rowdy crowd, they had somebody at the piano when I arrived and they were singing and shouting despite the fact there was no drink taken. "No, no," they told me, "There's not a drop of drink, this is all just high spirits." There was a chap going round with a rifle and on the end of the rifle he had a chamber pot hanging over the sights. He pointed the gun at various people and they were fined for having been late or not being at the last meeting or doing something minor like that. I was startled when one of the victims got up and said that he objected to paying his taxes particularly those which went to the police because they certainly weren't doing their job properly. He proposed that the chief constable, who was a member of their club, should be expelled and that they should pass a resolution that they would not pay any more police taxes. When the chief constable got up to reply the chap who had accused him also got up, drew a revolver and shot the policeman. He fell to the ground clutching his face with the bright red blood oosing between his fingers. He was carried out amid the cheers of the members of the Lions Club. Only then did it dawn on me that this was a charade and quite normal activity - the blood had been tomato juice.

However as soon as the lunch was finished and I was called on to speak I had a most attentive audience and they were most well behaved, and apparently this was just normal procedure for a Lions Club. The Kiwanies were nearly as bad. The Chamber of Commerce were probably next to the Rotary clubs the best behaved of the clubs I had addressed.

I learned one thing also on that tour... never to speak on subjects you don't know about. I was asked and stupidly agreed to speak on gardening. I think I knew a lot about farming but very little about gardening and I waffled my way through a speech on gardening to a lot of ladies. They listened politely but when they started asking me questions it was quite clear that I was way out of my depth. I waffled a bit more and then said I had to go and gladly escaped and never again have I talked about anything that I thought I didn't know enough about.

We travelled by plane, trains and buses. The Greyhound bus in America is a great institution. When I was there I was told they averaged sixty miles an hour between stops and that included a stop in between for coffee and a loo break although some of the buses had a loo on board even then. I was travelling by car between San Francisco and Portland in Oregon and we were going at about seventy miles an hour when a Greyhound bus went past us. I was amazed but my driver told me that was quite normal.

I went on a bus going down from Desmoines to Kentucky to speak to a 'mixed' youth group. Mixed meant sex and race to my surprise. They were all young people belonging to the youth organisations, church organisations as well as Boy Scouts, which I was going to concentrate on. The Americans are great for having receiving lines and I was at the receiving line with the president of the host youth club. He was introducing me to the leaders of the various clubs when there was a slightly horrified pause before I was introduced to the next guest. And I wondered at the pause and I looked up and there was this very black gentleman. I shook hands with him and was very glad to see there was at least one black man in this crowd. But after we had been introduced the Chairman apologised profusely for having me introduced to this black man. He certainly didn't know they were going to have any 'mixed' people here. It astonished me that even in 1949 they were still separated and it was not the done thing to have a black Boy Scout mixing with a white Boy Scout.

I remonstrated with the chap but he would have none of it. "Oh no, Mr Mackie," I was told in no uncertain fashion, "We don't do that sort of thing." After they passed the civil rights legislation it was astonishing how quickly that broke up really and I think they have got to give some credit to John F Kennedy for starting that although it was finally passed by Johnson.

Anyway, all sorts of funny things happened on that trip, or interesting things. I went by train from Portland up to Seattle through the Rockies and it's true that as you round some of the hairpin bends you look back and you see the end of the train coming round the corner that you'd been round a while before. Enormously long the trains were and very comfortable. Their short distance trains are dirty, disreputable and hopeless but their long distance trains, at that time, were very, very good. I understand that today they are not so good because everybody flies now, but it was not so common in those days.

Again I missed out when I was in Seattle. I should have been given a few hours off to see the big national park which stretched for miles and miles from Oregon up into Washington. I could have had an hour or two there but I they hadn't thought of that. That was one of the things I complained about when I got back.

In California, where they were having a premature heat wave in (I guess it was) the beginning of April. I remember passing a field of alfalfa which had just been irrigated in the early morning. I was being taken on a tour to a university to speak to some students and then to a farmer's union meeting in the afternoon. When I came back in the evening we came past this same field and I swear it had grown an inch since we left in the morning. Apparently they could get seven cuts in the year off this alfalfa which seemed to me to be pretty marvellous and they were feeding that to cows and getting very big milk yields. At least they were big yields for those days and certainly better than ours. It made me jealous to think you could grow alfalfa like that and cut it seven times a year and make good silage. And it grew on for six to seven years before they had to reseed it... marvellous stuff.

From Seattle I went by train to North Dakota. From the heat of California I arrived at Fargo, North Dakota at minus 30 degrees. People were walking about in the streets with little muffs over their noses and their ears. I don't like heat very much and I got out of the train and was sniffing this up and saying wasn't this glorious. The net result was that a few days later when I got to Desmoines I was feeling very ill. I'd had nearly a week in North and South Dakota where, at one of the meetings, my wife was entertained by the ladies while I was doing something else. During the course of her entertainment she was asked if she had any children and she said, "Oh yes, six."

And they said, "Oh, are you Catholic?"

She replied, "No, just careless." It so amused the ladies that that kind of news travelled fast and before I got back to her I was told at my meeting that I had a careless wife. We made quite a few friends in North Dakota but one of them was a university economist called Schickele. It was about the time that Macarthy was raising his nasty head and Schickele, who was a most excellent chap and was in line to get the professorship, was accused of being a communist and had to leave his post. Fortunately he was so well known for his writings and so on that he got a job in Rome with the Food and Agriculture Organisation and had a much better post. In the end it did him good to leave the rather small town of Fargo, North Dakota. Many years later I met him in his office and stayed with him one night in a beautiful home overlooking the town of Rome and very happy with himself, travelling all over the world on behalf of FAO.

I really had no problems with what to talk about in my lectures because I had been really well briefed with all the facts and figures about how Britain was doing its best to recover after the war. I knew the amounts we were spending to make the railways workable because, of course, they had been thoroughly overworked during the war carrying millions of tons of munitions, soldiers and what not. And I knew what we were doing about coal mines. As I used to have a pretty good memory for figures I could trot out all the facts about how much we were doing to recover from the effects of the war. That was part of the idea.

The British Information Services used to send about half a dozen speakers a year to America and they had doubled the number because of the wrong ideas the Americans were getting about Britain going to the dogs under a socialist government. They made me concentrate on talking to students of all kinds and youth movements, perhaps because I was involved in youth movements here, and farming groups.

I was amazed at the difference in the number of people employed on the land. At the time I had thirteen men at Westertown and when I came home I said to our men, "I've just come off a place where one man and his son are looking after a thousand acres, so which of you are to go?" They didn't approve of that. Of course when you stai ted to count up the yield per acre and the return per man we were beating them hollow. In spite of the large machines and contracting, their farming didn't seem to me to be very much fun. You had a great big bit of land in the wheat-growing areas and, once you had sown the crop, you had nothing to do until harvest so you went off to the Bahamas. You came home and did your harvest and then disappeared to a hotter clime again. It looked all very simple but I didn't care for the look of it.

I was taken to a club in Chicago. We went in our host's limousine covered by what Isobel assured me was a mink rug. The host did three loud knocks and three small knocks before a little window on the door opened. He was recognised and we were allowed in. This was because of the local drink laws which were very strict and this private club had to be very careful not to allow non-members in.

From Chicago I was taken to Valparaiso University. Compared with our university the staff were paid better and it seemed to me they were more serious about their work. They had enormous research facilities, for which our people would have given their back teeth.

From there we went back to Chicago. And on to Detroit where I saw the Ford motor works and the Ford museum. And most importantly I was introduced to Ernie Wilson. He was a most interesting character, the son of the famous grieve Jock Wilson from Balquhindachy of Methlick. (The one who sent the men to sow the manure with nothing in their happers). In 1918 Ernie was offered £5 to take cattle across to Montreal. From there he intended making his way to Detroit. Detroit was expanding all the time and he had been told there was a good chance of getting work on Ford's new car assembly lines there. So Ernie started asking how to get to Detroit as soon as he had delivered his cattle. Unfortunately, as it was French Canada, everybody he asked spoke French. He was a bit dejected at this until he saw a tall, red-headed man coming down the street and he said to himself, "Aha, I'll have better luck here. He's bound to be Scottish."

So he put on his very best English, which had no doubt been pretty broad Aberdeen, and asked this chap how to get to Detroit. The man looked down at him and said "Terribly sorry, old chap, but I don't speak a word of French."

However, Ernie found his way to Detroit and got a job on the line making cars. As soon as he got a job he wrote home and asked his girlfriend who was a housemaid at Schivas House to come and join him because he could now afford to support a wife. So she came over and they were happily married for more than 60 years. In the meantime Ernie was working on the line one day when a man approached him and said, "Are you Ernie Wilson?"

"Yes."

"Well you are wanted in the Finance Office."

Someone stepped into his place on the line and Ernie went in to the Finance Office, dejectedly expecting to collect his cards. There he was met by a man called Paterson, who was a Vice President of Ford Motor Company. He was holding Ernie's overtime card and he said to Ernie, "Where did you learn to write like that?"

"You wouldn't know sir, it was at Cairnorrie school, just out of Methlick."

"Oh, I know it very well. I come from Banffshire and I know Methlick and I know Cairnorrie very well. But where did you learn to draw two lines at the bottom of your total figure and a diagonal line left hand edge up to the bottom of the calculations."

Ernie said, "Oh I'm going to an evening class on book-keeping?"

"Oh," said Mr Paterson, "and would you go to an evening class that we would design for you?"

And Ernie said he would be delighted. The end result was that Ernie ended up with a degree in Engineering. Then Paterson sent for him again and said, "Would you like to run this such and such engineering shop?" It really was a glorified blacksmith's shop but the main job was in fitting up rows and rows of shafting and belts driving every machine and their business was contracting to Fords.

Ernie said, "But I don't have the money to buy this shop."

"Oh, no no, but we will lend you the money and you

can pay us back out of the profits." Ernie jumped at the chance and during his first few years he devised ways of automating the moving of one part of the car to the next stage of production. Eventually his company became known as the Wilson Automation Company, which is still a major company today, and Ernie Wilson became a multi-millionaire.

When I saw Ernie Wilson he had a machine which took a lump of metal, drilled out a hole in the middle, and turned it over bored holes, turned it over, bored more holes and finished up at the end ready for the electric wiring to be put on to make motors for refrigerators. He was selling these machines to General Motors, who made an enormous number of refrigerators, and that was one of the machines which made his fortune. He made so much money that he decided to take a year off and go round the world and he came to see me. He insisted, "Now if you are back in America you must come and see me." It so happened I was back in America the following year and went to see Ernie Wilson. He had a beautiful house with a lovely garden and pop-up sprinklers on the lawn. They came up at six in the morning, sprayed the lawn and then popped down again so that they didn't get in the way of the mower. He also had enormous suction fans with tubes in the corner of every room so if you wanted to dust you went swinging round the room making the dust rise and this was extracted by these fans and landed in a box in the loft. He apologised and said that he would have to be in the office at seven in the morning but that he would be back for breakfast with me at half past eight. "But Ernie," said I, "I thought you had retired."

"Oh Aye, but I left my son in charge when I had my year off and when I came back my profitable business was losing money, so I have had to take charge again."

His son was a salesman and could sell the machines, but he could not organise the work. So Ernie was back in harness and he said he was much happier than he was taking time off and kicking his heels. Ernie Wilson was very happy to see me and very hospitable and took me with great pride to his golf club. But it had all sorts of games, it was not just a golf club. I asked him what it cost to be a member there and I forget but it turned out that he only played golf about twice a year, so it was several thousand dollars per round, but of course it was a bit of show for his friends and also for the customers of his company. And Ernie, you may be sure, would make a profit out of it one way or another. He loved to talk with me about Aberdeenshire and who was doing what there. He used to come home maybe about every second year and he would appear with a great big Buick, Lincoln Continental or Cadillac. He said it was cheaper to bring a car over and drive it up than hire a car here and drive it up. But of course that was nonsense. All he really wanted to do was go round all his old friends and any enemies he had and show them his great big car.

A nice man.

He was latterly fond of a wee dram and maybe bit too fond, but Mary was very good for him and kept him from going over the score. Between the two of them they had a very happy existence. Unfortunately Mary died first and Ernie was again retired. He didn't last very long without Mary's restraining influence.

He was also a most amusing man. On another occasion I went back to see him and for some reason Big Wull Robertson, the Kincardineshire farmer, was there at the same time and we both went to see Ernie. It was amusing listening to the two of them, both exaggerating what they had done. Wull exaggerating how many acres he was farming and Ernie exaggerating how many machines he was producing. I have outlived them both and I am writing my book so I can out-boast them both now.

But back to my tour. I was now to do three weeks in Canada. There I went to see my cousin, John Mackie from Coullie at Udny. John had been my Uncle John's oldest son. When he left school in 1928, his father had been talking to Tom Hutchison of Barclay, Ross and Hutchison and asked him what he thought young John should do seeing he did not want to farm but was very good at mathematics. Tom Hutchison said, "Send him to Canada. My brother James is a CA in Montreal and I am sure he will give him a job as an apprentice." So John did his account-ancy with James Hutchison in Montreal. When he had just qualified he was helping with his first audit; of the books of the Canadian Schenley company, the second biggest distill-ers in America. The boss of that enterprise, a Mr Rosenthal – a great bully of a man but a great organiser, happened to be visiting his Canadian empire. He just happened to stop where John was working to say something. Once in the office he asked, "Who is that young man with the funny voice that I spoke to on the way in?"

"Oh that will be the Scotsman who is working for our auditors, James Hutchison."

"I want him."

And, since the Schenley account was one of James Hutchison's most important, he got him. So John moved to the Schenley distilling company and within a few years he was the treasurer. It was then that I called on him. I was particularly impressed when I was taken up to this big office. He had two telephones and a few buttons on the desk. As we were sitting chatting he suddenly sat up and pressed a button. I thought, "Ah! I'm going to see big busi-ness in action now." But all that happened was that a girl came in and he sent her out for a packet of cigarettes.

As it turned out, John did very well with Canadian Schenley. The boss told John he was tired of having to buy all his Scotch whisky through old Joe Kennedy who, while he was ambassador to Britain, managed to get himself the agency for most of the well known whiskies. So if Canadi-ans and Americans wanted to buy Scotch whisky they had to give a cut to old Joe Kennedy. That did not please Sch-enley so he said to John, "I want you to go and buy me a distillery in Scotland." So John went over to Scotland and bought the Inverugie Distillery at Peterhead and bought half the production of the Fettercairn distillery from Tommy Scott Sutherland. He went back thinking he had done a great job. Reported to Schenley and the boss said, "Well done, John, but that is not enough. Go back and build me a distillery and we'll have our own distillery and we can say goodbye to Joe Kennedy for ever." So John came over and built Tormore, the first distillery to be built

134

in Scotland since before the war. There they produced very good whisky. He used to take me up whenever he came home. I tasted the whisky when it was two years old and it was absolutely dreadful. At three years John, the expert, had decided it was going to mature fairly quickly and at seven years he started marketing it. I told him it was a mistake as I considered myself an expert in malt whiskies and, as it turned out, it was a mistake. They recognised it and took it off the market. It turned out to be a very good malt at ten and twelve years.

John told me that some whiskies need a little longer than others to mature, particularly those from the West Coast, but he assured me it was not worth buying anything or paying much more for anything above twelve years because they tend to go back rather than improve after twelve years or so. So I am never impressed when I hear that someone has bought a malt whisky of twenty years old.

John Mackie also took me to his club. I am not the greatest music-lover in the world, but they had a team of black singers there and they were absolutely fabulous and I enjoyed that immensely. I went back another time to see John and he took me skiing and that was the first time I'd tried it. He took us up into the Laurentian mountains. I was fitted out with skis and I tried it out a little bit on the gentle slopes at the bottom and thought it was so easy that I would just try the steep bit. So I grabbed a tow rope and glided gently up the hill, turned round and thought I would do what I had been doing on the gentle slopes and set off down the hill. I was doing splendidly but always gaining speed. Then I came across some skiers who were herring boning up instead of taking the tows and they expected me to swoop round them and were amazed at me shouting, "Out of the way, I can't turn." Then I was getting up to such a speed that I began to get scared and I fell down. Fortunately I fell down the right way, got the edge of the skis into the snow and stopped. I then realised that all I could do with my skiing was to get a little valley which I could swoop down at 45 degrees, slow down going up the other side, turn my skis and go down the other way. But I was so enamoured with skiing that when I got home I would go skiing at Aviemore or elsewhere. Just at the time my brother George broke an ankle on the slopes and was off work for three months, and my daughter Pat twisted a leg very badly. So I decided that I could do without the skiing.

I never got over to Western Canada. We were only in the Eastern Provinces. I did New Brunswick and then flew over to Prince Edward Island, where the first Provincial Parliament was started. In Quebec, the French speaking Province, I was met by one of the Extension Officers, which is the equivalent of our Advisors at the Agricultural College. He had arranged a nice tour for us and as we were passing along I saw a farm which looked interesting. I asked if we could stop because that looked an interesting building. He said, "Oh, they are French speaking. I don't know how you will get on."

But I said, "Oh well, let's go down and see." So down we went and entered this funny octagonal building. It was on two levels, the top level you could back in loads of hay and feed down to the animals below. We went round and didn't see a soul. There were cows in the building, and pigs and horses. It was very dark and dingy, but we were satisfied that we had seen all that there was to see and were about to leave when a fat little man burst in upon us with a torrent of French. We could clearly see that he was more than a little puzzled as to what the hell we were doing there. So with my twelve words of French permutated this way and that I tried to pacify him. I talked about "les chevaux" and "les vaches" and "les bonnes vaches." Every now and again as I was struggling the Frenchman giggled and laughed. And finally I turned to the man who was showing us round and asked what the hell he was laughing at. At this the Frenchman laughed even more and said, "Your French is very bad and my English is very good."

After that we became very friendly and he took us in to his home and we had coffee.

I had a quite different but just as extraordinary experience in Prince Edward Island. I flew in, the only passenger in a little light aircraft and we were told the airport was closed because of fog and we'd have to fly to the other side of the island. I asked the pilot what he'd have done if that had been closed also and he said he'd have to land anyway as he hadn't enough fuel to go back. I then had a car journey in thick fog across the island and arrived just in time for the meeting at seven-thirty. I was used at home to being told that Scotland was too small a place to justify having its own parliament and yet in a province of fewer than 100,000 souls with its own government I was met by the Minister of Agriculture and the Prime Minister. I had a very diverse audience of about three hundred who kept me going, without supper, until getting on for midnight. After that the Prime Minister, Walter Jones, and Minister of Agriculture Robert Shaw set about entertaining me. I had no hope of drink because I knew they had very strict laws against it but he would take me to a little fish-and-chip kind of cafe. In we went but out we came again because the owners wouldn't give us the booth farthest from the door. We had more luck at the next cafe and settled into the furthest-in booth, whereupon the Prime Minister asked the girl for a "set-up". I was quite out of my depth but I subsequently learned that that was a glass each, a jug of water and maybe a tonic or two. "Oh no, sir," she said, "not here." However glasses were produced and the Prime Minister then produced a bottle of Johnny Walker whisky and holding it below the table poured out three good drams. I had a most welcome surprise to which I believed I was fully entitled.

I thought it quite extraordinary that the Prime Minister should be reduced to breaking his own laws to entertain his official visitors, but that was their way. Everybody carried their own drink. It was called "brown bagging" because everyone could be seen carrying a brown bag with them and everybody else knew what was in it.

At the end of the Canadian tour I can tell you I was a little tired because I sometimes gave two or three talks per day and there was the travelling, speaking to strange people all the time and trying to be a good ambassador for Great Britain. I had the kilt with me because I thought it might take a trick occasionally but the only time I wore it was when the ambassador Paul Gore-Booth in Washington arranged a party for me before we left. Of course he said it would be evening dress. Nowhere else was I ever asked to wear evening dress until when we left Canada from Halifax on the dear old Empress of Britain, which was subsequently sunk - in Liverpool Harbour. It was a much smoother ship to travel in than the Queen Mary, but when we went aboard I discovered that we had an invitation to the Captain's table. So I put my kilt on for that as it was supposed to be evening dress. We were shown to our places at the Captain's table and there I got a message that the Captain had been delayed on the bridge but he was to give me a drink... and what would I have? I ordered a whisky which was brought and then our waiter came back and said the gentleman at that table over there would like to buy the Scotsman a drink... so what would you like from him? So I had another whisky and, because I was the only one wearing the kilt, I had seven whiskies lined up before the Captain arrived. So I told Isobel, "I'm going to wear the kilt every evening for the rest of this trip." It was a great success. I got free drink all the way and was poured off the boat at Liverpool after the most enjoyable journey. I was supposed to report to the British Information Services on all the things I had seen and done in North America and make any suggestions I had for future visits. I had intended to do that on the journey home. But seeing what fun was to be had on the boat I said, "To hell with the reports, I am going to enjoy myself," and joined in all the jollifications and games and so on and left the reports until I got home.

That was the end of the American journey except that we made so many contacts that for a long time afterwards we got telephone messages that so and so was arriving from America and was accepting our offer of hospitality, which was splendid, but sometimes they came at inconvenient times. Nevertheless I had had a lot of hospitality in America and was glad to return it here. So I did and still do.

But in the early sixties my associations with America were to become much more important... in more ways than one.

CHAPTER TWELVE

Charolais Cattle

ALONG WITH my brother John, Tony Harman and a few others I was busy in the late fifties and early sixties in trying to persuade the government to let us import Charolais cattle from France. The Government was being very awkward about it, though eventually it did set up a committee, chaired by Lord Terrington, who interviewed everybody. Of course all the established breed societies, the Hereford, the Shorthorn, the Aberdeen Angus and the Galloway, objected that it would be a tragedy introducing continental cattle into Britain, when the British domestic cattle had the world at their feet. I went up as a member of the Milk Board and argued that the Board should at least buy some bulls to inseminate the cows and produce better beef from the dairy herd. To my amazement sitting next to me, waiting to give evidence, was Willie (later Sir William) Young, the Chairman of the Scottish Milk Marketing Board, but also a great Ayrshire breeder, who was terribly against the introduction of any European cattle. He gave strong evidence that the boards certainly didn't want any bulls other than the established beef bulls. Terrington recommended there should be a trial done and twenty-four Charolais bulls were introduced. Willie Young was the first to claim some of the best of them for his Scottish Milk Marketing Board and after the introduction of the females Willie bought one of the best bulls in France for the Scottish Board and it made them an absolute fortune.

Anyway, the Government were being very stupid. A man called Craig Wheaten-Smith was even expelled from the country because he brought in some French semen without a licence. He managed to inseminate one cow and when the ministry discovered that, he was chased off to America and subsequently became friendly with the Four T Ranch which became leaders in America and which was to become very important in my story.

I had gone to America because I thought I would beat the Government ban on Charolais cattle by buying eight heifers and a bull, taking them up into Canada, getting them naturalised there and then it would be legal to import them... from Canada. After having done my research on Canada, I discovered that the best Charolais cattle were bred by the Four T Ranch from Texas. They were the founders of the Charolais breed in the United States. The French Ambassador to Mexico had imported a few Charolais for his own use and when he left the country his friend, a man called Poojoubait, was able to buy the herd. The owner of the Four T Ranches, Fred Turner, was an enterprising gentlemen, a Ford car dealer, but like a lot of Americans, he wanted to do a bit of farming and had bought the Four T Ranch. He was able to buy two or three of Poojoubait's cattle and take them into Texas. After his death Turner's wife, Pauline about whom more later, built up the herd with further Mexican imports despite the trade having been banned. She picked up one of the smuggled calves herself at a quiet airstrip and drove it home in the back of her car.

Fred Turner was one of four who pioneered the breed in North America. Another was Howell Thomas. They were crossing them with Brahmen Bulls which were particularly suitable for the hot climate in Texas and in no time the breed was into all states in America, because they were so obviously better beef producers.

So I arranged to visit the Four T Ranch. I flew to Dallas and called on friends I had met on a previous visit and they very kindly lent me a car with a black driver. He was called Robert and he was quite interesting about how clever they had been in Dallas with race relations. They had a nice house, lawn, sprinklers on the lawn and his daughter had a hairdressing business where his wife helped. He drove a car and did odd jobs, so he thought the blacks there had no complaints. I discovered later that this had been a very conscious policy of the powers that be in Dallas. They had met the problem head-on long before the civil rights thing got going. Robert drove me down to the Four T. I was to meet the manager, Carlos Holmes, in Georgetown, Texas. I used to tell people that when I got to the "L and M Cafe" it had half doors, like you see in the Western movies, but on a later visit I saw that my imagination had run riot because it just had ordinary doors like any other cafe in Britain. Anyway, I went into the L and M cafe which was peopled by stetson hats. I think the Texans slept with their stetsons. They certainly never took them off when they went into a restaurant. I asked around but there was no Carlos Holmes. They knew him, but he wasn't there. So a little later a lady appeared asking for a Scotsman. I discovered that she was Pauline the widow of Fred Turner. She had told her manager that she would meet the Scotsman.

So she drove me out to the ranch and we drove all round it. I must say I felt sorry for this woman, having to make a living out of this barest of bare country, sand and flat stones, cacti and tumbleweeds. I soon discovered that my concern was misplaced because what looked so bare of food became green immediately they got some rain and when the grass dried and looked dead it was just as good to eat as our dried grass. Anyway, they had most excellent cattle and I chose eight heifers and a bull.

We went with Carlos Holmes to a restaurant on the edge of the ranch and had the biggest steak I had ever seen. I, of course, ate all my steak and all the fat as well as I had been taught to eat "aa'thing that's put in front of you." But I watched in amazement as Carlos Holmes ate the heart out of the steak and left three quarters of it. I thought it the most awful waste. We then started haggling about the price of the cattle. We could come to no agreement. Pauline was asking ridiculous prices but then she was getting ridiculous prices in America for them. So I didn't get the cattle. She asked me if I would like dinner before I left and I said that that would be splendid.

So we sent Robert off with her Land-Rover because her daughter was away with her Lincoln Continental and her other daughter had her Cadillac. He was to take the Land-Rover up to the Stagecoach Inn, which had a club next to it. That was important because of the ridiculous drink laws that they had in Texas at that time. In this county you could drink in the club but you could not buy a drink in this famous restaurant. So I would drive the widow up to the Stagecoach Inn in the Buick which I had borrowed from my friends in Dallas. It had a buzzer which you could set at whatever the speed limit was so whenever you went over the speed limit it would let you know. I had it set at fifty and then sixty and then seventy and then eighty and then switched it off, because I was enjoying driving on these clear ways, straight roads for miles and miles and miles. Then Mrs Turner asked me if I would drive off the road and into a little village, where she bought a bottle of gin and a bottle of whisky, because she wasn't sure if she had enough in her locker. Every member of the club had their own locker where they kept their own drink. We got to the club where we had a splendid drink or two and went into the restaurant and decided midway that we could do with more drink and asked the waiter if he would go across to the club. But the waiter declined to go for the drink because he wasn't allowed to. That was another example of the ridiculous laws governing booze in the States at that time.

I was able to make my point about that some years later, when I was asked to address the Senate of Texas. Bedecked in my kilt and medal as a Commander of the British Empire I took the opportunity to say what a farce their drink laws were and the best thing the legislators could do was to change them. I am glad to say that that winter they passed laws saying that you could buy drink more or less where you like and I claim to have revolution-ised the drink laws in Texas.

Anyway, I went and got the drink myself and we had a glorious time. Meantime poor Robert who had to drive me all the way back to Dallas was waiting, but he was catered for and was having a nice meal in the establishment. So as the evening went on I got very taken with this lady and invited her to come and see me in Scotland. That she did the next year when she was over in France at the Vichy show. She came to Scotland on the way back and I toured her around Scotland and she says it took her two days to get me to ask her to marry me. That I did on the Beach Boulevard in Aberdeen. She was in favour of getting on with the job, but I said "No, but you'll need to go back to America, discuss it with your daughters and see what they say."

So a year elapsed before we eventually got married. That was in America and my brother George and his wife Lindsay came over so that he could be best man and I took three months off for a honeymoon going round the world. At the family dinner we had when I returned I thanked George for his services . He replied that it was not every bridegroom who needed his best man to go on honeymoon with him.

But back to the Charolais. One of Pauline's best customers was Stewart Grainger, the actor. When he heard Pauline was to be living in Scotland he said to her, "I'll probably see you in Fortnum and Masons next time we are in London." Now we didn't go to London very often let alone to Fortnum and Mason's but eventually we did and imagine our surprise when a voice said, "Pauline! How nice to see you again." It was Stewart Grainger.

Having got back from America and having failed to buy these expensive American Charolais, I used to say that having failed to buy the cattle I had married the owner in order to get the cattle. But in fact it didn't work out like that.

Pauline's son in law, Andy Williams, had come out of the American Airforce where he was a fighter pilot, and joined the ranch staff. In spite of being new to it he soon developed a stockman's eye for a beast and in no time was in demand as a judge of Charolais all over the United States. So he took over the management of the herd and after a few years had a great sale and gained the highest average of any production sale of any breed anywhere in the world. I was there and it was a most exciting occasion. I even made money myself. I had a ten dollar bet with a rancher friend of Pauline's as to what the average would be. After the first four cattle had been sold he passed over his ten dollars.

Unfortunately the Charolais prices started to fall and Andy left my step-daughter-in-law and she divorced him. With Pauline now living in Scotland with me it was decided to sell the ranch and the cattle, except for what Andy Williams kept as part of the divorce settlement. It was a sad end to what Pauline and her husband had built up.

However that was not the end of my interest in Charolais cattle as, when the import of semen was allowed in 1962 we tried some on our dairy cows. Also, as a founder member of the breed society, we got five heifers from the first importation from France and more in subsequent importations. We also went to the Paris Show and bought one of the champion bulls which we called Westertown Espoir and which made us a lot of money. We didn't make as much as we should have though, as what was needed was a dedicated beef cattleman. Such a man was Neil Massie of Blelack, and when he made us a suitable offer in 1971, because our main interest was in milk not meat, we sold out.

CHAPTER THIRTEEN

Around the World
on Honeymoon

ANYWAY, PAULINE and I were married and set off round
the world on a three month honeymoon. It brought out
some contrasts. My first wife got a week of a honeymoon
for a start. And then there was the question of rings. When
my father got engaged he went to have the jeweller put in
the initials inside the ring but for some reason he was embarrassed about that and gave a false name for himself. But
then when he said he wanted M M in the ring the jeweller
was astonished and said, "But you surely want your own
initials in the ring," whereupon my father had to confess
that he was indeed Maitland Mackie. Ah, well. I gave the
correct name but I did go to Perth to buy my first engagement ring and I was always able to tell Isobel that she
should remember that her ring cost a whole cow. I have to
admit that Pauline, my second wife, got a wedding ring
which cost more than a cow, in fact, even more than she
had tried to charge me for a Charolais heifer when I was
trying to buy them in Texas. We British tend not to spend
a great deal on wedding rings and I think Isobel's one was
thirty shillings or something like that and, as we were to be
wed in Texas, I asked Pauline's daughter Jan to buy me a
ring there. Little did I know that the Texans go in for
fancy wedding rings and she got me one with beautifully
inlaid diamonds. Instead of the modest bill, I was faced

With Pauline on our wedding day

with the price of another cow and a damned good one at
that. In fact I had a narrow escape even at that because I
had told my prospective daughter-in-law, "Oh, just get the
best wedding ring there is." Fortunately Pauline had toned
down her daughter's ideas or I could have been spending
the price of a whole herd of Charolais.

On the honeymoon we spent three weeks in New Zealand. I had relatives there and thought it would be fun to
visit them. They were relatives of my father and we used to
hear every year that they were coming home. But they
never made enough money until after we were there. The
son, who had become involved in Farmer's Union politics,
came on that business. But they were getting something
like fourpence a gallon, making some milk into butter and
were making a little profit but not enough to have a holiday
at home. We enjoyed New Zealand. We went right down
to Bluff Point and saw the sign post which points in every
direction including the one which points South, and that
one says that there's nothing between that point and the
Pole.

When we were leaving to fly home via Acapulco I had
noticed a man coming on board. I said to my wife,
"There's a Texan coming on board." He was wearing a
stetson and cowboy boots and he had a diamond tiepin in
the shape of a map of Texas so it wasn't an altogether
brilliant piece of detection. When we got to Hawaii, where
we had to stop to give the pilots a rest, I said, "Go and
speak to your fellow Texan."

So we got in touch with the Texan, invited him to
come and have lunch with us and asked what he was doing
there. He said he was on the way home from working at
the South Pole. Now, you don't meet a lot of people who
work at the South Pole so we asked what he had been doing
there. "We wanted to test a small atomic explosion in the
ice at the South Pole because we propose to use controlled
nuclear explosions to widen the Panama Canal which is
becoming too narrow for the modern traffic. The cheapest
way to shift all that earth would be a nuclear explosion. I
also promised the Australian Government that if they would
clear the area I could cure the problem of the port at Port

Headland being too small by using similar bombs. I'll give you a good deep port in one explosion."

All that had fallen through but I thought it was inter-esting and in the course of conversation I got into a bit of an argument with this chap about all the money America was spending on their attempt to go to the moon. I told him I thought there were other things they should be spending their money on. He said that he would like a chance to convince me that it was not a waste of money. "Would you like to come to Cape Canaverell to see the next launch?" Of course I thought he was just pulling my leg but he proceeded to tell me all that stuff about the spin-offs from the space programme, the non-stick frying pans and so on. I thought that would be the last we would hear from him but when we got back to the ranch from Acapulco, there was a message to phone Dr Maxwell. So I phoned him and he said, "I've got permission to take you to see the blast-off to the moon next week. Professor Somebody is coming up from the South. He'll pick you up, bring you up to Dallas and we'll take you down in one of my two airo-planes." I was to be a lucky chap again.

It all happened. We were put up in a hotel and at an un-godly hour (four or five in the morning) we were wak-ened up and went to see the launch. I was in the very front row, in fact, about three miles from where the space ship was, but that was the nearest anybody was except a poor chap who was sitting in a covered metal van with a metal rope up to the top of the ship down which, if anything went wrong the occupants were to skite. They'd have their fall broken by the rubber in this van which would then beetle-off before the whole thing exploded.

I was asked by Dr Maxwell to take some photographs. He had loaded three cameras for me and there I was with them on the bench at the ready while the count-down went ahead. When they came to "Ignition" the whole thing dis-appeared in an enormous cloud of steam and I thought, "Oh, good God! The whole thing's exploded." But what had happened was all part of the plan. When they light eight of those enormously powerful engines (and they hold them down for a minute and a half until they all develop full power) all this blast is going down into a pit and would melt the whole thing. So they poured forty thousand gallons of water into the pit. After the water evaporated she was let loose and the thing rose into the air.

I was introduced to some of my fellow spectators including Von Braun, the German who was largely responsible for the Buzz Bombs during the war and for the development of rockets strong enough to send men to the Moon. He seemed a nice modest man. I also met one of my heroes, Charles Lindberg, the first man to fly the Atlantic solo. Also Teddy Kennedy, though I'm not so sure that that was such an honour.

Then we were the first people to nip over to the site and it was extraordinary to see just a few puddles of water left out of the forty thousand gallons which had been in the pit. It had all evaporated in a minute and a half. It was no wonder that I had thought it had exploded... but I did manage to take Dr Maxwell's photographs despite my consternation. It was a majestic sight to see this polished silver thing coming out of the steam and gradually gathering speed. Then one bit of it was discarded and dropped into the Gulf, then another and off it went to the Moon. On that occasion they went to the Moon, detached the lunar landing craft and went close enough to prove that they could likely land on it next time, hooked on again and then came home. The next time they were able to land safely on the Moon because they had already practised so much of the procedure.

I subsequently spent a couple of days going round all the things on show and I was then convinced about the value of the project because they had already sent satellites into the sky from other launching pads. It was a great development. What was interesting was the enormous shed in which they built this thing. They took it out at one mile an hour and loaded it at the launching site. The whole effort was an engineering marvel. Most exciting, and it was nice to be able to say, "I was there."

Dr Maxwell then showed us round a number of people whom he had cured of cancer using "cobalt bombs." They were naturally very glad to see their saviour and poured out splendid drams for the good doctor and his Scottish friend. It was the time of year when, in Florida, the trees are hanging with grapefruit and oranges and each of our hosts insisted that we take with us a large citrus bag. When we got to the plane the crew were concerned. It was overloaded without four inebriates each carrying half a hundredweight of oranges. However they eventually decided they would be able to take-off and did so. During the flight I would have been alarmed, but for our jolly condition, by the sight of one after another of the crew coming along and shining a torch out of the window. I wondered if they were checking to see if they had remembered the wings but decided they were paid to do the worrying. When we landed I learned that the wings had been icing up and the weight of ice and our oranges was forcing us down into the Gulf of Mexico. The pilot had saved the day by searching the skies until he found a warm current of air which melted the ice. After we landed I would help Dr Maxwell transfer the oranges to his smaller plane. All I could see in the dark was the light from the hold where the oranges were to go and I ran into a wing splitting my head as well as breaking my glasses. I made a sorry sight when I arrived home, bleeding from the head, with broken glasses and the better of drink. My excuse that I had hit a plane was regarded as weak.

And so it was back to farming at Westertown, though by this time I was doing more and more public work.

Four generations of Maitland Mackie

CHAPTER FOURTEEN

Politics

IN 1957 I was getting so involved in things outside the farming world that I was very glad to see my elder son, Maitland, finished with his degree in agriculture. Like my grandfather and my father before me, I thought the best training for him would be to become grieve on a farm but I also thought it would be a good thing for him to see a little of the world before he started. I decided that he should take a year off and go round the world and he was quite excited to do that. I arranged with John Sleigh (the man who all those years before had given us the idea for the parachute and who was now involved in the export of Shorthorn cattle) that my son would take some cattle across the Atlantic to Montreal. I think Maitland was to get a free passage and that was all, but I gave him £50 and said, "You can work your way round the world but if you ever get absolutely stuck for money I will wire some money to you. It's up to you." When he got to Montreal he got a job taking some horses overland right across Canada so he also saw a bit of Vancouver. After Vancouver he crossed the American border with some difficulty because they didn't see how he was going to manage to support himself. He had only a back-pack and sleeping-bag and he didn't have a job waiting for him. His next difficulty was he didn't know where to go. I had given him some addresses of people I had met on my tour of America and the first address was in Portland in Oregon. It was beginning to get dark when he arrived there and when he rang the doorbell nothing happened, but a neighbour told him that they were away on holiday. So using some of his hard-earned cash he called a cab and said, "Take me to the nearest bit of open space."

That must have been one of the most curious instructions the taxi driver was ever given. As it was now dark the cabbie told him, "That's open space over there at the other side of the road."

So he was able to save his money, climb over the fence, find a nice spot, roll out his sleeping bag and fall asleep. He woke in the morning feeling rather uncomfortable to discover he had fallen asleep behind a huge ant heap and the ants had started investigating his sleeping bag so there was the curious spectacle, which he was glad no one else saw in case he landed in the jail for indecent exposure, as he shook out the sleeping bag and took off all his clothes and put them on again after he had picked all the ants out of them.

He had lots of adventures and moved all around the south and three or four months later landed back at Montreal. He was waiting there for a ship which he had looked out to take him down to the Argentine when he got a telegram from his mother saying that I was in the middle of an election and she thought he should come home and help. At two o'clock in the morning I got a phone call from him asking for ten pounds with which he would come home. I stupidly sent him the ten pounds so he came home and helped valiantly with the election which we lost anyway. I suppose the experience of fighting an election might have been better than another nine months going around the world, but I very much doubt it.

Anyway it suited me fine because after the election Maitland took up his duties as grieve. But in effect he really became manager. He had a short spell as a working grieve perhaps not long enough because I do think it's a very good training working as grieve and organising the work. But soon he was my manager and another working grieve was employed. That left me free to do many other things.

At the University Maitland Jnr had become engaged

to one Haldis Ramm who was a Norwegian student doing medicine. She had been the Charities Queen and as he was the convenor of the student charity effort he felt that it was only right that they get together. Now that Maitland was home with a job they decided to get married, although Haldis had a few years of her medical degree still to do. We did up the farm house at Eastertown for them but the wedding was held in Norway.

In order to make it easier for my friends and relations to go to the wedding I chartered an aeroplane from Dyce to go to Bergen and there is a lovely photograph of at least three of the guests marching up onto the plane with, on their shoulder, a box very clearly marked Bell's Whisky, and I can tell you that all the whisky was needed for the spree and a good many of us stayed on after the wedding... for nearly a week. The wedding feast was held in a restaurant up on the top of the hill which was reached with a rack railway. It was a most marvellous banquet at which we were somewhat taken by surprise by the Norwegian tradition of clearing away the plates after each course and bringing you some more of the same again. This shook us a bit because we all took very liberal helpings for the first course and struggled a bit with the second. But luckily the banquet lasted a long time so all was well. Liberal amounts of alcohol of all kinds were taken and my uncle Bruce Mackie from Milton of Noth - even he - was visibly the better of drink. On the way down on the rack railway Bruce took it upon himself to go down to the front of the carriage and conduct the singing with an umbrella and I looked across at my father to catch the amazement on his face at the sight of his younger half-brother conducting himself in what old Maitland would have considered an unseemly manner. But it made a splendid finish to that part of the wedding.

I've been fond of Norway ever since and have been back a few times. Of course my daughter-in-law has a holiday house on an island in the Bergen fjord and my wife and I have holidayed there and enjoyed it immensely. The only way to get to this island is by sailing boat so they keep a variety of boats and I had my first lesson in sailing there. It was very successful and I was complimented by my son on picking up the elements very quickly, but as we drew alongside the little pier which gives access to their home he stepped on to the quay taking the weight off his side of the boat. The boat then tipped over to my side and I slipped gently into the water to the great hilarity of everyone concerned. No great harm was done... not even to my pride.

After the marriage Haldis continued to do her medical degree. She had to pass a British test to drive her car and on one occasion she was stopped by the police because the number plate on the little mini she was driving had fallen off. When she was asked to produce a licence she only had a Norwegian one. The policeman phoned me from Oldmeldrum and said that this was really a difficult case that he didn't suppose that any of his colleagues would have had a case like this involving as it did international law. Anyway Haldis got her licence and got her degree and I always thought that was very clever to come from abroad and do a difficult degree in a foreign language. She has continued to do well in medicine and is now the senior partner in the Insch practice, her original partners having died or retired. Doctors seem to me to get a reasonable fee for their job and no doubt that has been welcome insurance in these difficult times for farming.

We continued to live in the house at Westertown for a number of years after that but it seemed to me that, as I was doing less and less farming, I should retire and we bought a house in Rubislaw Den in Aberdeen, which was considered very up-market. That was in 1974 and we lived very happily there for ten years or so. At first it was strange to be living in a town but I soon got used to it. It was much more convenient than having to drive, sometimes twice a day, the twenty-five miles from the farm into Aberdeen so it was often a hundred miles a day just to go to meetings. It was a waste of time. I had never thought I could live in a town, but since I was so much involved it wasn't as much of a wrench to leave the land as I had thought and of course I still had a financial interest in the business and could see what was going on.

At that particular time I had, like my father before me, thought that it would be a pity if I were to die and leave anything to the tax man... to the Queen. Perhaps that was a mistake but I had made the farming concern into a limited company with the shares. So I gave away all the shares to the six children and it was therefore Maitland's responsibility to see that his brothers and sisters were catered for in later years. All that has worked out reasonably successfully although the company later turned out not to be a very good plan for tax reasons. But that's now young Maitland's responsibility and as long as he keeps me in the style to which I have been accustomed that's all I ask of the business. I remained chairman of the company with a salary for a number of years but retired completely in 1982.

Looking back over the farming years I now recall another lesson that I learned from my father. I had sent some sixty of the best of the year's crop of lambs to an early sale in Aberdeen and went in to see them sold. I watched the sale beginning but I was a long way down the ballot and it didn't look like a very good trade so in my wisdom or lack of it I thought I would be pleased if I got about forty shillings per lamb. Now, one of the dealers, a man called Andrew Shearer, came up and said, "I see you have a pen of lambs for sale laddie. Now, what would you be needing for them?"

"Forty two shillings."

And after a deal of bargaining I sold them for forty shillings, supposing I had done quite well and thinking there was no need to stay around the mart, I went off to do some other things like visiting my girlfriend, the celebrated Miss Ross. So I booked the sale into the office, got my cheque and went off. My father phoned and asked what I got for the lambs and I told him I had sold them privately for forty shillings. My father phoned the next day and said that he thought I'd be interested to know that Andrew Shearer had put the lambs back through the ring at the end of the sale and had got forty three shillings for them. So I learned that maybe I should have stayed at the ringside and studied the thing a bit longer, as had the wise ones.

Although my parents were not great politicians except for farming politics, their family, for some odd reason, became very politically minded and they were mostly left wing. One sister, Mary, went as far left as she could be becoming a communist and marrying a communist. Later, after the Hungarian uprising in 1956, they made a great display of burning their cards, which took place on the steps of the Lincoln Cathedral, deciding they'd had enough of that and joined the Labour party, where Mary became a Labour councillor and very nearly won the Grantham constituency for Labour at the General Election when she stood against the then Minister of Agriculture, Joseph Godber.

Many people thought it extraordinary that a family brought up in a reasonably comfortable existence as we had been should turn socialist. But, in fact, apart from Mary, none of them believed that the means of production, distribution and exchange should all be in the hands of the state according to Karl Marx. What they did believe was that the world was ill-parted. We, as a family, could easily see round about us poverty and we could read about poverty and they were not so much socialists as people with a social conscience. The only way they thought their conscience could be attended to was by joining the Labour party. In fact I've always believed that the Labour party was comprised of two main groups; one group who may well be believers in Karl Marx and the other group of well-intentioned people who, like my brother and sisters, had a social conscience and felt that Labour was the only party that could redress the imbalances in society. On the other hand, at the University, I was tempted both ways, admiring my parents and they being Tories (though I discovered much later that my father had voted Liberal many times until Bob Boothby became our MP; all the farming community voted for Bob Boothby). My mother was the only real Tory in the family, she didn't know a lot about politics but she intuitively knew she was right. In all the family arguments about politics the only one who got really excited was my mother. She would burst out on us and tell us we were talking nonsense. But we had a tacit agreement that on such occasions we would change the subject and leave politics alone.

There was, of course, at the University, a diversity of opinions and I just adopted the Liberal view because I

think I've been a Liberal all my life. The Liberal philosophy seemed to suit me and I've never changed my view.
The Liberals were also the only party, it seemed to me,
which was totally against the party whip system whereby
you are expected to vote for the party no matter what you
really believe. The number of times a free vote is allowed in
the House of Commons you could count on the fingers of
one hand in any one year. That seemed to me to be another very good reason for joining the Liberals. I became
semi-active and, in 1951, the West Aberdeenshire Liberals
asked if I would stand against the resident Tory MP, a
Spence of Spence's knitwear factory in Huntly. I agreed.
We were a bit late into the field and we didn't have a very
good organisation but we had some keen workers and I got
thoroughly excited that we were doing awfully well. It was
very hard work, with as many as five meetings a day, getting home tired, having to organise the farm as well and
then back on the trail next morning.

Isobel worked hard canvassing and sitting on the
platform like a good candidate's wife. I've always thought it
must be dreadful for the candidate's wife to listen to the
same speech five days a week for three weeks. She did
sometimes get off to go to supporting meetings and drive a
car. On one of those occasions she went off to a meeting at
which Sir Archibald Sinclair was supporting me. She went
with him and joined me at the last meeting in Insch. Sir
Archibald made his usual speech in support of me at Insch
and Isobel told me later that she had studied him very
carefully and he had his speech written out in double type,
large type which he held in one hand and changed the
cards always at exactly the same moment in his speech. He
took off his glasses and held them out with a wave of his
hand at the appropriate moment, exactly the same performance each time he gave the speech. Like Churchill he
practised his speeches. He was one of the old fashioned
orators and it was really quite a performance when Archy
Sinclair came. He somewhat spoiled his performance however when he came to Inverurie. One of the reasons that
he had lost his seat was that he had attended to other
people's campaigns instead of his own up in Caithness and

Sutherland. He was so tired when he came to Inverurie that he opened his speech with, "I'm so glad to be in Turriff again." He did recover from that but it does show how tired you can get.

Surrounded by your supporters you think you're doing far better than you are and, of course, we didn't have a very good method of judging it was all just a question of feel and the feel of course was the feel of your supporters because that was who was surrounding you. So when the result was announced we were desperately disappointed to have come second but miles behind. That was the election when you got tired of hearing on the radio, "...and the Liberal lost his deposit." The next day I met Lady Tweedsmuir, the Tory MP for South Aberdeen, in the Caledonian Hotel. She was always very pleasant and she told me, "Next time, if you'll just stand for the Tories, you'll easily get in, Mike."

I might have but I didn't.

I said, "The reason that I stood against the Tories was that I don't believe in them," and at that point another message was received over the radio, "and the Liberal lost his deposit." Lady Tweedsmuir said, "See what I'm telling you?"

In retrospect I don't think it was such a bad performance because there were only six constituencies in the country in which the Liberal vote was increased and we were one of them. At any rate, that was some comfort to our supporters who were very disappointed. That was a lesson and I thought, "Politics is not for me."

Mr Spence was a good businessman at the time and, as Tory MPs go, I suppose he was good enough. But he apparently was not good enough to get any job in the Government. I think he was a rather colourless sort of character. He was quite a popular MP but he didn't know a lot about agriculture which I thought would be an advantage for me but at that time in rural Scotland a Tory MP was sure to go in on the nod.

My next venture was a good bit later in 1958 when Bob Boothby was elevated to the House of Lords after 30 years of being a very popular MP in East Aberdeenshire.

The only time when Bob might have been defeated was in 1945 when my brother-in-law John R Allan decided to have a go at him on behalf of the Labour party. That was the one time when Bob might have been defeated because there was the so-called scandal of the "Czech gold" when there was a fairly condemnatory report produced by a select committee of the House of Commons which went to the constituency party. Bob had spoken in the House of Commons on this issue concerning Czech funds held in this country and had failed to acknowledge that he had an interest in the matter. A report was sent to the constituency party but the constituency party, led by Gardy Duff of Hatton and Lord Aberdeen, were persuaded by the smooth tongued Bob that there was nothing in this report and that he had nothing with which to reproach himself.

At any rate, John Allan decided to take him on and I went to hear them both speaking when they came to Rothienorman, oddly enough on the same night. I listened to John R Allan and he gave a good speech and then fifteen minutes later Bob arrived and the same audience listened to Bob and he gave the most socialistic speech that I have ever heard a Tory give. He almost repeated word for word what John Allan had said half an hour earlier. I knew Bob reasonably well and after the meeting I went up and said "Bob what a splendid speech. When are you joining the Socialist party?" and he said "Oh, well. When they write off their ridiculous rules about MPs always obeying the party whip. If they would change their rules so that you didn't have to vote for the party no matter what you thought I would join them." The first thing that Attlee did when he got into power was to change those rules and when I met Bob, not very much later on the train coming up from London, I said to him, "Bob, you'll now be joining the Labour party because they changed that rule. You said that was the only thing stopping you." But he said, "No, no. The case being altered, that alters the case."

So Bob remained as the very popular MP for East Aberdeenshire. Now anyone who knew Bob knew that he was never in all his life a Tory. But, as a young man, he had been keen to get into politics and it is said that he and his friend Walter Elliot were both offered seats and when Bob's telegram came offering him the seat his reply was "Yes. Which party?" Bob Boothby was an excellent MP for the North East. He worked hard for the fishing community and for the farming people and it was no wonder that no one succeeded in getting him out. However, when he accepted a seat in the Lords the possibility of capturing East Aberdeenshire for the Liberals became a real one, or so I thought. I was persuaded to stand by Johnny Bannerman, the former captain of Scotland in rugby and then the leader of the Liberals in Scotland. We were on our way to the adoption meeting, as I thought, to adopt Sir Andrew Murray the former Lord Provost of Edinburgh as the Liberal candidate. Johnny did his best, at high tea before we left and all the way up to Peterhead, to persuade me that I should stand because Sir Andrew was a splendid chap but would be no good for a rural constituency and really a local man would have far more chance.

But I said, "We canna go to his adoption meeting and tell him that I'm to be adopted instead of him. Who's going to tell him?"

"I'll tell him," said John Bannerman.

And indeed, when we arrived at his adoption meeting, Johnny drew Sir Andrew aside and gave him the bad news. I took my hat off to Sir Andrew then because he accepted that that was the right thing to do and seconded the motion that I be selected as the candidate. He stayed the whole three weeks of the campaign used his office to write out envelopes and was a great supporter.

That was a most interesting campaign. I, of course, had a lot of Tory friends but it was a by-election when people are inclined to cross their normal party lines so a lot of my farming friends said, "Oh yes. We'll vote for you." So it seemed to me that what I should concentrate on was canvassing the Labour Party supporters in Peterhead and Fraserburgh. I made great efforts to persuade the trade unionists in the Cross & Blackwell factory in Peterhead and the Fraserburgh Toolworks and I had persuaded them that the best thing for them to do was to vote for me in order to keep the Tory out. I had even got the trade union leaders to agree to canvas their own membership in support of me because the Labour man didn't have a hope in hell of getting in. He was a very nice chap and a good man but a union man from Glasgow, which couldn't have been a worse background for fighting East Aberdeenshire. This time we had a very much better organisation and we had people who did so-called polling to see how we were getting on and they were getting more and more excited that we were going to win this seat. I think maybe we were in front but, at the beginning of the last week, the Tory Central Office sent up a man called Fraser who was to report on this important by-election. For some reason I took him down from Peterhead to Turriff to interview the editor of the local paper and he had apparently told the editor that it would be a good thing if he (Fraser) wrote the editor's leader for that week. The editor had said, "but why on earth should I let you do that?"

"Well, I must remind you that most of your income comes from reporting for Associated Press and another of the major news-agencies and we control them and maybe you might lose that job if you don't allow me to write your leader."

So the leader that week was to the effect that Maitland Mackie was such a good man that he was needed in local government and that he knew nothing about national politics. He should stay in Aberdeenshire. That annoyed some of my valiant supporters but there was nothing they could do about it. Then the next dirty trick came on the Wednesday morning. The headlines in the Aberdeen Press & Journal, which was controlled, of course, by the Kemsley family who were closely allied to the Tory party, gave Fraser's estimate of how the election would go. The headline was "Socialist to win East Aberdeenshire - Tories a near second - Liberals a distant third." Of course it was too late to do anything to counter that but my Tory friends immediately abandoned me to try to make up the same leeway that the Tories allegedly needed to win and my Labour Party supporters from Cross & Blackwell and the Toolworks believed that their party did have a chance after all so they abandoned me as well. We did a count that night and we reckoned that we lost half our votes. So the result was that Fraser's count was quite right and we did indeed come third, although we had been leading according to several polls, and the Tory did indeed win.

It was quite extraordinary that the successful Tory candidate was Patrick Wolrige Gordon, a twenty-three year old student at Cambridge. He hadn't even done a degree. He really didn't know Aberdeenshire, only coming to Aberdeen in his school holidays. He had never done anything except go to school, hadn't even had a job, and yet he was elected in preference to a highly respected electrical engineer from Glasgow and myself with all my knowledge of the area and wide experience. But the Tory Party was very strong in those days and their man Fraser showed what could be done if you had the right political 'nowse'.

Having been beaten once I had said to myself, "I'm not going to be involved in that again." But it did seem that the inexperienced student would be an easy target and I was persuaded. Having been beaten a second time I was determined never to try again. During the campaign I had a lot of help from a lot of people and I remember that my brother George came up to help me from his farm in Kirriemuir. He was a valiant worker and on one occasion he and Dick Pirie, a friend of mine from the University days, went canvassing in Turriff. They came back to Westertown after the meetings. I had been home for some time and was having a wee dram. Dick and George came in and appeared to have had quite a few drams already. They were recounting how clever they had been at the meeting they had been at and the clever things they said to some of our prospective supporters. I think they probably lost me more votes than they had gained. But they had had fun and during an election you needed a bit of fun. One experienced politician came up and spent a day with me and he said, "You've got to get out and just walk down the street and stop everybody and be bold and say 'I'm Maitland Mackie and I'm standing and I hope you'll vote for me'."

I found that a little difficult for a start but emboldened by this chap I latterly got up to this business and paraded myself up and down with my large rosette and encouraged folk to vote for me. At the end of the day I thought we were going to win but the newspaper tactics of the opposition defeated us.

One thing that happened during the election amused. me particularly. One of my county council colleagues Alec Bell was asked if he was going to vote for Mike Mackie. He said, "Na, Na. Mike's jist like aa the Mackies They're just like whales. They maun aye come up tae blaa."

I thought this was a very funny remark and a little later at a County Council meeting when I saw Alec in the company I retold the story which was greatly enjoyed by all the councillors except poor Alec who was kind of hiding behind and lowering his head and I said, "Oh, you shouldna hide yer head Alec. I've enjoyed that story and I've told it many times. Thank you very much." In fact that story has been much enjoyed by all my family.

Alec Bell was a great big man and when the thirty shilling tailors came to Aberdeen he went in to get a suit. But when the tailor measured the girth he said he thought he couldn't do this size for thirty shillings. But Alec held them to it, pointing out that it was well advertised that you could have a suit for thirty shillings. So Alec got the suit. When he was paying for it he said, "Well now. Since you've been so good as to stick to your word I'll tell you what I'll do. I'll send the three laddies in to get a suit." So next Friday the three laddies, also huge men, all appeared to get a suit for thirty shillings.

The Bells were all great big men and they put that to good use in their own tug o' war team, which ruled the roost at the shows throughout the North East in the thirties and forties. And we had the temerity to challenge the Bells at the first Turriff Show after the war. We chose all the strongest men from Eastertown, Westertown, Thomastown, North Ythsie and Little Ardo and after a hard day's work they met at North Ythsie for training by a retired sergeant from Forresterhill. He taught them that the strongest bit of the body was the back muscles and if they would all straighten their backs at once they could pull anybody over. Our team was called Mackie's Milk. Alec was watching closely and when our men started to pull the Bells Alec came dancing in about and I had to restrain him. We were as bad as the modern day football managers when the thing gets too exciting. Anyway we won in two straight pulls and were absolutely exhausted though very delighted. So was I and, of course, it was a great advertisement for Mackie's Milk.

It lent substance to our slogan;

"Look at me sae big and strong
That eence wis thin and wirey.
If ye wint tae look like me
Tak yer milk fae Mackie's Direy.

For his funeral Alec Bell needed a great big coffin. All his county council friends were at the funeral and after the service in the church some of the elders were to carry him out but it was an awkward church with a nasty corner to get round to get into the vestry and they had a bit of a struggle getting this enormous coffin manoeuvred. The mourners were delighted to hear them saying, "We'll jist hae tae coup him up."

My neighbour turned to me and said, "Alec was an awkward bugger when he was alive and he's still an awkward bugger now that he's dead."

At any rate, from the 1958 election on, I decided to stick to local politics which I enjoyed for many, many years.

Of course I was always interested in national issues and one big excitement in my lifetime was the Suez disaster. The Egyptians had nationalised the Suez Canal which belonged to Britain and Britain, France and Israel set out for their separate reasons to invade Egypt and restore the Canal to British ownership. I was totally opposed to this escapade, which was led by the British Prime minister Anthony Eden. It seemed to me that, having struggled for years to get our troops out of the Middle East and out of Egypt and having come to terms with the ownership of the Suez canal passing to the Egyptians, having come to terms with the fact that the British Raj couldn't throw its weight about all over the world and that people had some rights in their own country, I was utterly against the British project to take the Suez Canal back from the Egyptians who had nationalised it. With one or two of my friends we decided we should do something about it and I phoned Bob Boothby and asked him what he was going to do. He said, "Well, at this moment, we've got fifteen or twenty Tory MPs and we're discussing what steps we can take. You can rest assured that we'll do all we can to stop this bloody nonsense, but what you should do is to get people roused up in Aberdeen."

So along with the Provost Graham, who was a socialist professor at the University, and JJ Robertson, the headmaster of the Grammar School, I held a great public meeting in the Music Hall.

I phoned the Provost first and he agreed entirely with me. "What are we going to do?" he said.

"Well I think we should call a public meeting."

So we called a public meeting and we all made fiery speeches against the Government's actions. There were, we thought, enough people there to really spread the gospel, and we received good reports in the papers the next day. Then the nasty phone calls started. People who thought I was being a renegade and even my own cousin Alice from Coullie, a most generous, warm and happy person, phoned to tell me that I was a traitor to my country. But Suez was a fiasco and I didn't feel I was being much of a traitor. They said they were going to keep the Canal open for the benefit of the free world but by the time our soldiers had landed it was already totally blocked. It stayed that way for months and months. And the British organisation was hopeless. The troops that were supposed to be getting in there quick were loaded from Cyprus and it took them hours to get there. The whole shambles really finished Anthony Eden's career.

Cousin Alice, who was a true blue Tory and believed that everything the Tories did was right, pro-Mackie family as she was, was very angry with me. I was a traitor and I ought to retract and apologise. She was very excited about it. But it took them months to get the Canal going again and since they got it opened the Egyptians have done what the Tories said was impossible - they have run the thing with perfect efficiency. So maybe it was a lesson to the Tories.

Another quasi-political activity of mine was the Campaign for Nuclear Disarmament. It was a very big issue at the time, the question of nuclear bombs, and a lot of us got excited that we were going to destroy humanity. Thousands of people joined CND and I joined and was quite enthusiastic and listened on one occasion to their great leader, Canon Collins. He was a brilliant speaker and influenced many people. He certainly influenced me and I wore my badge reasonably proudly until all sorts of weirdos joined the movement. At that stage I got tired of them and sent my badge back saying that I would have no more to do with them. I have not regretted backing out of the CND movement because I think they were more than a little naive.

While I was wearing my CND badge I got my leg pulled a great deal but it did not bother me too much. I never got up on a CND platform. I did intend to go on the first Aldermaston march but I took influenza at the time and so I didn't go. I rather regret that because it would have been nice to look back and say that you were on the first Aldermaston march.

CHAPTER FIFTEEN

Local Politics-
Chairman of Education

MY FIRST venture into national politics in 1951 coincided with the start of my work on the Aberdeen County Council. My father said (with a twinkle in his eye, I thought), "It would be a bad job to be a stucken MP *and* a stucken Councillor."

Although I was busy enough at home I was already taking quite a bit of interest in things outside the farm and was on the local Community Council in Aberdeen, which dealt with community affairs. I was also on the Local District Council with my friend Sam Niven, who was the County Councillor and never did anything on the Council - never spoke and wasn't really very active. A lot of my friends said you should stand for the County Council but I said, "Oh, I can't possibly stand against my friend Sam." But when Sam decided to retire I was then pressed to stand and of course I couldn't very well refuse as my excuse for not standing previously had gone. The other man who had done a lot of work for the local community was Jimmy Simpson of Brownhill. He decided that he too would stand for the council, so we had a real fight on our hands. But I did get a team together and I think both Jimmy Simpson and I called on every voter, or nearly every voter. I had one or two friends like Wallace Wight from Mill of Saphock, a great worker and anybody I hadn't managed to call on he went to see. Jimmy Simpson was a very popular local farmer and had really done a lot of work locally so I wasn't at all certain that I would win. When the polling booths closed I had some of my valiant workers back at Westertown having a dram and to discuss how we had got on and what the prospects were. Wallace Wight said, "Oh great God! I went back at the last minute to pick up that auld manny when we discovered that he hadn't been to vote and I took him there and he voted just a minute before they closed and I've just suddenly remembered in all the excitement that I hinna voted masel." And I remember saying, "Well, Wallace, if I lose by one vote you'll never hold your head up again." But we won fairly handsomely.

The reason that people wanted me on was that Sam, bless his heart, never really represented the people when there was anything needing doing. For instance, there was always trouble with the water supplies to various places, the roads were in a mess and there was all kinds of things that people thought an active councillor could get done... and they were right. I was quite successful in getting these sorts of things done and I think I made a reasonable councillor. But people are not as interested after the elections. One of the things I promised in my great campaign was to have two meetings every year, one in Fyvie and another in Rothienorman, which was a fair division of the constituency. The idea was to tell my constituents about what I had done and what I hadn't managed to do and answer any questions they had about the council. For several years I held these meetings with the number of people attending going down every year until the last two years I suddenly realised the Rothienorman meeting was being attended by about ten people and, when I looked round, I realised they would all much rather have been at home. They were there just because they felt they couldn't have their county councillor having a meeting and nobody go. So I stopped the meetings and made it plain that my door was open and my telephone was ready for anyone who wanted.

So really, after the excitement of the election there was a great deal of apathy with nobody caring a damn. But I thought it was a very good example of local democracy and one of the things that I liked about the old Aberdeen-shire County Council was that we had no party politics. That was quite different from the very highly politicised Aberdeen City Council. I was boasting to my brother John, who was a socialist MP at the time, how wonderful it was that no one was forced to vote for a political party. We just voted for what we thought was right. He immediately said, "What damned nonsense, you're the biggest lot of bloody Tories that there ever was."

I was forced to say to my brother, "Well that's the biggest lot of bloody nonsense, because here I am, I'm now Convenor of the Council, and I've been a Liberal all my life, the Vice-Convenor who was previously elected Chairman of the Finance Committee is one of the few socialists on the Council, so you'll just need to take your words back John."

I really enjoyed the Council because we really were doing something. I often felt that my brothers in the House of Commons slaved away and attended at all the most curious hours and couldn't really look back and say they had done anything when in opposition. It was different of course when John's party got in and he got a job as a Parliamentary Private Secretary to the two Ministers of Agriculture. He had to train them because they knew nothing about farming. He could then look back and think he had actually done something. But the back benchers would slave away and never get anything done and although I had tried twice to get into the House of Commons I'm glad that I did not succeed. I can look back at my County Council work and see the schools and the halls that we had done up and the roads we made and all sorts of things.

Mind you, we weren't always successful. One of the biggest disappointments in my life was the failure to get the Cabrach water scheme going. In fact for many years I used to waken up at night regretting that great failure. As far back as 1929 there had been proposals to go along with Banffshire and build a great big dam up in the Cabrach and run the water into Banffshire and all over Aberdeenshire. Eight million gallons a day was the first proposal. Banff-shire, however, were a bit slow. When I joined the Council it was decided that we should resurrect this scheme because we were by now really needing water. So the great scheme was updated. But then we ran into the opposition of the fishing community. Gordon Duff of Drummuir ran a campaign saying, "Of course it's not the fish we're worried about it's the money you're putting on the rates with your scheme. Who on earth thinks that Aberdeenshire will ever need eight million gallons of water? You'd better go for a different scheme." Against the opposition, we went ahead with the planning but they forced us into a public enquiry. We were very badly represented at that by our engineers. The opposition on the other hand were very well represented and produced an alternative scheme. Our scheme was to cost six million pounds to get eight million gallons per day which would have run all round Aberdeenshire by gravity for the rest of the life of the scheme and, had we needed more water, by adding three feet to the height of the dam we could have got twelve million gallons per day. However, at the public enquiry the opposition's scheme, which certainly was nothing to do with the fishing, proposed taking water from the lower Deveron or the Don. The Don was at that time one of the dirtiest of rivers but their scheme was to take five millions gallons of water from further down the Deveron at about Turriff. That would only cost three million pounds and would save a great deal of the tax payers' money, so they said. The commission included The Earl of Mansefield, The Earl of Cromarty and Neil Carmichael the Labour MP, with a Conservative lady, Betty Harvey-Anderson, who made a good job of chairing the thing. When the opposition produced their facts and figures for this scheme, I got a telephone call from the MP who was sitting on the commission and who knew my brother John. He said he was staying at the Caledonian Hotel and if I happened to be around in the hotel at ten o' clock, he usually went down and had a pint of beer before he went to bed. So I made it my business to happen to be in the Caledonian Hotel at ten o' clock and he came over and said, "I just thought I would tell you that if you don't pull your fingers out tomorrow and defeat the figures we were presented with today, you're going to lose the case." So I got on to our engineers and the finance committee treasurer and said, "You have to make a better job than you have up until now and attack these people's figures."

The reply I got was, "Oh, no trouble at all, their figures are totally all wrong and we'll have no difficulty." In fact they made a total mess of our presentation and we lost the case.

The end result was that they took someone else's advice and we had to pump all the water from the Deveron at Turriff. Instead of sand filters, we would use permutit filters, which were new at the time, would cost much less than sand filters and would do a better job. So we would get our five to six million gallons. Eventually all the pumps were in place and even at that stage the cost of pumping was to be quarter a million pounds a year against our scheme which would have cost nothing. In the end, when the pumps were set going and there was to be five million gallons ready to rush all over Aberdeenshire, it was discovered that the filters would not produce more than three million gallons and they had to put in sand filters after all. The cost of the scheme by the time it was finished was between seven and eight million pounds, whereas the Cabrach scheme could have been done for six million and would have, like the Aberdeen water from Invercanny, run for ever and ever, amen. And of course the system is now overloaded. Far from five million gallons being too much they now need nine million gallons. Had they gone for the Cabrach all they'd have had to do was raise the height of the dam. Jock Leith of Glenkindie was Chairman of the Water Services and the County Clerk, James Craig, and I were so disappointed at losing the battle we bought a bottle of Glenfiddich whisky and went up to the Cabrach where we had a little dam across the Black Water to measure the run of the water. We filled a water jug from the wee dam and drank the bottle of whisky, felt relieved and went home.

Another great cause celebre in my time at the County Council was the sacking of Dr Trapp the headmaster of Gordon Schools, Huntly. We had found him really impossible to deal with. He had crossed swords on several occasions with the Director of Education, he didn't get on too well with his staff and there were various incidents which annoyed the Education Committee. For instance, he kept using the telephone to contact the office and his telephone bills were the highest in the whole Education Authority. As most things in a local authority had to be written down on a piece of paper in order to be put to a sub-committee and then a committee, he was told to write a letter since very few things were urgent enough to require the use of the telephone anyway. So he said he would do that and his next phone bill was considerably smaller. But then it was discovered that all he did was phone up one of the other departments, reverse the charge and ask these other departments to transfer him to the education department. Of course when the telephonists received this call from the Rector of the Gordon Schools Huntly, they accepted the charges and it was transferred and so did not appear on his bill. But since a reverse charge call cost more than an ordinary call, the situation was worse, not better. This was not regarded as a satisfactory solution to the problem. There were a lot of things like that but what brought things finally to a head was the question of the new headmaster's office. We had spent a lot of money giving the school a fine new hall and various improvements, including a new office for himself. Dr Trapp had always argued with the Local Authority that the telephone exchange must be in his office because he didn't like anyone having phone calls which he did not know about. The Director of Education had told him in no uncertain fashion that they did not regard this as a suitable job for a headmaster, answering the telephone - that was what he had a secretary for.

However, on the new plans there was to be a new office for himself and a little office next door for his secretary and the exchange was to go in the secretary's office. A little later the Director of Education was in Huntly and looking for the headmaster. There was no one in the headmaster's office and the janitor said to the Director, "Oh, but Dr Trapp is in his own office." "Oh, where's that?" said the Director. "He's established in one of the staff rooms." It transpired that the headmaster had put himself in one of the staff rooms, while the staff crowded into another room.

He, in the meantime, had asked for another extension phone to be connected to the staff room to save the staff always having to come to the office to make a phone call. The purpose of the scheme of course was that this new extension was now the sole telephone in and out of Huntly Academy. He had blocked off the fine new exchange. This led to the silliest sorts of things, for instance, when the cooks or the school meals department wanted to order something they had to go up to the headmaster's room and get him to phone for an extra stone of sugar or whatever.

Prior to that, he had phoned me and said that we were making a dreadful mistake in the plans for the new school and he wanted a change to the plans. I remember saying to him "Dr Trapp, one thing I get a row for in the council is changing plans at the last minute because that's always expensive and we're just about finished with the plans for Huntly, but I will come up tomorrow to see what we can do." That I did and he then revealed that he wanted a change in the office plans. I said, "But Dr Trapp, the architect informs me that that is your own planning of the office with the room for your secretary."

"Oh, yes," said he, "but it would be much more convenient if it were in another part of the school."

I said, "We really can't do that but I will bring a sub-committee out to hear your story because I think we're in dead trouble if we ask for big changes at this stage." So a very high powered deputation went to see Dr Trapp. There was myself as Chairman of the Education Committee, the local member and Alec Young, the Director of Education. We listened to Dr Trapp's story and the county architect's story. He produced the plan which Dr Trapp himself had drawn and showed how he had amended it to make it slightly bigger than Dr Trapp had asked for. Dr Trapp was then asked to leave the room and the committee, after discussion, were unanimous that Dr Trapp be told that he must occupy the headmaster's room as per the architect's plans. So he was called in and I said, "Dr Trapp, you will not like the decision of the committee, but as a loyal servant you will have to accept that we think we have done the best thing."

He said, "Oh, well. Yes I am disappointed." It was after that that the Director went to see him and found that the rooms were not occupied. At that point the committee lost patience and the local member and Provost of Huntly, Alexander Gordon, proposed that Dr Trapp be given the sack. That was carried with only one vote against.

It was quite an event. It's very, very difficult to sack a teacher and a headmaster is a bit special. It's one thing that I thought about many times; that the only way you can get rid of a teacher is if they are caught with their fingers in the till or if they are guilty of sexual impropriety. But for incompetence in teaching or in administration it was very, very difficult to sack a teacher. Nor, apparently, could you sack a headmaster for not doing what he was told. It lead to a great controversy because he got his union, the EIS, to act for him. There was a public enquiry into why we were sacking this well known and well qualified man. "You appointed him why should you now sack him?" we were asked. The poor Director of Education was in the box for about fifteen hours and I also got two hours grilling for my part. However, the finding was that we were entirely justified and poor old Dr Trapp duly left.

My part in the whole affair was somewhat complicated because, prior to the actual sacking of Dr Trapp, when we were having rows with him there was a report of a caterpillar being found in the milk which we supplied from Thomastown to Huntly schools. Somebody had complained that there was a strange, foreign body in his little bottle of milk and Dr Trapp, instead of complaining to us as suppliers, immediately sent the bottle of milk to the sanitary inspectors, who had to report it to the committee. Then there were further complaints of unhygienic milk and I was taken to court for supplying it. The first complaint was of a chrysalis of a butterfly in the milk and subsequently there were complaints every day of various things in the milk. The last straw, and the one which really annoyed me, was when there were pencil shavings and various bits of things in the milk which you would have been much more likely to get in a school than in a byre or in a dairy. What happened, of course, was Dr Trapp told the children that if they found anything in their milk they were to take the bottle to the headmaster's room. We thought it likely that this was a great distraction for the kids as it was very easy in those days to squeeze off the top, put something in the bottle, put back the disk and then get great fun in taking this to the headmaster.

So the case against me was that I sold milk with pencil shavings in it and one with a chrysalis. There was also one complaint which I thought was legitimate; that a piece of glass had been found in one bottle. Every dairyman gets a bit of glass in the bottom of the bottle now and again and that is very difficult to prevent because when the clamp comes down on the bottle to put on the seal a sliver of glass can be broken and it falls to the bottom undetected. So when the case came up I was to plead guilty to the glass and not guilty to everything else. I was represented by a QC and we thought we had made quite a good defence. The sheriff, to our surprise, took the case to "avizandum" and he would give us a result the next week. During that week he was walking down the road with the late James Donald of the theatre, who lived in the same street, and had told him that he was finding in my favour and that I was not guilty. Jimmy Donald phoned my solicitor and I was informed that in due course I would be found not guilty. However, fiscals don't like losing cases and when the sheriff told the fiscal of his intention he had badgered the sheriff for the rest of the week, contending that he couldn't and he shouldn't let me off. So on the Monday morning, I was on holiday I remember, I got the phone call from Harry Forbes, my solicitor. He told me that I had been found guilty on all counts except on the one thing to which I had pleaded guilty. As you can imagine I was very annoyed about this but there was nothing I could do about it. It was a cause celebre at the time and my fine was twelve pounds, not a big item beside my legal fees of one hundred and fifty pounds. One witness that I had not called was the Huntly minister. He had told us that he had been in the headmaster's room the week when all the complaints were coming in and there was a lot of Mackie's school milk bottles in the headmaster's office. As we delivered all the milk to the classrooms and none to the headmaster's office, we did wonder what all this milk was doing there.

I think some people thought my part in the sacking of Dr Trapp was me getting my own back for the milk business but that really had nothing to do with it. It was his many instances of direct refusal to do what the Education Committee wanted him to that were his downfall. It was an accumulation over the years of little things, like the decision to buy a new electric organ for the new hall. It was probably a good idea but to finance the purchase of the organ all the income from the various trusts for the benefit of the school would have to go to this one project. We had been telling Dr Trapp that he would have to consult his staff more, and we told him to tell them that the reason they were not getting money for their other projects was because the money was required for the electric organ. We discovered that he hadn't asked the staff if they approved of putting all the endowments into one project, so the Director told the headmaster that we had no objection to the purchase of the organ but that the staff must be consulted. We expected that some would be disappointed that all their endowments were going on one feature. That would include all the money raised from the highly successful annual concert at which the staff had all worked so hard each year. Dr Trapp then sent a letter saying he had consulted the staff who were unanimous that the organ be bought. Subsequently we found that he had called a meeting but hadn't consulted the staff. He simply had told them that he was buying an organ and that the proceeds of the annual concert were required to finance it along with the endowments. So his sacking had nothing to do with the famous milk case.

But Dr Trapp was a very determined man and, when he was sacked, he went to Edinburgh University and took a law degree and proceeded to fight his own case in the courts. He found that he couldn't appeal against his dismissal but that he could sue us for defamation. In the meantime, perhaps because he was running short of money, he applied for teaching posts in the Edinburgh area and he got some temporary teaching. Then he went to Mr

Frizell, who was the Director of Education in Edinburgh, and said that he was now ready for a job and that he had honours maths and honours science and a PhD and now had a law degree. But Mr Frizell was a wise man and knew all the history and said to come back in a few days by which time he would have found out what vacancies there were. He phoned round his secondary schools and said he had got an honours maths and science man available and they all said, "Oh, yes. Let's have him," until they were told it was Dr Trapp from Huntly. Then all of them said, "We don't want to be selfish, there's a terrible shortage of maths and science teachers and we're managing not too badly there must be other schools in greater need than we are." So when Dr Trapp appeared back in Mr Frizell's office to find out if there was a job for him or not, Mr Frizell was forced to tell him that there was no vacancy. Dr Trapp then made the remark which I felt deserved a good mark for him , "Well, well. Alone I have done it."

"What do you mean alone you have done it?"

"Alone I have cured the shortage of maths and science teachers in Scotland."

He subsequently took out a case against the Director of Education, the County Clerk and myself as Convenor of the Education Committee. That never came to court. It was his contention that we had committed perjury during the inquiry. But perjury being a crime, only the Procurator Fiscal could have instituted a case against us, and he refused. Dr Trapp then pursued the Director of Education and myself jointly and that was also refused in a sheriff court.

He was then given permission to sue me personally for my part in the business on the grounds that I was motivated by revenge for the milk case. I was sued for £20,000 damages to his professional reputation. That was eighteen years after the milk case. The case was heard in the sheriff court and I didn't even attend. It was refused and Dr Trapp had to pay the Council's expenses. But Dr Trapp wasn't beaten yet. He appealed and that went to the Court of Session under three Law Lords and again I was represented by the County Council and again Dr Trapp lost the case with expenses. But of course you don't pay expenses if you appeal and he appealed again. By this time I was out of Council work because the reorganisation had taken place and I was afraid I was going to have to find this twenty thousand pounds if I lost and I don't know how much expenses out of my own pocket because Aberdeenshire County Council, in whose name I had been acting, no longer existed. So when I was informed that the case against me was still up and running I hurried to the convenor of the new council, Sandy Mutch and he said, "Oh, but we will take on the responsibilities of the old Aberdeenshire County Council and we'll engage council to defend you."

This time I decided to go to the case. I thought it would be interesting as it was to be held in a committee room of the House of Lords with five Law Lords pronouncing. So I went up to hear the fun and it was most interesting. The chairman, Lord Diplock, was very kind to Dr Trapp, who again represented himself. He would word something in a way that was not allowable and Lord Diplock would say very kindly, "Dr Trapp, you may not say that but what you could say is this," and then he would rephrase it for him. I thought he really did very well and did the most for a case which was really as thin as a case could be. Then the Law Lords withdrew and within a very short time they were back and Lord Diplock said, "I am sorry, Dr Trapp. You will not like the decision but our verdict is unanimous and you will get our various reasons in due course in writing."

And that was the end of the case because twenty years had elapsed and you cannot go beyond twenty years. I did go up to him on the day of the case. He was sitting in a corner of the North British Hotel before the case was heard and I said, "Dr Trapp, I must take off my hat to you for persistence at least. Although I don't think you have a hope in hell of winning this case, you do deserve a medal for persistence." He gave a little smile.

He was a strange man, Dr Trapp. One of those brilliant chaps who just had to have his own way.

I was very proud of the things we did during my time

on the Education Committee. Funds were in fact more and more available and we always had plans ready if there was any spare cash. There was a silly system in operation whereby if councils hadn't managed to spend all their money they were not allowed to carry it forward. You had to get it all spent by the end of March. We really set about getting as much of the surplus funds as we could. For instance there were a great many schools with rather crude outside lavatories and one of the things that we did was to give every school in Aberdeenshire inside lavatories. We were very proud of that and in his introduction to the Third Statistical Account of Scotland John R Allan said of the Education Authority; "But no effort is spared. However little can be provided for the brains the very best is provided for the bowels."

I was proud of the many new schools we built and all the repairs to old ones. All the secondary schools got good gymnasia and halls. And latterly we started putting in swimming pools. There was a regulation that you could only have a gymnasium or a swimming pool. You couldn't finance both. But we often got round that. The first time we got round it was in Cults and when the County Clerk came to the open day and saw the swimming pool I had a lot to answer for as to how we had managed to get both a gymnasium and a swimming pool. But I was quite unapologetic about it because I thought every bairn should have a chance to swim. I had had a terrible struggle learning to swim. It was miserably cold and muddy in the river Ythan and it was not very good even when we went to Cruden Bay or Collieston for holidays as children. Because I had to learn to swim for a Scout Badge I went to the public baths with my friend Alec Giles, who could swim, and some other friends who could also swim. I was standing at the deep end putting my toe in to see if the water was as cold as the Ythan when some of my friends just pushed me in. I was coming up struggling for breath for the third time and all my friends were roaring and laughing and thinking I was putting on a good show when Alec Giles came out and said, "Where's Mike?"

"Oh, that's him in there putting on a show." Alec

Giles then dived in and pulled me out, for which I was very grateful. I then moved from the Beach Baths to the pool at Mile End school where a nice old man who, despite being seventy, could still do a hand stand from the end and dive in cleanly, taught me to swim so that I could do my five hundred yards to get my King's Scout badge. So I thought it would be a very good thing to have swimming pools in as many schools as possible.

Our last effort before money started to run out was to build the secondary school at Aboyne. That was a great achievement because it had a theatre with raised seats and dressing rooms and what not, a swimming pool and a gymnasium. It was opened by the Queen Mother. That was the first time that I had worn the full regalia of the Lord Lieutenant and I was a little embarrassed waiting for the Queen Mother to come from the powder room (You always have to provide one when you have Royalty around). When she came out I said to the Queen Mother, "I hope I don't lose my spurs or get tripped up with my sword because this is the first time I have worn your daughter's uniform." The Queen Mother said, "Oh, you'll just get on fine and if you don't you'll not be the first to get mixed up with their sword or lose his spurs because the other day Lord Mountbatten did just that." So I thought I was in good company. But the Queen Mother was astonished when we took her round the school to find this theatre and also the little community room in which there were old men playing draughts and chess. They delighted the Queen Mum. So that was a kind of crowning achievement.

I don't really remember how we managed to swing the money for the extra amenities, but the credit should go in any case to Alec Young, who was my Director of Education. He was adept at that sort of thing. There were occasions when, for the whole of Scotland, there would suddenly be spare money and we always had plans ready if money was offered and other counties could not take it up. Our plans were always ready to be taken off the shelf. Sometimes we got a swimming pool because we were ready to go. The best example of our preparedness concerned the Stonehaven by-pass. We had been agitating for years for a by-pass round Inverurie but there was never any money and never any money. Kincardine was also agitating for a by-pass for Stonehaven and suddenly there was money for the by-pass at Inverurie but we very gallantly said, "No, no. The situation is much more desperate at Stonehaven. They can have this money." They were delighted of course but it turned out that they hadn't even a plan drawn of where they wanted the by-pass to go, not even a line on a map. But they didn't tell us that until it was too late and of course it takes years to get the planning permission to get the land bought and all the objectors satisfied, so the money was lost and Inverurie did not get its by-pass until years later... and neither did Stonehaven.

It has always been said that there were a lot of people involved in Local Government work, and it's true. We lived in seven very crowded offices. The main one was in Union Terrace and one day the late James Stephen was standing at the bottom of the stairs at half past three with the then County Clerk, Mr Hornall, when a crowd of young men and women came flocking down the stairs to the canteen to have their afternoon tea. Mr Stephen said, "Good Lord, Hornall, how many people have you working here?"

"About half of them."

When I was Chairman of the Education Committee, Alec Young, one of the great Directors of Education in Scotland, had two deputies. There was James Gordon, the senior depute responsible for primary and secondary school work, and Norman Nicol the junior depute, who was in charge of further education and youth services. Then there was James Cowie, an administrative assistant. The mail was divided up as appropriate between the two deputies or the assistant and Miss Violet Chisholm, the Youth Club leader, and Miss Grant, the school meals organiser. By the time I came in Alec Young always seemed to have a clear desk and everything at his command. He was a great administrator. Nowadays there are many more deputies and assistant deputies. That's not to say that the work load has not increased because of regionalisation and ever more theories about education. I still wonder if we didn't do as much with a much smaller staff. I was very fond of Alex Young apart from admiring his work. I think that may have been because we shared a love of a good dram. So, latterly, if I was in his office after five pm, and the office staff were away, he would produce a bottle and we would toast each other and plan our next success.

When Alec Young retired we engaged a James Michie, who was at that time an Assistant Director in Dundee. He was a tremendous worker, non-stop, going to carry all before him. I called him and said, "At the end of the year we want a live Director of Education, not a dead one. At this rate you'll be dead afore your time." But he was something of a workaholic and didn't stop. Some years later he went on a mission to examine education in Australia and he worked so hard there that when he came back he had a small stroke just through overwork. Fortunately he recovered and carried on till his retirement.

Before I leave the education committee I must tell you a bit about my predecessor, Sir Ian Forbes-Leith of Fyvie Castle. He retired because he said he could no longer hear but he could hear perfectly well when he wanted to. He stayed on as a councillor and was most helpful and friendly to me. If he disagreed with me he would phone up and say *we* should change our mind and occasionally *we* would agree.

He stayed on until reorganisation and was a most influential member of the Finance Committee. On one occasion he objected to a proposal but got no seconder, which was unusual for him. He said, "I must warn you that I will raise this matter at the full Council." To prepare for his objection I had the Chairman of the Committee, Charles Christie, and Alec Rennie, the Chairman of the Housing Committee, lined up to make speeches in favour of the proposal and then I was to support them. At the meeting I read out the proposal and asked if there were any amendments, but Sir Ian just kept his head down looking at his papers. I gave him a second chance but he still stared deliberately down at his papers.

Questioned later he said, "Well Mike, I knew I would lose anyway so it was fun thinking of you all tearing up the fine speeches you had prepared."

CHAPTER SIXTEEN

Convenor of the County

I BECAME Convenor (which I always thought was a nice name for the chairman of a committee - we didn't have Mayors in Scotland or even Lord Provosts in the county authorities, the chairman was called the Convenor). On one memorable occasion Paul Miller from Balmedie, who was elected councillor for that area, at his very first meeting raised various points and sent a letter then to the County Councillors suggesting that we do half a dozen things. One of them was that we should run a lottery which was, at that time, illegal. Most of the other suggestions had been so well discussed that I thought that we ought to take this man into the office and tell him how we thought he could be useful because it sounded as though he was at least enthusiastic. So Mr Miller came into Mr Craig's office wearing dark spectacles and I had to tell him that of his six suggestions, one was illegal and the other five had been discussed interminably over many years with people who have been involved much longer than him and he should just take his time. I also told him that if he wanted to know something the staff were very willing and would be helpful. He never took these dark glasses off and I had to say, "Mr Miller would you please take your glasses off so that I can see what you're thinking." We became good friends after that despite the fact that he didn't take the specs off at that time.

Some time later my wife, Pauline, had got excited about the countryside and planting wild flowers, so one of the first things to do was to get somebody to take this on.

We thought up the slogan "Keep Grampian Beautiful" but who would take charge of it? I said, "I know the very man, Paul Miller." He has been the most active chap in Keeping Grampian Beautiful that you could imagine and has kept the campaign in the news. He has planted trees and shrubs himself, cleaned up the Balmedie Beach many times and often turned up hoping volunteers would be there to plant bulbs and what not. On one occasion, he told me, nobody turned up because it was a bit wet so he planted all the bulbs himself before he left. The County Clerk was quite pleased to give Mr Miller this job and Mr Miller took it all very seriously, using the facilities of the County Council to get letters written and pamphlets put out. Some months later Mr Russell said, "You'll need to put a brake on your man Miller because he's occupying half the County Council staff writing letters and phoning and getting papers duplicated so that we can't get on with the rest of the Council work for improving the environment." It was nice to see someone with enthusiasm taking this thing up. Incidentally, in pursuance of a better environment, I thought it would be a good thing to plant daffodils up and down the roadsides. So I said to Bob Milne of Dykelands, who was one of the first to grow daffodils commercially in the North East, "You must have some daffy bulbs that you're ready to throw out?"

"Oh, yes. How much would you want?"

"Oh, well, I'll take half a tonne. What price are they?"

"Oh, well, £12.50."

"Well, I'll take that." I got my half tonne and planted them and they were quite a good show. The next time I met Mr Milne I asked him if he had any more bulbs and reminded him that he still hadn't sent me a bill. "Were they still the same price?" I asked. "Send me another half tonne," said I, "and send me your account and I'll pay it." So he sent me another half tonne and I planted them but when the account came I discovered that it was £12.50 per cwt instead of per half tonne. So instead of the bill being £25.00 it was £250.00. However, I felt that I had had £250 worth of pleasure and a lot of other people seeing the daffodils got a lot of pleasure too. I then invited the members of the Roads Committee out to Westertown to see the daffodils and they agreed to give me £100 every year to plant more. The Department of Leisure and Recreation were to plant these bulbs at random round the countryside but at first they made the mistake of planting them in diamonds and circles. When those came up they were told that that wasn't the idea at all, that they were to throw the bulbs out and then plant them where they lay. I was very pleased about that because in the City of Aberdeen they spent a lot of money on the environment and made a great effort with the public parks and so on but the County really didn't do anything, so the daffodils were a start. After people started phoning to say how nice the daffodils were the Finance Committee started to allocate a bit of money and they now do very well really.

I used to write an article for the Farming News every week and on one occasion I suggested that as farmers didn't really have time to dig the corners of their fields they should plant an apple tree in the corner of every field. A scathing letter was written to the editor saying, "How ridiculous can you be? Don't you realise that if you grow apple trees in the corners of all the fields, all the loons in the countryside would come and eat them." In the next article I wrote that it would be a splendid thing if there were all these fine apples for the boys to eat on ground that was useless anyway.

Pursuing her interest in sowing wild flowers all over Grampian to make it beautiful, Pauline had bought a packet of wild flowers on her visit to her home in America. She got a lot of her friends quite excited in the project and they were all going to put up money to buy a huge number of these seeds, so she phoned the company in America from whom she had bought the seeds and they said, "Yes, yes. And how much will you need?"

And Pauline thought and said, "Oh, well. Maybe a cwt."

"Goodness me, and where do you want all these seeds delivered to?"

"Oh, I want them in Scotland."

"But why on earth would you come to us for the

seeds? We buy them from Thomson and Morgan in England." So we got a lot of wild flowers from Thomson and Morgan and saved the cost of transatlantic shipping fares twice. The idea was that we would make stopping places like they have on the great long roads in America, where you can get off the road and have your picnic with tables and chairs provided and among the nice wild flowers. We got the roads committee to agree to make a lay-by at Pitcaple, the first one in our neck of the woods. It was nicely done with shrubs and little alcoves where you could have a picnic and eventually we got a dry lavatory put in. We had a great do to open the first lay-by and a little metal plaque screwed on to the first table saying "Gifted by Mrs Maitland Mackie." Within a month someone had unscrewed it and taken it away. But the lay-by has not been taken away and it has been a tremendous success. At the opening we had a great bowl of planter's punch made to Pauline's American recipe and we had a very jolly time after the opening of the lay-by. We then proceeded to a party at Westertown, where the Councillors got even more jolly. At the end of the party we poured at least two of the Councillors into their cars and arranged for someone else to drive them home.

A great number of people wrote saying what a splendid thing the picnic areas were and there are now many lay-bys so converted in Aberdeenshire. Pauline can claim some credit for that and I am going to claim some too because I got the County Council to cough up the money to do it.

When I was in the County Council there used to be complaints all round the countryside about the delays in getting planning applications processed and, with the support of James Craig, who was the first County Clerk I had to deal with, we sorted the problem out. He was a very good administrator and he insisted in the planning committee that every application had to have a reply within three days as to what was going to happen to it and an answer, yes or no, within a month. By and large we managed to keep to that. Of course there was all the usual debate about sporadic development and I must say I didn't agree with a lot of it. When a man who had made a million went back to his home village and wanted to build himself a house on the top of a hill overlooking where he was born, he would apply to build a house and the planning officer would say, "No stop. That's sporadic development, a terrible thing. There's a gap site in New Pitsligo or New Byth and you could build there."

That sort of thing used to get me quite annoyed and I'd say, "but this man doesn't want to build in a gap site, he wants to build on the top of a hill overlooking the place of his birth and he'll be doing no possible harm."

It is interesting today that a lot of applications are being granted in the countryside and I think it's rather nice to see new houses dotted around the countryside. The argument that if you grant permission to one it'll just encourage someone else to apply is nonsense. You needn't say yes to them all and if you get to the stage when there are too many you can always start refusing. If people are asking you to install a public sewage scheme and other items of public expenditure, that's the time to question whether a development is appropriate or whether people should be directed to a gap site in New Pitsligo. But if a man has made arrangements to dig a well for water to provide himself with his own sewage system, let him get on with it and I'm glad to say that that seems to be approved of these days.

In 1972-3 there was the great Wheatly Commission inquiry into local government organisation. They decided there had to be a reorganisation of local government in both Scotland and England. The great debate in Scotland was whether there should be a two tie or a single tier authority and the Wheatly Commission agreed on a two tier authority. The old authorities were asked for their opinion. Our council - Aberdeenshire - influenced by Sir Ian Forbes-Leith, supported the establishment of a two tier system. I didn't think that was a good plan and put in a minority report saying that I thought it should be single tier and it is interesting that almost twenty years later they are now talking about going back to single tier authorities. I thought that the single tier authority which I had worked in for many years worked well. We co-operated very happily with neighbouring authorities but I never thought the recommendations of the Wheatly Commission would work because there were not sufficient lines drawn as to who did what. Both authorities were given some responsibility for planning and some responsibility for leisure. It was the same with libraries, museums and whatever and since then there have been continual demarcation squabbles. The worst case is planning, which I think it is obvious must be in the hands of one authority.

It was decided that there was to be a regional authority and having been thoroughly involved I stood for a seat on the Region. My constituency was from Rothienorman to New Deer. I was opposed by Mr Dingwall-Fordyce of Brucklay, who stood as a Conservative. Business had to go on as usual and as Convener of the County Council I couldn't give full attention to the election with canvassing and so on. Perhaps I was a bit too conceited, thinking that with all my years of service on the County Council I would surely get re-elected. In fact I should have remembered what somebody said when I appeared at a meeting in Boddam. There had been a complaint about our proposals for sewage from Peterhead being piped out to sea. The Boddam folk thought it would all flow back into their harbour. I explained what was happening and explained that the officials had told us that there would be no danger to the Boddam beaches. And to add force to what I was telling them I said that I had been a long time in local government.

To that a voice at the back replied, "Aye, ower lang." Maybe I should have remembered that.

Pauline, as an American, was rather amazed at the method of election. But she did go round an area she didn't know very well canvassing for votes for her husband and on one occasion she was visiting a little farm on a rainy day and she had to go round to the back door when no one answered at the front. She was waiting, as she thought, ankle deep in mud and the lady came to the door and apologised saying,

"Ye see, we've an affa lot of dubs."

Pauline said, "Oh. Is that a good thing?" She had never heard of the stuff.

At any rate, three weeks later I was intensely disappointed to find that I had lost the seat by some sixty votes. I received lots of sympathy all round. But really I was better without it. I thought I had arranged with my friends in the old Aberdeen County Council that if we got elected we would have no nonsense about having any party politics on the new Council. Although they were Tories they would act in the best interest of Grampian and act as Independents. I had stood very definitely as an Independent but the voters expressed their preference for party politics and elected the Tory. Although I was a Liberal I detested party politics in local government and I told them I would be an Independent if I were elected. To my surprise, the day after the election, all my one-time friends who had been successful in getting elected to the new regional authority had given up the idea (except for Paul Miller and Angus Pelham-Burn, who declared themselves as Independents at the first meeting). The others swiftly divided along party lines, since the Aberdeen City members were already organised on party lines. So, after being terribly disappointed at not being elected, I was delighted since I would have stuck to my guns and been an Independent and I would never have got a job on the new Council. A lot of people said that I would have been Convenor of the new Grampian Regional Council but instead Sandy Mutch, a Conservative from the Old Aberdeen City Council, became the first Convenor.

I remember for my comfort what my brother John had said about being a Labour Member of Parliament out of power. He spent his days making up speeches on every conceivable subject but was never called to speak and how totally frustrated he felt about that. Of course it was different once his party got into power and he was made a Parliamentary Private Secretary. He was then able to influence events. At least he had one foot in the corridors of power then and could really do something. I think I would have suffered the same frustration had I been in a politicised Grampian Regional Council.

But I was to receive more comfort for my defeat from a quite unexpected quarter.

CHAPTER SEVENTEEN

Lord Lieutenant of the County of Aberdeen

IT SO happened that almost immediately after the election I was on one of the Milk Board tours to India to attend the International Dairy Federation meeting. I thought it unfair that we should welcome the Indians when they came here but not go to India when they were hosting the meetings. We had been on a sight-seeing tour and when we got back to our hotel at night there was a message from my son to phone home. I immediately thought that my old father had died or was seriously ill so I phoned home. But if you try phoning home from India (in those days, at least) it isn't very easy. Lines were always engaged or out of order and it was some unearthly hour in the morning when I finally managed to get through. My son had opened a letter because he thought it might be important. It was from the Scottish Office saying that the Queen would like me to be her Lord Lieutenant in Aberdeenshire in succession to Lord Aberdeen who had died. My first thought was that this was not my cup of tea since Lords Lieutenant throughout the country seemed to me to be from the aristocracy or Brigadier Generals and, being neither a blue blood nor a top military man (although I was still very proud of being a lieutenant in the Home Guard forty years earlier), I could

not be said to be of the usual mould for the Lords Lieutenant. Although flattered by the offer, my first inclination was to decline. My wife and friends thought otherwise and I was not difficult to persuade. I decided that, in spite of my pedigree not being quite right for the job, I would enjoy doing it. I did it for twelve years and I was quite right for I enjoyed it immensely.

Of course I had already been a deputy Lord Lieutenant for many years but deputies don't do very much. They are rarely asked to do anything in Aberdeenshire although I do remember when Lord Aberdeen was Lord Lieutenant at the time of the Winter of Discontent when all sorts of demonstrations and strikes were being held against the government, he called his deputy Lords Lieutenant to a great meeting.

"You never know, you may be called out to prevent riots." he told us.

I couldn't imagine myself back in my old Home Guard uniform trying to prevent riots in Daviot. I thought it was rather exaggerated. There were things happening in the rest of the country which looked slightly alarming but I didn't take the warning very seriously myself.

Many people wonder what on earth is the use of Lords Lieutenant. Well, I remember being told very early on that one of our jobs was to support the monarchy and there were murmerings here and there against the monarchy. The great Willie Hamilton was the arch antagonist of the monarchy, active and quite influential in the Labour Party until his wife told him the score. But we were to support the monarchy on occasions where it was needed and, if such occasions didn't arise, we were to make occasions when we could show our support for the maintenance of our Royalist tradition. So there we were. Our job was to tell people what a good thing it was that we still had a Queen. That gave me very little difficulty and one reason for that is that I have not been impressed with the political system in the United States despite my many visits. It seems to me that their system of Presidential election costs the earth and that politicking for the Presidency takes up about half the time of each Congress. They do a bit of work for two years and then for the rest of their four year term they're trying to get re-elected. The great thing about the monarchy is that there is no election for the head of state.

We have been very lucky indeed both during and after the war with the quality of our monarchs. George VI and his daughter have been a splendid example and at times inspiration, as well as a unifying force in the country.

So what does the Lord Lieutenant do? Well, I did discover that there were some things that I had to do. One of the first that I ran up against was putting names in for the annual garden party at Holyrood House. I discovered that there was a thing called "The List" and The List consisted of a number of people who expected to be invited every year irrespective of whether they had done anything during the year or not. I had a look at it and immediately thought I could see no reason why these people should be on every year and I turfed a good few names out. In that I was before my time because the next year I got a letter from the Lord Chamberlain saying that the Queen's wish was that the invitations should be spread over a wider range of people and ages. So this encouraged me and having made up my mind to score off some names I proceeded to score off a good many more. One man who I scored out wrote a very peeved letter saying that he had not received his invitation to the Garden Party and he understood the invitations were out. He always went to the Garden Party and he arranged always to meet his friends at the Garden Party and what was I going to do about it? So I wrote back that the Queen thought it right that the invitations should be spread more widely and that was what I had done. I got a nice letter back saying that he quite understood and he thought that the more people that were invited the better. I was so impressed with this nice letter that I put him back on The List and he has been invited ever since.

The names that had been on The List were all the county families and their relations and their families because the previous Lords Lieutenant had all been from the county families themselves. Maybe it was more difficult for them to suggest names from the lower orders than it was for me.

Another of the Lord Lieutenant's jobs is to chair the committee that elects Justices of the Peace. I remember how carefully Sir Ian Forbes-Leith, who was the first chairman I served with, did his job. He supervised the choices. Having been on his committee I knew the score and we took great care to choose people who would be available to ordinary folk to take their forms to be signed and so on. On the form we had to fill in for presenting someone to be a JP we were required to state their religion and their politics. But latterly a lot of people didn't want to say what their politics were but in theory we were supposed to balance the JPs as between the various political persuasions. One of our problems was it was difficult getting enough people with Labour sympathies who were suitable and willing to be JPs. By suitable I mean available to the public as witnesses for passports, legal documents and so on. One year when Sir Ian Forbes-Leith and his committee drew up the list of proposed JPs, the Secretary of State sent it back and said that he would have to take more care to balance things with more Labour members. Sir Ian got really angry at this and told James Munro, who was secretary to the JPs committee, to write back and tell the Secretary of State in no uncertain terms that the committee had spent a long time making up the list and that if the Secretary of State was not pleased he could come and suggest some names himself. Without further ado the names were accepted.

I continued the same method of allocation and scrutiny as Sir Ian and got people on the committee who would know their own districts and who would know suitable people to suggest as JPs.

But of course most of the Lord Lieutenant's duties are ceremonial and surround the Royalty. It was a most pleasant part of the job to meet and (in theory) look after members of the Royal Family when they came into Aberdeenshire. The Royal Family's annual holiday at Balmoral was a most important occasion for the Lord Lieutenant. At that time the Queen normally arrived in Aberdeen on the Royal Yacht. There she would be met by the Queen's representative in Aberdeen, the Lord Provost of the City of Aberdeen. The Lords Provost of the four cities in Scotland are also

Lords Lieutenant so I had to be very careful not to step on the Lord Provost's toes, though, in fact, I never did have any trouble in that respect. I didn't meet the Royal Family until they got to Balmoral. It was my job to be at the gates of the castle, dressed in the kilt, accompanied by my wife and accompanied for all the time that I was Lord Lieutenant by her neighbour at Balmoral, Captain Alwyn Farquharson of Invercauld and his wife Francine. I thought it a nice touch that the neighbours also met the Queen when she arrived for her holidays. The bridge over the Dee was lined by whatever regiment was guarding the castle and there was another company of them drawn up beside the lodge and the band which played marching music behind the gates. Every inch of standing room was taken up by crowds of people who came to see the Queen arriving for her holidays.

The Royal car or cars would arrive and the Queen would step out, come round and shake hands with me and I would introduce her to Pauline who, through time, she came to know, and she knew the Farquharsons. So there were handshakes all round, a little chat (not much) and then she would step across - a lonely looking figure standing in the middle of the square by herself - while the major in charge of the guard stepped forward with his sword and did all the usual things. I am the least military of gentleman and never understood what the officer in charge was doing with his sword when he raised it and lowered it and kissed it and eventually held it erect in his hand and marched round like that between the ranks of the soldiers with the Queen while she inspected them. Then he would look casually at the band who would strike up God Save the Queen. After that the officer in charge would do a bit more fancy work with the sword and the Queen would come back to where we were standing at the gate. There she would chat a little, perhaps introduce us to the rest of the Royal Family if we hadn't been speaking to them already.

Princess Anne might be there, Princess Margaret and once Prince Edward and Prince Andrew were in the car with her. On that occasion she had several corgi dogs and one got out of the car and was being a nuisance and wrapping itself round the Queen's legs when she whispered to Prince Andrew,

"Get that damned dog out of here."

So the dog was eventually extricated and put into the car. When she was saying goodbye, Andrew was still outside the car and the Queen said to him, rather sharply, I thought,

"Get in the car."

To which Prince Andrew replied, "I can't get into the car for dogs."

"Well get round to the other side, you silly ass," she said.

So he did that and all was well. But when they were driving off the Queen wound down her window and said with a twinkle, "We've only seven dogs in here, you know."

So it was each time. They would get into the car and drive through the gates and that would be the end of the performance. I always used to think, 'She'll be kicking off her shoes and saying, "Thank goodness for that. Apart for going to church I won't have to appear in public again for a whole six weeks".'

Their Balmoral stay was really regarded as their holiday and her representative in Aberdeenshire was well warned to discourage any requests for public appearances during that time and quite right too. It must be a terrible job to be on public display all the time and have to be nice to everybody.

I must say, the Queen really captivated me.

During the last two years of my Lord Lieutenancy it was decided that I should have an esquire to be picked from the territorial army cadets. The first one was a sergeant from Aboyne and I presented him with his letters of appointment, a signed scroll that he was now my chief esquire. I told him, after the formal doings, that I was not the kind of chap who would call on him to attend on me at functions because that would be a total waste of his time but I would ask the Queen if my esquire could meet her at the beginning of her annual holiday. She wrote that she would be delighted. Mr Gatt was told to be on parade and there he was on the appointed day looking very smart. Both his parents were employed by BP and I told him to bring his parents and their camera so that they could photograph their son being presented. And I told him where to get his parents to stand so that if the press were taking photographs his parents would be in the picture as well. And indeed BP sent a special photographer just to get this picture, parents and all, and that was a great success.

The next year the cadets decided a girl from Peterhead was the best cadet and so I had a girl appointed as my esquire. She turned out to have a splendid record. She was the best shot and had won lots of athletic competitions and was very smart. So I told her the same thing; that she wouldn't have to accompany me to public functions but I would ask the Queen again if she could come. Which I did and that was all arranged. But on this particular year it was the hundredth anniversary of the making of a special waiting room for Queen Victoria at the old Ballater Station and the great North of Scotland Railway Association had all sorts of nostalgic things to do with railways. They decided that this ought to be recognised and would I ask the Queen, instead of meeting us at Balmoral, if she would stop and inspect the old waiting room which they had all tarted-up and the walls bedecked with old photographs. The Queen agreed, so I told the girl, my new esquire, to come good and early and I would see that she would be introduced to the Queen. There was a lot of arranging as to who would be there and who would not. The Queen arrived at the back of the old platform at the station and was introduced to various people on the district council, etc and came through the pass that led into the station square. At that point I had arranged that my esquire would stand beside a pillar just before the band and I would ask the Queen to stop and say hello to her. So that was fine. I came through the pass chatting very naturally to the Queen and then reminded her that this was where she was to meet the esquire. To my horror there was no girl standing there and I was forced to say to the Queen

"Maam, I fear I have lost one girl cadet."

However, the Queen then went round to inspect the guard. At this point I hurriedly said to the Chairman of the

Railway Committee

"For God's sake, go and find my cadet. She must be here somewhere. I told her to stand there."

He came back in a minute or two and said, "She's nowhere to be found."

Since the place was swarming with police I told a policeman, "For goodness sake, go and find my little cadet."

"O, yes. I'll find your cadet."

But a minute or two later the policeman also came back and said, "Sorry, I can't find your cadet either."

I told him keep on looking and I'll keep the Queen engaged for as long as I can. I introduced the Queen to some people who were standing by the door.

You had to remember the names of the people you were talking to and on that score the worst experience I remember was at the opening of the gas terminal at St Fergus by Total. There were a lot of Frenchmen and their wives there and the first to be introduced was the Chairman of British Gas, and that wasn't so bad until I came to the French lot. I had been careful to memorise the names but I did have a squint at a little postcard which I kept in my hand if I forgot a name. But I was very pleased to remember all the men, about seven, and their wives. The only thing that I did lose there was my spurs. As I was quite unaccustomed to wearing the fancy uniform (the Lord Lieutenant with spurs but no horse) the damned things fell off. However I had warned the police by this time that they were to come behind me and pick up my spurs and anything else that fell off.

But back to the poor little girl at Ballater. Having been introduced to everyone I could see that I knew, the Queen went into the waiting room and was most interested and took a while to come out. But even then there was still no cadet. So I decided to keep the Queen going a little longer. As she was getting in the car there was a great crowd and I saw that quite a few people in the crowd had bunches of flowers, so I said, "Maam, I think it would please the crowd if you went round and picked up the flowers that they have brought."

And the Queen turned to the future Duchess of York to be who was with her and she asked, "Do you think we should do that?"

The answer being "yes" the Queen and the Duchess of York spent another few minutes doing that. But unfortunately they came back and I had no other reason to delay the Queen. So they departed and I went to look for my cadet myself. By this time the guard were marching and when the band marched off there was the little girl. She had been totally hidden by the great big burly members of the band. When I asked the girl why she had not been standing where I asked she said she thought I would come for her. I thought she would be in tears but no, no she said she had really enjoyed seeing the Queen and it had all been really interesting. But I thought this was so sad for the girl and I wrote Buckingham Palace and said that it would be very nice if the Queen could write a letter saying that she was disappointed not to meet my esquire owing to some misunderstanding and I got a letter back saying that they would do that. So, in the end, she was probably better off than her predecessor as she had a letter from the Queen saying she was sorry not to have met her.

It was always pleasant meeting the Queen and I also had an opportunity to meet various members of the Royal Family.

The Dean of St George's Chapel at Windsor was a great admirer of the Royal Family and a man who thought that Lords Lieutenant ought to use their influence for the good of the country in various ways, and that we didn't throw our weight about enough in our own communities. He held a weekend conference every year in St George's Chapel library. He had turned St George's house in the private square leading down to the library at Windsor into suitable accommodation. There were rooms there for a company of thirty or thereby and my wife and I were present at several of these meetings. They were most interesting. The Dean would get each Lord Lieutenant to speak about his own particular interest and on one occasion we had been impressed with a trade union speaker and a local government speaker and then Dean Mann set us off into small groups to discuss how we could do our job by liaising better with the local authority people and the trade unions. Our little group was led by the Lord Lieutenant of Nottingham and we repaired to a little room and were discussing our duties when someone (I thought rather foolishly) said, "You know we're being asked to do all these extra things, we'll be using the telephone a lot more and using our cars a lot more. Who is going to pay for the extra expense?"

He got no reply to that because, just at that point, the door opened and in came the Duke of Edinburgh who often came to these things and listened to our discussions. At that the chairman repeated his question about who was to pay the extra expenses and the Duke without giving it much thought said, "Well, if you can't afford that you shouldn't be a Lord Lieutenant."

And that put an end to that discussion. Next morning at breakfast Dean Mann said that the Duke had sent his apology that he had spoken without thinking and that of course Lords Lieutenant should be reimbursed for their expenses and that he understood that, with current high rates of taxation, to pay for these expenses out of taxed income was unfair. So maybe it did some good but I don't think the authorities heard for I never got any expenses for being a Lord Lieutenant.

I don't know what it did cost me but the only expenses people claimed were for the one meeting in the year held in the House of Lords. In fact I didn't claim for that because I always tried to work it in with something else. That meeting, just one a year, was rather fun though I don't know whether we achieved much. Most of the hundred of us turned up and it was interesting to meet the other Lords Lieutenant. They didn't all attend but you got to know quite a few of them and others sent deputies who often turned out to be just as interesting as their seniors. They really were a lot of highly placed aristocrats or military gentlemen plus Mackie. In fact there was another Lord Lieutenant at my humble level. He was a former president of the National Farmers Union of England and Wales, Willie Swan, and even he had been a Major in the army which compared favourably with my Lieutenancy in the Home Guard. So after that meeting you could claim expenses but there was a long form and I could never be bothered filling it up. So I really don't know what it cost me to be Lord Lieutenant but I do know it cost me an awful lot to get the uniform.

Having decided that I would take the job I had to reply to Buckingham Palace. After it had appeared in the papers it transpired that Lord Aberdeen, the previous Lord Lieutenant, who had died in office, had left instructions that I was to be given his uniform because that uniform had been given to him by Sir Ian Forbes-Leith his predecessor. Now, this uniform had been made specially for Sir Ian Forbes-Leith who had a very big body and was six foot six inches tall. When Lord Aberdeen got it, all he had to do was cut a couple of inches off the legs and it fitted him fine because he also was a big-bodied man. I collected the uniform in a box from Lady Aberdeen at Haddo House and on the top of the box was written, "This uniform to be used for Lords Lieutenant" and signed by Sir Ian Forbes-Leith's daughter Anne. (She married Angus Pelham Burn.)

So, quite excited one day, I got the uniform out and dressed up. First of all the hat wasn't big enough which confirmed what my friends had told me for a long time - that I had a big head. The uniform itself was far too long in the leg and the tunic was far too big. When she saw me in this Pauline roared and laughed so I took it to my tailor in Aberdeen. He took one look and said, "Oh, no. I wouldn't like to tackle that. I see it's been made by Moss Brothers in Edinburgh. You should take it to them and perhaps they'll be able to do something with it."

So I took it to Moss Brothers and they said, "Oh, no, Mr Mackie. You'll have to get a new tunic because all the pockets are made in relation to the size of the tunic and we could never alter it."

And of course the boots were size thirteens. I would have had to run a while to get into the toes so I had to buy a pair of boots. They had to be very special boots because they had to have a hole in the heel into which the spurs fitted with a prong and two little clicks where the two sides of the spurs fitted. Even at that time the blooming boots cost me thirty something pounds. I was more fortunate with the tunic though. Moss Brothers found a second-hand tunic which was more my size but it still cost the earth because all the badges and buttons had to be changed. Then I discovered that the uniform had been made in the time of King George VI and, as there are King's buttons and Queen's buttons, all the buttons had to be changed. Fortunately the very expensive epaulettes fitted and all the other very expensive paraphernalia transferred quite satisfactorily. Then there was a very fancy sash with silver threads and gold threads. Luckily it was alright because if I had had to buy a new one it could have cost several hundred pounds.

And then there was no sword as those had been the personal property of those previous Lords Lieutenant. Again I was lucky and somebody came to me and said, "Don't tell anybody but this sword belonged to my wife's uncle and if you want a sword you can use this one." So I got a sword. It wasn't quite the pukka sword for the job because it had a leather sheath whereas it should really have been metal. However, nobody ever said boo to me and I got on fine with the leather scabbard and its sword.

At long last I was equipped with a uniform and I must say it did lend a certain something to the Lord Lieutenant's image. Another of the duties of the Lord Lieutenant is to present British Empire Medals, Memberships of the British Empire when the Queen has not enough time at investitures to present them. And there are other special awards of various kinds that the Lord Lieutenant presents. When people were unable to go or were not invited to an investiture the impressive uniform helped to make it more of an occasion. The first one I did was a man who was employed by Shell. I asked Shell to lay on a cocktail party with tea for the wives and asked them to bring along some of their top directors as well. As that was my first I tried the gimmick of saying, as I handed over the letter from the Queen apologising for not being there in person, "But you have a representative of the Queen here. Its not Maitland Mackie but the Queen's representative who gives you this and this is the same uniform that is worn by every Lord Lieutenant so if you have a photograph with me it is a photograph with the Queen's representative and nothing to do with Maitland Mackie."

That always went down very well and I think people enjoyed the photograph taken with the uniform and I always made sure that there was a photographer present so that they had a memento.

A great many people were astonished with my appointment as Lord Lieutenant and certainly a lot of my friends, although congratulating me, did wonder why they should appoint a farmer as a Lord Lieutenant. I didn't know and still don't know. But having done it for twelve years I'm conceited enough to think I did the job well. Everybody seemed to accept my approach to the matter and many people have said that it was a change from past Lords Lieutenant. By that I took them to mean that it was a change for the better. The appointment, which I still have hanging in my office, is a great big document, and in the wonderful old language it says, "To my trusty and well beloved Maitland Mackie and so and so hereby appointed until the sixteenth of February, 1987." And that is a new feature. In the old days Lords Lieutenant and their deputies were appointed for life. The Queen had so many doddery old men not quite fit to do the job that she decreed that Lords Lieutenant should only be appointed until they were seventy-five. She hadn't made the same regulation about deputies so that some of them who were appointed before that time would still be deputies until the day of their death. However, new deputies are also appointed to resign when they are seventy-five... and a good thing too.

There were among the deputies, both to Sir Ian and Lord Aberdeen, some who may well have thought they could or should have been elevated but nobody ever said anything openly to me about that. And I must say, after their initial astonishment, they were all very loyal to me. It is not very often that deputy Lieutenants are asked to do anything in a population of our size. I could have used a deputy on some occasions but I made it my business to do it all myself because, if it was a presentation of a medal or to be present at some particular occasion, they didn't really want a deputy they wanted the Lord Lieutenant dressed up in all his finery and none of the deputies had a uniform. So I never really used them. There was one exception; when we were asked to raise money for the Queen's Jubilee present. Then, after a meeting, we divided Aberdeenshire up into areas and gave each of the deputies a target and all my deputy Lieutenants, except one, reached their target and some beat the target. I was able to raise the money myself in the case of the one who failed; he was ill at the time and could hardly be faulted for that.

Another job that the Lieutenants are supposed to do is to recommend people for honours or to give an opinion on a recommendation made by someone else. It's one of the most frustrating parts of the Lord Lieutenant's duties. I always thought that Freddie Green, who was the first secretary of the Oldmeldrum Sports, should have got something. He ran a most efficient show, made a profit every year and had given, over the years, forty thousand pounds to local and national charities. Freddy started the sports in 1931 in aid of the fund which bought cocoa for the school-children in the middle of the day in the hard times when there were no school dinners. It later became a major supporter of all local charities and more than half the credit was due to the secretary, Freddie Green... the last oatmeal miller at Foresterhill near Oldmeldrum.

Anyway I asked Sir Ian Forbes-Leith when he was Lord Lieutenant if he would get an honour for Freddie and Sir Ian thought he could but he died and Freddie still hadn't got an honour. So I put it to his successor, Lord Aberdeen, that I had thought that Sir Ian was going to get Freddie an honour and would he please see to it. "Oh, yes. I think Freddie thoroughly deserves recognition." Again nothing happened. So when I became Lord Lieutenant I resolved that the first thing I would do was make sure that Freddie Green got an honour. Still nothing happened and Freddie died so it was too late but I thought I should do something about other people and I tried with almost complete lack of success. So the annual meeting of the Lords Lieutenant at the House of Lords in London, was my opportunity. The first year like a good new boy I didn't say anything but the second year I asked what the drill was for making recommendations for honours because my experience had been of complete failure and I wondered if I was doing it wrong. Meantime we had a new chairman of the Lords Lieutenant Association, Lord MacLean, the ex-Chief Scout, and I had known him in my Scouting days and I tried to impress upon him that something should be done. Since you only meet once a year it is very hard to get any pressure put on but the next year I raised the question again and asked if my experience was singular or if the other Lords Lieutenant were failing to have any of their recommendations acted upon. It is a meeting at which very little discussion takes place but eventually one or two other Lords Lieutenant got up and protested that they also had had no success with their recommendations and that they thought that Mr Mackie was right.

Lord MacLean said that he would take the matter up with the Queen's Honours Committee so we had to be satisfied with that. Next year I raised the matter again and Lord MacLean said that he'd had a very useful meeting with the honours committee and they had agreed that we had good cause to be dissatisfied and if we would document our applications properly they would pay more attention to them. That annoyed me because I had always documented any application I had made but I made dead sure the next time I put somebody up that I had a long list of people backing the recommendation, full details of what all he had done and why he was a deserving case. Again nothing happened.

I missed the next year's meeting so it was two years before I was back at the Lords Lieutenant's meeting at the House of Lords. Again I raised the questions and I asked what the experience of the other Lords Lieutenant had been... had there been any improvement? Several got up and said that there had been no improvement. At that Lord MacLean said, "Well I think you're right, and, as a matter of fact, I haven't had much success myself."

I thought there was little point in me putting people up if Lord MacLean couldn't get any honours for his people because he, as well as being chairman of our committee, was the Queen's Lord Chamberlain. So I gave up and I was very disappointed at that because I feel that if the Lord Lieutenant is doing his job he does hear who is doing well in his own particular area. But I did ask the next year a specific question. "How many honours were granted in the previous year as a result of recommendations by Lords Lieutenant?"

So Lord MacLean said he would try and get those figures. So the next year I got the figures and it absolutely astonished me in the whole of the United Kingdom four OBEs had been granted and six MBEs as a result of our recommendations. After that I never put up anyone else because it was just a waste of time.

When I read the list of people who have got honours each year I am always disappointed that some of the people that I think should have got haven't got anything. But of course I can never tell whether the people who have got the honours really deserved it more than the people I recommended. But on the whole I think the honours system is quite good and I've been very proud to receive the honours which I have been given though I have no idea why I got them or who recommended me for them. I got a CBE from the Queen and then a Knighthood so who am I to complain about the honours system? I do know that the people to whom I have presented MBEs have always been terribly pleased and proud to get them and in every case deserved to be recognised and that they were all people who were well thought of in their own district. There must be cases where people have got one and people in the district have said, "What on earth for?" But not in my experience. The problem is that a lot of people deserve it like Freddie Green and don't get it. And it did disappoint me that the Lord Lieutenant, who was doing his job, had no power to recognise the people who he was in such a good position to know deserved public recognition.

I did, as Lord Lieutenant, have the power to bestow one honour however, and even when I exercised that I ran into trouble from the establishment. The Lord Lieutenant recommends who shall be his deputies. Now one of my first jobs was to recommend four additions to the list of deputies and in this I departed a little too far (in the opinions of some) from the tradition that deputies should come from the county families. One of my recommendations was Marc Ellington, a Canadian-born musician who had taken British nationality and settled in the area. He had made a wonderful job of restoring the sixteenth century castle at Towie Barclay, and taken a great interest in the musical and architectural heritage of the area. I was therefore astonished when I was visiting the chief civil servant in Scotland, Kerr Fraser, on another matter to be told that there had been complaints by some people in Aberdeenshire about this recommendation and that it should be dropped. I told him in no uncertain terms that I knew exactly the sort of people who were objecting and that Marc Ellington had done more for Aberdeenshire than any of them and that I would on no account change my recommendation. No more was said.

Those who are lucky enough to be asked to go to Buckingham Palace to an investiture enjoy quite an occasion. You're allowed to take three guests. When I went up to get my CBE I took Pauline and my daughter Pat. It was a very well organised occasion. The Queen did over one hundred and sixty presentations and managed to say a few words to each of us. I remember when I stepped forward, the Queen said, "I am right that you're main interest in Local Government has been education?"

And I wondered if she had been very well briefed or if someone whispered something to her when they handed her the medal because she managed to say something to everyone. I was even more pleased when I was Knighted when, as well as Pauline, my daughters Isobel and Mary came with me. There is a stool for you to kneel on and a post for the old and infirm to pull themselves up on and I gather if you're too old and infirm you don't have to kneel nowadays, but I am pleased to say that I managed to bend the knee before the Queen hung the medal round my neck. On that occasion she said, "Its nice to give a medal to someone you know." And I thought that that was the nicest thing she could have said to me.

One of the perks of being Lord Lieutenant was that

we were invited to two Royal occasions. The first was the
Queen Mother's Jubilee which was held in St Paul's Cathedral. And the second was the wedding of Prince Andrew to
Sarah Ferguson, this time in Westminster Abbey. Pauline,
of course, got a new dress and a new hat specially selected
for the occasion. Just before we arrived Pauline said, "Is my
hat box here?"

I thought for a minute and said. "No. Your hat box is
in the boot of my car in Aberdeen." There was a flurry and
she determined that she wouldn't go to the wedding without a hat. My brother John who lives in Essex and had
offered to come in and drive us to the wedding said that
this would be no problem and that he would bring in a
selection of his wife Jeannie's hats. This was done and he
arrived with, as he said, "a bagful of hats." One was chosen
and all was well. We were interviewed by David Dimbleby
and told the story of the hat and all Jeannie's friends said
they recognised the hat which seemed to be more important than the wearer.

But that was a great occasion. The organisation was
perfect. We were sitting in the Abbey with a TV monitor
and we could·not only see all the guests arriving and being
shown to their seats but we could see the Royal Party getting into their carriages to come to the service. Every guest
had a little brochure saying, to the minute, what should be
happening. And if you looked up at the monitor you could
see each carriage arriving and leaving dead on time. It was
beautifully done. I felt privileged to be there. I'm sorry the
good start seems to have had a bad finish.

One feature of the Lord Lieutenant's dealings with
the Royal Family was the requests to get a Royal to come to
various functions. If you're running an event and you want
a Royal to come you get the Lord Lieutenant to write up to
Buckingham Palace saying where and when and what you
would like them to do. And you can't ask for just any
Royal, you've got to ask for one in particular. You have to
say if you want the Queen or Prince Andrew or the Duchess
of York or whoever. So again I was making trouble at the
Lords Lieutenant's meeting in London by suggesting that
there should be a clearing house for such requests. I said I

thought we ought to be able to describe the occasion to a committee at Buckingham Palace and leave it to them to decide whether the event was worthy of a Royal and what level they could provide and whether the level in question was available. It was very unsatisfactory that every member of the Royal family had their own secretariat and you had to make up your mind which you wanted and write to them. So you might write and ask for the Queen and be refused whereas Prince Andrew was kicking his heels that day. My idea was that, that committee having looked at your event would be able to say to you;

"Well in our opinion you won't get the Queen and we know that Princess Anne is busy that day but you could try for Prince Charles." You could then write to the appropriate secretary. Strangely, I never got a request from Oldmeldrum Sports for a Royal opening and they took great care to have some famous singer or actor or television personality. Of course from time to time their arrangements fell through and on such occasions they always called on me as a stop-gap and I am the only person who has opened Oldmeldrum Sports three times.

One of the pleasant duties was to meet the Queen when she came to the Braemar Gathering as she did every year. The drill was that, about three o' clock, the Royal cars entered the field and the Queen got out at the Royal Pavilion to be greeted by the Lord Lieutenant - not this time dressed in his Lord Lieutenant's uniform, but in the kilt. I would introduce the Queen and then shake hands with the guests in the Royal party - Princess Royal, Princess Margaret - whoever was there. The first time I met Princess Diana was at the Braemar Gathering. Then they had to climb the steep little slope to the Royal Pavilion and I was always rather afraid that someone would slip on it but in my time no one ever did. There the President of the Braemar Gathering was introduced and the three patrons and their wives, Captain Ramsay of Mar, the Queen's cousin, and his wife Lady Saltoun, then the Duke of Fife and then Captain Farquharson of Invercauld with his wife Francine. Then the Queen took her seat and we arranged ourselves in the second row and might occasionally be asked a question by the members in front.

The Queen and the Duke always managed to look very interested in what was going on but I think some of the younger Royals were sometimes rather bored because if they had been there before they thought it was all just the same again but the Queen comes every year and although it may look all the same she manages to look as though she's fascinated by the whole thing. She charms everyone and hands over some of the cups to the winners and about four o' clock the Royal family prepare to depart. That's always done after the last appearance of the massed pipes and drums. The Lord Lieutenant walks down to the car with the Queen and the rest of the Royal Family, shakes hands and says goodbye. Then they all get into the cars which move right round the field again before leaving. The first year that I was Lord Lieutenant the police explained that if I wanted to get away they would bring my car round behind the Royal cars because after the Royal Party left there was always a terrible crowd in the village and if I was in a hurry I would need to follow directly after the Royal party. It seemed to be a tradition that the Lord Lieutenant would be invited by Captain Farquharson to have a cup of tea at Invercauld House. Since their cars were at the back of the pavilion they were out and away immediately after the Royal Family. Since I had to say goodbye I couldn't be ready in my car if it were round the back so the police brought it down and Pauline and I got in behind the Royal party and followed them, as I thought humbly, round the ring. But, since I had my window down and every now and again somebody would roar out, "Aye, aye Mike," and other people I knew were waving frantically at us, I suddenly realised that we were being frightfully snooty so I started waving and my wife started waving. In the end we were behaving just like Royalty. Of course a great many people there would have known us but the bulk of the people had no idea and presumed that we must be Lord and Lady Something-or-Another and were all waving to us enthusiastically. It was all rather fun to be receiving the plaudits of the crowd, however undeserved they may have been.

There was a theory that the Lord Lieutenant would arrive in time to share the taking of the first salute to the massed pipes and drums. So I was asked to be there for 11 o'clock. Pauline admits she was a bit late in getting dressed and we hurried to Braemar to be caught behind the band which was marching from the Invercauld Arms so there was no hope but follow them slowly into the field and hope that we could get quickly to our car park in time to nip out and take the salute. We were crawling behind the band when, outside the Fife Arms, the car died on me and wouldn't restart. I didn't know quite what to do but to my delight a Police Landrover appeared coming the other way. I stopped it and explained my predicment. I asked if they had a rope which they had, "Oh well, pull me in."

So the crowd were entertained to this somewhat infra-dig spectacle of the Lord Lieutenant being pulled in the ring to take the salute. We passed the press tent and I thought the photographers missed the photograph of the year. I was too late to take the salute anyway but Captain Farquharson had been there and he had taken it.

On the whole I was impressed with the Royal Family. I was most in love with the Queen Mother who is a very remarkable lady. I remember on one occasion we were invited to a cocktail party run by the Guards in the Royal Ballroom at Balmoral. The Queen, the Duke and some members of the family came down the double staircase that leads from the Royal apartments and on this occasion the Queen and the Duke of Edinburgh split up at the foot of the stairs and went round different ways speaking to as many people as they could and the Queen Mother stopped and spoke to me. We were slightly in the way of the people passing at the bottom of the second stair that leads up so I said to the Queen Mother, "Perhaps we should get out of the way," and stepped two steps up the stairs and so did she. We chatted away for some ten minutes and she's very easy to chat to but I suggested that perhaps I ought to let her go and she might want to go round and speak to some other people.

She looked at me and said, "Are you tired of me?"

I hurriedly assured her that I would be delighted to

stand all night with her and she chatted away for a few more minutes and left but she's very good at talking to everybody and anybody.

In common with other people I thought that Princess Anne was slightly stand-offish the first time I met her, but then, for all the few minutes I met her, it was very difficult to judge. I must say that the last time that I met the Princess she was most charming and I think that she has perhaps changed in her attitude to the public and she appears to charm everybody now. I had to meet her once at the Highland Show and take her round and introduce her to various people. Then we were asked back to lunch. On that occasion Princess Anne was being very dry. At three o'clock we were asked by Lord Arbuthnott, the Lord Lieutenant of Kincardineshire, to take Princess Anne down to the Royal Box to watch the Grand Parade of livestock. After the parade there was show jumping in the ring and her husband, Mark Philips was competing. John Arbuthnott who was the senior vice-president while I was the junior vice-president of the Royal Highland and Agricultural Society, sat down first with the Princess. After about twenty minutes he came and said,

"Mike, you come and take my place. I'm exhausted."

So I went and sat down and thought I would try and make conversation. Knowing nothing about horse jumping myself didn't stop me, and I said, "Is this a difficult course?"

"Not really."

End of conversation. A little later when what seemed to be a little horse did what seemed to me to be a high jump I said, "Was that a high jump for that little horse?"

"No."

End of conversation. Then Mark Philips came round. He just needed to clear the last jump and he would have been second in this particular competition but the horse baulked and the Princess at last got excited and said, "My goodness me. He's done that too often. Wait till I get hold of him."

"Maam," I said, "I wouldn't get at him for that. Have you never had a horse baulk with you?"

"O well, yes."

"Well I think you should let him off in this case."

To my great relief she smiled and we were reasonably friendly after that.

The Duke of Edinburgh can be forthright and sometimes almost curt. I had one experience with him at a lunch in Holyrood Palace. When this invitation came in I was of a mind to refuse but Pauline said I couldn't possibly refuse. I told her there'd be a thousand people there and it'd be a bit of cold ham and a glass of sweet sherry. But I was persuaded and I remember when I arrived somebody came out and parked my car and that doesn't often happen to me. I was then led in by Lady Airlie, who was the Queen's lady-in-waiting.

"Glad to see you, Mr Mackie, would you like to see the guest list?"

This turned out to be only five other guests. One of them was Max Harper-Gow the Chairman of Salvesens and I remember when we were going through to the lounge to have our coffee he said to me, "Well, Mike. If we don't spill our coffee on the floor of the lounge we'll have aquitted ourselves quite well." In fact that had been made very easy for us because of the way they conducted the meal.

When we arrived in the drawing room we were told that the Duke and the Queen had been held up and sent their apologies but they would be ten minutes late. So when they did arrive we were all lined up and were introduced. The Queen was at her most charming and she had at least three of her corgis with her and she demonstrated one of her corgis which had either no leg or a bad leg. It ran in and, on the Queen's command, it lay down and rolled over and got up again and that was greatly approved of as a trick. I admired the Queen's corgi and then went over to the Duke of Edinburgh because I wanted to ask if he could come to Houston to back up the North East Development Association mission there. I did ask him and he said, no, that he'd been in Houston before. Then the Queen said, "I think we'll go in to lunch" and, as if by a miracle, the corgis disappeared to the right and we disappeared to the left into a dining room.

I did admire the way the Queen handled that lunch.

Lady Airlie sat at one end of the table and the Duke's equerry at the other, the Duke of Edinburgh and the Queen sat opposite one another at the middle of the table and the guests were arranged two on each side of the hosts. At one stage she said, "I hear my husband say such and such" and then she would turn to the person diagonally opposite and say, "What do you think about that?" and soon she had the conversation going round the table which I thought was very clever. It doesn't always work that way. Once I was at a dinner party in Holyrood Palace just after I was knighted and Pauline and I were next to the Secretary of State for Scotland, George Younger, and his wife. The Secretary of State was on the Queen's right and I was on the Queen's left and I thought now they'll just do the same as they did at that previous lunch. I was prepared to talk with the Secretary of State's wife but keeping half an eye and half an ear on the Queen thinking she would start a general conversation again. But the first course passed and the second course passed and I was totally ignored by the Queen who was talking to the Secretary of State. I'm sure I was a very bad companion to Mrs Younger because all the time I was expecting the Queen to want to speak to me. The Duke of Edinburgh had done exactly the same to Pauline on the other side. Her partner had said to her, "I hope I'm not keeping you from the Duke." And she said, "He hasn't even looked near me yet." At the end of the main course the Queen then turned to me and the Duke turned to Pauline and they totally ignored the guests they had been speaking to in the first half from then on. Pauline was a bit worried because there was fruit being passed round and she didn't know what to do with the grape seeds but she was left in no doubt by the Duke of Edinburgh who just spat them out onto his plate.

Another contact I had with the Duke of Edinburgh was when I was asked to propose the toast to him when he was visiting the Chamber of Commerce in Aberdeen. We were raising money for some charity and it was one of these £20 per plate dos. When it came time to propose the toast I said that I had read the speech made by my opposite number when the Duke had attended a similar dinner in Glasgow. He had said he was an ideal person to propose the Duke's health as he met him regularly every fifteen years. I said that I could make a similar claim; that I had met the Duke regularly over the last thirty years. The first occasion was when I was on the finance committee of Gordonston school. I was standing at the school door with one or two of the other committee members when the headmaster, Kurt Haan, drove up and stepped out with the Duke and came over to us and said, "Don't go away gentlemen. I want you to meet the Duke." I was introduced as a farmer and when he asked whereabouts.I told him it was Inverurie thinking that would be easier for him than Rothienorman.

"That's in Kincardineshire, isn't it?"

And I thought, "What an ignorant fellow. Doesn't know where Inverurie is?"

Next time I met him was at Holyrood Palace after a lunch and he was arguing with Shaw, who was Chairman of the Crofters Commission and would have known all about Blackface Sheep. The Prince had been at Glensaugh, the college's hill farm and, as he picks things up very quickly, he thought he now knew a thing or two about Blackface sheep and was inclined to argue with Shaw.

I broke in and said, "I'm sorry your Royal Highness, you've got that all wrong. The facts are..." at this point the Duke called me an "argumentative.beggar."

So I repeated.all that at the dinner and then added, "Mind you, I don't think that that was the exact word he used."

When he got up to reply the Duke said, "I would like to assure the audience that beggar was the word I used... What else would you call an impecunious farmer?"

Despite that I enjoyed my contacts with the Royal Family and I think that Lord Lieutenancy is a job that will continue for a long time because it is useful to the Monarchy. I am very proud to have been Lord Lieutenant of Aberdeenshire for twelve years.

CHAPTER EIGHTEEN

Highland Hydrocarbons

I GOT involved with a friend of mine George Stokes and the late Pat Hunter Gordon in a great business venture. They were trying to get some spin-off from the oil business up to the Highlands and the Cromarty Firth and they had the bright idea that very soon governments would stop the use of lead in petrol - a substitute would be needed. So great plans were laid and a company formed called Highland Hydrocarbons. We booked land in the Cromarty Firth and great plans were laid for a loading pier to bring in the raw materials we needed - the methane and ethane which were the main constituents from which we would produce the additive for lead-free fuel. Everybody got very excited about it, long hours were spent arranging the deals to make this possible. One priority was to get enough ethane and it was thought that we needed a) some financial support and b) some of the raw materials from the oil companies. I had made a lot of contacts with the Total people in Aberdeen and their boss in Paris, M Renouard, was very interested and it looked as if they would put money, and by money I mean many millions, into the project and provide some of the raw materials. The oil companies do things in curious ways and I had arranged to meet M Renouard at his office in Aberdeen one day at five o'clock.

At that time the administrator of Total was Andrew Armstrong who is now the manager of the North Sea operation in Aberdeen. At five o'clock I received a telephone message that the French party were held up. They were the operators of St Fergus (the gas terminal) and had been out to see how things were but had got held up. The message was "Tell Mr Armstrong to give Mr Mackie a drink." So I got a drink and twenty minutes later another phone call, "Apologise to Mr Mackie and give him another drink because we're going to be even later." At about five thirty the party arrived with profuse apologies but refused to do any business that night, "You'll just come to Paris and we'll organise it."

I thought that was a good thing because I hadn't been in Paris for some time so a little later Mr Armstrong came on the phone again. Could we go to Paris on Friday and stay the weekend? M Renouard would deal with me. My wife was invited too and Mr Armstrong and his wife were to accompany us and see that our journey was comfortable.

I said, "I could go, but I have a meeting in Edinburgh in the morning."

"Oh, that will be no problem. We'll get a private plane to pick your wife up in Aberdeen, take her to Edinburgh to meet you after your meeting, and then take you over to Paris."

So that was done.

On the way a tragedy occurred. For once I was a distinctly unlucky chap. Pauline and I had had a great argument about what we should take as a present to our hosts. She suggested that I take a gallon bottle of Glenmorangie which I had been given some time before. I had demurred at this because I had been looking forward to drinking the gallon of whisky myself. So that was left undecided or at least I thought it was undecided but Pauline had in fact decided that, whatever I wanted to do, the gallon of whisky was going to France. When she was preparing to leave and waiting for the taxi to come, Pauline took the gallon bottle and set it down on the tiles in the hall. At this the whole ring of the bottle became detached and she was left aghast as waves of Glenmorangie swept over the hall. She suspected that I might kill her when the news reached me. However, the thought of the gallon of

Glenmorangie was so overwhelming that all thoughts of retribution were overlooked. In fact I was more amused that anything else. As it had cost me nothing, I had lost nothing except a lot of beautiful whisky.

When we arrived in France two limousines were waiting for us. The second was because Pauline might want to go shopping in one direction while I might want to go to their offices. That night the chairman's wife cooked dinner for us in their flat. His main hobby was old books and he had a fine collection of some of the finest French books that had ever been printed. He was more interested in that even than his job. He was looking forward to the day when he could retire and give his full attention to his hobby.

It was arranged that next day we would have our long delayed meeting in the hotel where we had been given luxurious accommodation. Indeed it was the most luxurious that I had enjoyed; in the King George V Hotel, one of the best in Paris. We had a suite in the hallway of which, to greet my wife, was a most enormous bowl of flowers and on the sitting room table a beautiful bowl of roses and as a gift to her, not just a bottle of perfume but an enormous bottle of perfume and a silver cigarette box to me. All this I thought a bit over the odds and I said to Mr Armstrong, "We really can't accept all these gifts."

Mr Armstrong said, "I know. I've told them several times that they overdo the hospitality but that's the way they do business and if you refuse you offend them."

So I said, "Oh. well. That being the case..."

At ten o' clock we had our delayed meeting to arrange for financial support for Highland Hydrocarbons. Within the hour we had reached satisfactory conclusions. They were going to invest in the company and also supply most of the raw materials that were going to be needed. That was a great breakthrough and we were all very excited about it.

The success of the proposed company depended on the government, and indeed all the governments in Europe, setting firm dates for getting the lead out of petrol because nobody was going to invest the many millions of pounds needed for the development of alternative fuel until they did so. The market would certainly have been there had they made the decision at that time but none of the countries would set a firm date so sadly, after investing a good deal of time and a good deal of money, we had to fold up Highland Hydrocarbons and a dream went bust. I still think it would have been very successful and a very, very good thing for the Highlands, if we'd been able to get ahead with that project.

At any rate we had a nice time in Paris and after the negotiations they proceeded to entertain us by taking us out to Versailles. Since both Pauline and I had been through Versailles we thought this something of a duplication but it was said to be a treat. To our surprise it turned out to be so because they had arranged a special guide to take the six of us through Versailles and we walked past all the queues to get into various rooms and we got into rooms which no one else was allowed into. So it really was a fascinating tour. Then we went out to lunch, a little more sight-seeing and then we were taken to dinner at night. Again we were entertained royally. We went to the Tour d'Argent restaurant which specialised in duck. So, of course, everyone had duck, and each of us who had duck got a certificate saying, "This is the one million one hundred and forty eight thousandth... duck served in the restaurant." On top of that the ladies got a beautiful ceramic duck as a memento of having had duck at the Tour d'Argent.

The two limousines were at our disposal throughout and the next morning we went shopping and sight-seeing though we always used only one of the limousines. We were tempted to take a limousine each when we were returning to the airport to fly home... but we didn't.

During the oil business I was lucky enough to be taken out to the oil platforms. They are really an amazing sight. I was on the Oxy platform before it was blown up and later I was taken out to one of the Forties platforms. I was absolutely amazed at how they could crowd on so much machinery. I was speaking to one platform manager and I said to him that I was amazed at how much stuff they managed to get on to the platform. "Not any more amazed than I am," he said. "Although I know all the jobs of oil production most of my experience is in the deserts in Saudi Arabia and elsewhere and there we take forty acres to lay out all our machinery and its a marvel to me that we've got it all here in this concentration on the platform."

I was also fortunate to meet Arnold Hammer on one or two occasions. I was invited out to the launch of the fire fighting ship, which later turned out to be not so useful, when the Piper Alpha burned, but the Duke of Edinburgh was quite amusing. He was the chief guest along with Red Adair the firefighter who was there to say how wonderful this would be for firefighting. The Duke said, "I don't know why I'm here. It has been commissioned. It has been named. It has been working but I am just pleased to see it." And so was I.

That was typical of the trips we made to the oil companies and that was typical of the way they entertained. It fairly opened my eyes to how the top brass spread their wings and live well.

But we could get nowhere with Highland Hydrocarbons without a date for going lead-free, so I took the opportunity to raise the matter with Mrs Thatcher when she came to power in 1979.

The Lord Lieutenant gets invited to all sorts of things and one year we were invited by Mrs Thatcher to 10 Downing Street (and in fact she repeated it the following year). At first I thought we should refuse because in those days of austerity Maggie would give us a glass, or maybe even half a glass, of Australian sherry and a soggy cheese biscuit. However we had a second thought that it would be nice to see inside 10 Downing Street.

Far from half a glass of sherry there was all the drink you could imagine and better still, a nice Irish lassie who came round with the drinks said she liked my voice and poured me a very large Glenlivet. From then she followed me round the room keeping the glass well filled-up. So it turned out to be a most excellent occasion.

Maggie didn't waste much time with you at the door. She thrust out a hand which seemed to be about six feet long and pulled you into the room. We then shook hands with Denis and on to the drink. Later on I saw Maggie standing speaking to the Duke of Buccleuch and now fortified with Glenlivet I thought I would need to tackle her about Highland Hydrocarbons. I walked up and said, "Prime Minister, I know this isn't the time to talk business but you do know, I think, about our problem with Highland Hydrocarbons and I don't think your Ministry of Energy are being as helpful as they should."

"Oh, yes. I know about your proposed company but have you talked to the Secretary of State for Scotland?"

And I said, "Mercy yes. We had an hour's meeting with him last week."

At this she pointed to a spot on the floor and in a commanding voice said, "Stay there." and marched over to the fireplace to where George Younger was talking to the Tory party chairman at the time, Lord Thorneycroft. She was back in about a minute flat to where I was standing as though to attention and she said, "Keep in touch with the Secretary of State." and marched off. I then walked over to where George Younger was also standing to attention and, after he had introduced me to Lord Thorneycroft, I asked George what he was going to do for us.

He said, "Well Mike, I've had my orders anyway."

We chatted for a while and then I said, "Well gentleman, I mustn't keep you. You do know that I am not of your party but I do wish you well because you have lots of difficulties."

Almost with one voice the two of them relied, "Ah yes, but now we've got leadership." They were both almost saluting.

I left them to their leadership and their difficulties. Half way across the room, and greatly to my surprise, Pauline said, "There's Willie Whitelaw. I think I met him in Northern Ireland and I'd like to go and speak to him." So we went and introduced ourselves. "You won't know me but you may know something of my two brothers who are in the House of Lords..." He at least said that that was so. After we had chatted for a while I again took my leave saying, "I must circulate and not monopolise you. I am not of your party but I wish you every success because you have many difficulties."

Again back came the reply. "Yes. We have difficulties but now we have leadership." And he was almost saluting. So we circulated and enjoyed lots more of Maggie's hospitality.

We did seem to make further progress with the Ministry of Energy but in the end we failed because we never did get the British nor the European Governments to set a date.

Two or three times I've been invited to the great annual dinner at the Grosvenor rooms in London where all the oil companies and service companies have a do. It's quite an occasion and only the Grosvenor rooms can handle it because there are some sixteen hundred guests who all sit down to dinner. On one such occasion I felt very sorry for the maitre d'hotel. The custom was that the Minister for Energy would address the company and on that occasion Peter Walker was the Minister. Anyway we were just about to have our steak and you can imagine the organisation that went into having sixteen hundred steaks just perfect all at once. The maitre d' hotel has a walkie-talkie where he is in constant contact with the chef and the waiters. It's all a split second job, and then, just when all was ready, the chairman got up and said they had received a message that the Minister had to go away to the House of Commons to vote on some urgent issue because the Labour Party had refused to pair. So they would just have the Minister's speech now to let him away and he had asked the kitchen to take the steaks back for an hour and we would get them after the Minister's speech.

I can only imagine the words that passed between the maitre d' hotel, the table managers and the chefs when everything had to be rearranged. And yet, an hour later, we were served with steaks and whether they were the same steaks or new steaks I don't know but a beautiful steak appeared in due course.

Lots of cynical people wondered what I got out of being in local government. Apart from those trips which were first rate, what I got was a lot of interest but not in the financial sense. It cost me a lot of money to be spending hours and hours on local government work when I should have been at home paying attention to my own business.

When the great oil rich companies came to Aberdeen I certainly got nothing out of it except an enormous amount of interest and the big oil companies to whom I had been very helpful in getting planning permission and so on were very good to me although not in a monetary way. For instance I was out in Japan at a Milk Marketing Board Conference and BP suggested addresses of their people in Japan and Australia and all over the place and they told me that if they could be helpful in any way then I would just need to contact these people. Also they suggested that I flew back from Japan via Alaska and they would meet me and take me to the North Slopes where BP and Arco were just developing their major Arctic oil field. So on the way home we stopped in Alaska and BP were very good, they took us in an executive jet up to the North Slopes. There we saw the beginnings of the great pipeline and with astonishment looking out to sea, which was completely frozen over, I could see a barge stuck in the ice about three miles out with a great load of pipes which they wouldn't get in until the sea unfroze. There was only a month or two of each year when they could bring the loads of pipe in because the sea was frozen the rest of the year. Other things were flown in by big transport planes but the pipes had to come in by sea.

It was amazing to see the development there. It was a lovely sunny day and Pauline, thinking we were going to the North Pole, had bought a parka made of seal skin and fur with a furry collar and what not and while I was discussing things with the BP people in their office she would go for a walk in her parka. When I eventually caught up with her she was carrying the parka because it was so hot amid all the snow and ice.

That was an enormous project and I felt very proud to be there because not many non-technical people had seen it. I commented then on the fact that my wife's parka wasn't much use and the chap who was looking after me said, "You should be here in the winter when we're all covered up with layers and layers of clothing and if you want to have a pee there is great difficulty in finding the apparatus because the cold has made it smaller and smaller and we have to wear about six inches of clothing."

That day, when we flew back on the lovely executive jet we were caught in a great storm. I had just learned to fly myself at that stage so when we were coming in to land the pilot had me up in the seat behind him so that I could appreciate landing this plane. There was really a tremendous wind and it was really a skilful piece of flying to land because the wind was blowing across the runway. We were buffeting about and he had to go round twice before he managed to get her down. That was the storm in which Congressman Dobbs' little plane was lost in the snow. I was quite glad to get back safely.

So that's the sort of thing that I got out of my public work and the friendship of a lot of the chief executives of the oil companies and I was very proud when I resigned as Lord Leiutenant (mind you, resigned may not be the word as when you reach the age of 75 you are put out to grass whether you want to go or not). Sixteen of the big oil companies invited me to a dinner in my honour in Fyvie Castle. They had taken the castle for the night. BP sent their liason man with a limousine to pick me up and take me out to the castle. There, a piper and a man in a frock coat and white gloves showed me up the stairs to a room where lots of drink was taken and then to the dining room where we had a super meal and lots more drink was taken and then back to the little room where more drink was taken and then very kindly they had thought, "We can't send this man home with so much drink taken. We'll give him a bed for the night at Towie Barclay Castle." So the limousine appeared and picked up the chief executive of BP who had organised this bit of it, their PR man Peter Finch who hadn't been at the dinner and myself. When we got to Towie Barclay the poor chief executive was invited in, as though we all hadn't had enough drink, and we had more drink with Marc Ellington, the Baron of Towie Barclay. I got to bed about four o'clock and at eight o'clock woke refreshed and went downstairs. Mrs Ellington was away for the weekend but her two children were there trying to get their breakfast ready so I made breakfast with them and a little shamefacedly Marc appeared about quarter to ten slightly recovered from the night before. At 10 o' clock sharp the limousine appeared to take me back home. So a sober gentleman then was reunited with his wife. I thought that was a splended finish to my oil connections.

I spent some years on the Scottish Council Development and Industry and many years later was honoured with three others by being made one of the Council's first fellows. I think there was no doubt such a council was needed in Scotland and was very well run during my time by Peter Balfour who subsequently became chairman succeeding Lord Clydesdale who was at that time Chairman of the Royal Bank of Scotland. I think Scotland is indebted to a lot of people for the work they put into the Council because it was the voice of the people who were involved in the industry of Scotland. Because they were in the Council they had access to the Secretary of State for Scotland. When there was any real problem they were able to go and tell the Secretary what the businessmen of Scotland were thinking. The politicians listened to the SCDI because of the calibre of the people involved in it and because it was so representative. As well as businessmen and local authority people, there were representatives of all political parties and the trade unions. So, if they came up with a view, the politicians were likely to listen as they were fairly sure that the main interested parties would support it.

For some years I chaired the Aberdeen Committee of the SCDI and I was well served on that committee by Bill Adams. When I retired he wrote me a nice letter suggesting that I write my memoirs so he is partly responsible for this review of this lucky chap's life.

After I had been involved with the oil business for some time it occurred to the head man of Shell, the head man of BP and myself that it would be a good thing if we had a charity which would be seen to be supported by the whole of the oil industry in Aberdeen. After a meeting in the Shell premises it was decided that we would form a charity called the Oil Industry Community Fund and I became the first chairman of that until I was eighty when Alec Mair the late head of Grampian TV agreed to take over from me. This charity has been fairly successful because every oil company and every service company is inundated with requests to support local charities and all they can do is throw most of them in the waste paper basket since they would hesitate to send £5 or £10 to each charity that came looking for a £1000. Our idea was to have a hundred companies giving us £1000 each; a total of £100,000, so we'd be able to give a hundred pounds or so to small charities which would mean every oil company would be making a contribution but wouldn't have the administrative job of deciding what to support and what to file in the wastepaper basket. We never did achieve the hundred members but I still have high hopes that, now there has been a resurgence of wealth in the oil industry, we will get more subscribers. The most we've had up to now is thirty-eight but it has been very useful. Three times a year we distribute and over the years hundreds of charities from the Highlands and Islands to Montrose - any place where the oil companies have any sort of interest - have benefited. Now where any oil industry member feels they can't help they just refer the charity to the Oil Industry Community Fund.

For instance we helped the Inverurie people who were trying to raise money for a taxi cab to take people who were in wheelchairs to the hospitals. We helped a good many village halls including the one at Daviot. There was some hilarity when I suggested we help the Daviot hall since I had been chairman of that hall committee many years previously. But that's one of the advantages of having a committee of seven or eight who know the area and everybody makes some attempt to find suitable applications of the funds. We give quite considerable attention to them and I think fair play is done. We've helped a great many community centres and struggling play groups have had toys and what-not bought for them. (In the case of Daviot the whole hall had to be rebuilt and we gave them £500. In some cases we give £50 or £100 but the biggest donations we've given was over a £1000 to the great scheme to add a new wing to the maternity hospital for the Special Nursery for looking after premature babies and £2000 towards one of those new body-scanning machines.

CHAPTER NINETEEN

Other Extra-Curricular Work

ONE OF the things I did when still involved in local authority work was to spend ten years on a sub-committee of the University Grants Committee. I found that very interesting because at the time they were starting to run short of money for the universities and they thought that there were too many of them teaching the same things. I was on the agricultural sub-committee and those dealing with forestry and agricultural economics. The UGC committees and sub-committees do a visitation every five years. Those were really rather fun especially as the universities really laid down the red carpet. We would start off with a marvellous meal with the chancellor all his senate and all his big wigs telling you what a marvellous job the university was doing and telling you what you'd be seeing next day. Then next day you go round and again everything would be laid out to impress you and then you interview all the lecturers and some of the students.

The odd thing is that sometimes the ballyhoo had the opposite effect and you would start to say, "Gosh that canna aa be true."

And although it seems impossible to judge a university's work on a two day visit, you did get some sort of a feel for the university and I think the members of the committee who were used to judging that sort of thing managed to do a fairly good job. It was of particular interest to me when they decided that there were far too many universities teaching agriculture. We went the rounds and agreed that there were indeed too many and that three universities should stop teaching agriculture. It was decided that Glasgow, Cambridge and Leeds should close their agriculture departments. Of course there was an immediate uproar from all three. In the case of Glasgow the Secretary of State, Willie Ross, was brought into it and he wrote a personal letter to me saying that this was a terrible thing to do to Glasgow. However the sub-committee report to the main committee and the main committee supported our recommendation. Now, although you can't tell a university what to do, you can withdraw its financial support. So, in the case of these universities, the plan was that they would lose the financial support given for their agricultural facilities but if they wanted to, they could, of course, close down another department or make other economies and continue agriculture. Glasgow cheated to some extent. What they did was to appoint two agriculture lecturers to science departments where they continued to teach agricultural botany or agricultural chemistry or whatever it was. We were somewhat annoyed at this but the wise ones on the committee said, "It won't work, it'll soon fade out because they won't be able to produce the kind of graduate that other universities with agricultural schools can produce."

And that, as it turned out, was correct. Cambridge, on the other hand, took it very well and did stop teaching agriculture totally. They didn't, of course, sell the land they had and that included some very nice farms in the prime lands round about Cambridge where they did some very good research projects. But since they were making a lot of profit out of their farms at that time those didn't bother the committee.

Leeds, under Professor Bywater, were very angry and they tried to do the same as Glasgow, but with the same result. They found that no one would now go to Leeds to do an agriculture degree.

The next visitation we did was on forestry and again it was decided that there were too many universities teaching forestry and because of the Commonwealth Bureau, we couldn't touch the little bit of forestry that Oxford taught but that there was no need for Edinburgh and Aberdeen both to teach forestry. But having had a look of the initial information we had from both universities it was more or less decided that if we liked what we saw in Aberdeen, which we were to visit first, Aberdeen would stay open and Edinburgh would close. We visited Aberdeen and were favourably impressed. Of course they had very close contact with the Forestry Commission and the big estates were collaborating with them and really we were very impressed. On the way down on the train to Edinburgh for our visit the next day, it was confirmed that in our opinion Edinburgh would close. When we arrived in Edinburgh, to the surprise of the committee, and why we didn't know beforehand I don't know, we were astonished to find that the forestry department in Edinburgh were into a fine new building with wind tunnels in the basement and fine new labs and Professor Black who made a splendid spiel about what they were doing in Edinburgh and what they could do. The result was that, on the grounds that Aberdeen had very bad out-of-date buildings, their decision was reversed and it was decided that Edinburgh with its fine new buildings should be kept open and Aberdeen should be closed. I argued for Aberdeen as forcibly as I could (and, even as a graduate, I think I was being objective) but the committee thought otherwise. However I said, "I don't often do this but I wish to present a minority report to the main committee."

So I wrote a minority report to the main committee suggesting that this decision had been taken for the wrong reasons and that the main committee should agree to close Edinburgh and keep Aberdeen open. And the committee accepted my minority report and Edinburgh was told to close its forestry department.

The department and the faculty in Aberdeen were very pleased with this result and I was invited some time later to a very fine dinner in the refectory in Aberdeen with all the university silver on the table. Nobody said it was because the forestry department had remained open but I said to the principal afterwards. "It's a good job you didn't do this before the UGC visitation, that really would have been bribery." Professor Matthews told me later how pleased they were that they were to be left to carry on the good work. And I felt I had really done something worthwhile.

Another very interesting bit of work I did was ten years on the National Trust for Scotland. I found that very interesting. They have on the council a fair number of people from county families. They're very useful because they are used to living in stately homes of the type that the Trust was taking over and these county people could tell us where we could get suitable furniture for our properties and so on. People used to say that the National Trust was a snooty, aristocratic organisation but it's almost bound to be because these are the people that really know about the types of properties they are looking after. Not being very aristocratic myself I found that they were really friendly and I got on very well on the Trust.

One interesting job I did for them was for Crathes Castle, which had been left by Sir James Burnett to the Trust on condition that, on his death, his wife would be allowed to stay in the castle until her death. It was somewhat ambiguous as to whether this tenancy would follow on to the family. In my opinion it did not. But the truth was that some of the committee believed that the public like to think that the building is occupied by the owners from way back. I took the opposite view because I have never liked paying half a crown to see round a house when the owners were living in it and have nearly always refused to do so. Anyway Crathes Castle had at that time a wing called after the Queen Anne. It had been built much later than the castle itself and it had been three stories high which hid one turret of the main house completely and some of the corbelling of the castle. Sir James' grandson, a bachelor in his early twenties who had changed his name to James Burnett so that he could continue the Burnett connection and inherit the estate, occupied a flat on the top storey of the Queen Anne wing. He had had a party one night and the wing had taken fire. The guests all escaped in the middle of the night and the fire brigade extinguished the blaze before the main castle was damaged at all. That was a

Godsend as Crathes Castle is unique. But then the great
decision had to be made about rebuilding the Queen Anne
wing. The discussions went on for a good few years while
the insurance money gathered interest in the bank. The
main argument was whether to build it as it was before or,
as I suggested, take it down altogether and have another
Craigievar with just the one upstanding square tower.
However, Schomberg Scott, the Trust's very good architect,
persuaded me that, in the original plans of the building,
there were 'laich biggins' and if we wanted it restored to the
original there should be a low building at the side but at the
most there should be two stories which was eventually the
plan. James Burnett of Crathes, wanted that flat to be for
his occupation and that it should have five bedrooms, three
bathrooms, and a large entertainment room. The Trust
wanted the ground floor to be for the reception of visitors
and the top for the use of staff. So the great debate was
what to do about Mr Burnett's request for accommodation
within the castle. I said that he had no right to the castle
and that when the nation received these estates it was to the
benefit of the successors because it saved them paying death
duties and had Sir James not given the estate to the trust
Mr Burnett would not have had very much left. I suggested that he be given £25,000 of the insurance money
and a site on the estate and told to go and build a house for
himself. The committee said they would agree to that if I
could persuade Mr Burnett to agree.

I remember standing with him at the front door of
the ruined Queen Anne wing on a cold, windy day trying to
persuade him and I think what finally persuaded him was
when I said, "You're a bachelor now but no doubt you'll get
a wife and she will not bless you in years to come if you ask
her to live in a house with three hundred thousand people
coming through it every year."

So his determined stubbornness was overcome and he
finally accepted I think £35,000 from the Trust and built
himself a nice house which must have cost three times that
amount. So he can now come round the corner and say
that was my grandfather's house and I think if he were
honest he would be very pleased that he made that decision

instead of having a flat in the original house.

I have also been involved in a number of charitable trusts. Two in particular are worth a mention. The first was as chairman of the Victor Cook foundation. He was chairman of the firm of Barry, Henry and Cook, who made castings in Aberdeen. They made most of the brander covers in the city for example. It was a very good business but in 1970, with the coming of the oil, Mr Cook sold out to Seaforth Maritime for a very good price. He invested the money and all his investments did well... even better than the company would have done. He was then able to pay full attention to his one great interest in life which was to see that children were educated in the proper way to live. How he thought he knew all about that was hard to understand for he was a bachelor with no children (that we knew of) and a mother complex but nevertheless had a fixed idea that he could tell teachers how to educate children about living properly.

He had already given about £200,000 to the Victor Cook Foundation and I was a very early member and tried to help Victor all I could. But he was a very determined man and difficult to advise because he thought he knew exactly what was needed. He had some very good trustees like Jack Marshall, the ex-Gordon's College headmaster, and Dr Bill Gatherer an ex-director of education in the Lothians and latterly Peter Clark the former head of the Robert Gordon's Institute of Technology and Charles Skene one of Aberdeen's great entrepreneurs. Then there was the Rev Derek Henderson. He had been his minister and came down from Inverness for the regular meetings.

Victor used part-time teachers to help him produce log books to give out to children and leaflets and he gave prizes for the best essays and all sorts of things. All this was planned at Countesswells House where he lived on the outskirts of Aberdeen. Most of his ideas were quite good except that they were out of date. They related to his experiences at school and we found it very difficult to get him to accept the fact that he ought to employ somebody active in modern education to help him make up his leaflets and log books relevant to up to date problems. That used to make him quite angry. Nevertheless we all liked Victor and we wanted to help.

We eventually succeeded in persuading him to get into the colleges of education and get those who were going to be teaching the young to put over his material. We recommended that he should work through the Scottish Education Department and persuade them that this was a necessary part of education. So he gave the Scottish Education Department a quarter of a million pounds to finance a committee who would see if Cook's views constituted a teachable subject or not. They have done very little with his £250,000 except produce a rather sketchy questionnaire-cum-report which has gone to all schools asking their opinions. That'll take a year then another year of discussion, nevertheless we did succeed in giving Victor's ideas an opening into the Scottish education system.

At this time when we thought we were making a little progress the dear old man had a heart attack and died and I was left as chairman of the executors and chairman of his trust fund. He had left the whole of his estate, Countesswells House and grounds and all his investments totalling three and a half million pounds to the fund which had already grown so that the fund is now worth four million pounds. So I now had an embarrassment of riches with which to pursue a somewhat uncertain objective. However, we employed a chief executive, Bill Robb, who was a lecturer in education at Glasgow University, and he seems to know what is wanted. We are subsidising research at all three colleges of education into what needs to be done to educate young people in the art of living. There are a lot of people who think that this four million pounds could be used to better effect and that it's the government's job to do that sort of research. But we have no leeway in the matter. The will is quite explicit that we have to pursue "values education" and who is to know what long term benefits may flow from Victor Cook's beneficence. Certainly there is no shortage of people who would like to spend the money for us. One of the jobs of the trust is to try to sort out which suggestions might be worthwhile pursuing and which are unpromising. It is possible to ask the Secretary of State to alter the terms of the trust but only on the grounds that we have found it impossible to pursue the terms of the will and, although we have found it difficult, that has not yet proved an impossible task.

Then there was the Sharpe's Trust. Mr Shimmie Sharp left his estate land in Rothiemay with the proviso that the income from the estate be used to give five pounds to the poor of the parish of Rothiemay. Because he had had some connection with the parish of Fyvie, the poor in the parish of Fyvie were to get a fiver as well. As the representative of Fyvie on the County Council I was asked to join the Trust just after the war. The rest of the money was to be used to encourage children aged thirteen to stay on at school and to pay their expenses to stay at school. But by this time the state was paying the expenses of education beyond thirteen right up to university age so we had to go to the Secretary of State and get permission to change the rules a little bit. At that time architects and even lawyers used to work for sweeties for a year in the course of their apprenticeships and this often discouraged students from going into those professions. We used to help one or two and that was of some use but we needed to be able to give more to the poor. The original bequest only allowed us to give five pounds between all of the poor of Fyvie and Rothienorman so even in the days before the Welfare State this five pounds was unable to make life for the poor appreciably better.

The income from the estate was very little. In those days, if landlords fulfilled their responsibilities by maintaining buildings and so on, they were lucky if they could get one and a half per-cent income on the capital value. So I persuaded the Trustees to sell the land and invest the money. This trebled the income and we then had a really worthwhile charitable fund to dispense. I did the same thing in the John Gordon Trust. John Gordon, a merchant in Aberdeen, had left money with instructions to buy land and his executors had bought three thousand acres of land in the Mintlaw/New Deer area. A lot of it was very poor land and the income was very small. It was administered by Davidson and Garden, a law firm in Aberdeen. I was asked

by the late Roger Fleming and Quentin Forbes Irvine of
Drum if I would join their committee because nobody knew
very much about land and they thought I would be useful
to them. At the very first meeting I was a bit dismayed that
the only information I had was three years' accounts up to
date and none of these were audited. I went in about five
minutes early to be told by Quentin and Roger that I was to
be chairman.

I said, "That sounds a bit unfair because this is my
first meeting and I know nothing about the Trust. Why
don't you do it?"

"Oh, no. We're not going to do it and if you don't do
it Ronny Dean, who has been handling the affairs, just
automatically takes charge and that's not right because it's
his firm that administers the Trust."

So I accepted the job and discovered that we were far
too good landlords. The first thing I persuaded the committee to do was to double the rents. That didn't make me
too popular with my farming friends and I then proceeded
to persuade the committee, and they were not difficult to
persuade because the income was so tiny, to sell to the
sitting tenants. They were on a good thing because land
was not at a good price and in retrospect if we had waited a
few years we could have got a lot more. But then the shares
that we bought shot up as well and the income, which had
been fifteen hundred pounds per year off the three thousand acres of land (a good deal of that, of course, went to
the law firm) shot up also and thirty years on the trust was
making £70,000 a year.

Under the terms of John Gordon's will, we were to
assist domestic servants of good character who had, "served
their masters well and faithfully for not less than fifteen
years". When I joined the trust forty or fifty ladies of good
repute were getting ten shillings per week extra which
wasn't very much. But we are now able to give the ladies
(and we got permission from the Secretary of State to include gentlemen which let us assist some old butlers and
chauffeurs) £300 per year which is a considerable help. So
I was very proud of that and the large income which we
now have allows us to give a lot of money to charity. For

the last few years we have given a cheque for £10,000 to the Voluntary Services Organisation because they know where the needs are and they're very pleased to get this decent chunk of money from this charity. I retired from the Trust in 1992, when at eighty, I thought I had done enough.

Another of the Charitable works I was involved in was Cancer Relief. I was the local chairman and I got the job of raising a quarter of a million pounds for the first Roxburghe House in Aberdeen. I thought the easiest way to do that was to get some of my rich friends to promise me anything from a thousand to five thousand. I got a few of those and I then said to each of them, "Now you've been a sucker. You go out and get another two." I thought that would be a good way to get the money because a quarter of a million would take a long time in coffee mornings. It worked very well and was all done on a personal basis.

One man I wanted particularly to get was Dandy Wallace of Candacraig. I remembered that the late Tom Adam of Denmore was friendly with Dandy. I had got a contribution from Tom because he had just sold some of Denmore for housing. "Now Tom, Dandy Wallace, I think you should get a minimum of ten thousand pounds from him." Tom assured me that if he could get Dandy in a good humour he would approach him. Time passed and nothing had happened so I phoned Tom. He said he had never found the right moment to get his bid in. I thought Tom was maybe just putting it off so I decided to do it myself... after all I did know Mr Wallace slightly. I wrote quite a nice letter saying that I thought that ten thousand would be a suitable contribution from him.

Quite by coincidence, about ten days later, I was coming up from London and sat next to Dandy. It was a noisy old plane and we couldn't hear each other so we read our papers. When we had got off the plane and were on our way into the old reception place at Dyce he stopped me on the tarmac and said, "I got your letter Mr Mackie."

"Oh good," said I. "I hope you'll be able to help us."

"I suppose you knew my wife was dying of cancer."

I was appalled to hear that but also angry. "Mr Wallace, if you think I would be such a bloody fool as to write a letter like that if I had known your wife was dying of cancer you think less of me than you should. Just forget about it." I said and walked away.

Next morning, in the post, I got a cheque for fifteen thousand pounds. So I rang him up to thank him and asked if he would think me terribly impertinent, after getting such a splendid contribution, if I asked him to sign this as a single covenant and then I'd be able to get the tax back on it as well. "I'd have thought you a damned fool if you hadn't. In fact I've discussed this with my bankers and they say that at my age they advise me not to sign a covenant." And he was right. His wife died about a month later and he died about four months after that.

We did raise the money and it was one of the most satisfying things I ever did. The number of families who have come up to me and said they appreciated having uncle Joe or mother, or granny or daughter, or whoever able to go to a place where they would be cared for without hope of cure. Doctors and nurses are trained to cure people but on the whole they are not so good at helping people to die in comfort and with dignity. And I have visited the hospices in Inverness, Glasgow, Edinburgh and Dundee and they are fullfilling a very important need. One of the lectures I went to on the subject told us that there is no need for the dying to suffer pain and at Roxburghe Houses we are able to make the ends of people's lives at least comfortable and painless. In fact you get the curious impression that the residents are on holiday.

I got involved also with Hanover Housing through Lord Glenkinglass who I had known when he was Michael Noble the Secretary of State for Scotland. I had always liked the way he did things so when he asked me to join a committee he was forming I agreed. Hanover Housing was an old established housing association in England and they decided to expand into Scotland. The money comes largely from Government funds and we built in Aberdeenshire, Elgin, the Borders, Edinburgh and Glasgow. I became chairman eventually and we were even able to build in my native village of Tarves. The main idea was to build sheltered housing for old people. It is a very satisfying job when you see a scheme finished, the people in and the appalling waiting list down a wee bit. I remember particularly the opening of a scheme of houses in Elgin. On the way round I said to one old lady, "Now tell me. We're nearly all men and the architects are all men and some of my women friends tell me that there should be women architects because men are no good at designing kitchens. So, now that you have been in here a month, what mistakes have we made in the kitchen?"

She just looked up at me and said, "Mr. Mackie, this is the first hoose I've been in wi runnin water and het water and I'm in heaven and there's nae mistaks been made."

I went as an observer to the great World Environmental Conference called One World, in Sweden in 1973. Pauline decided she would come but was unsure about her wardrobe. "Is it the sort of thing where you would need your evening dress?" I told her I didn't know but that there was to be a briefing meeting in London with Peter Walker and Eldon Griffiths and that I would ask what the appropriate dress for observers would be.

When Peter Walker asked, during the briefing, if there were any questions I said, "I'm not sure about the status of an observer. If I feel that I want to contribute to the debate, what do I do?

"You go outside and have a drink." I totally forgot to ask Pauline's question. However her question appeared to be answered when, two days before we were due to leave, I got a message to take a black tie. Pauline said, "I told you so," and packed evening dress for us. On our first evening we went to a party at the British Consul's wearing bright clothes and were astonished to find all the women were in black dresses and all the men in dark suits with a black tie. The hostess did her best to put us at our ease, but it turned out that the black ties and the sombre clothes were official mourning for the Duke of Windsor which was to last until the next day

At the conference I got quite friendly with the representatives of Trinidad and Tobago and they kindly took me around in their limousine. One of the papers was to be given by Shirley Temple, now Mrs Black a US Senator, and she was to tell us all about how to save the alligators in the Everglades. For some reason I didn't quite get into the hall but was seated in the bar when those who had been more conscientious came out. One member of the press said, "Oh man. You fairly missed yourself. Shirley Temple made a very good job of delivering her paper but it was somewhat marred by the fact that sitting on the table in front of her was her handbag made of alligator skin."

Having been a great admirer of Shirley Temple when she was Shirley Temple, I stopped her one day as she was coming down the stairs to tell her that I had been an admirer of her film performances but she cut me off very smartly with, "Good-morning," and passed on.

One of the things I found very interesting about this conference was that the finance bill was going through the House of Commons and the Labour party had refused to pair with Eldon Griffiths and Peter Walker. They had to fly back to vote in the House of Commons at half past ten and then fly back the next morning to lead the British delegation to the conference. The net result was that they couldn't go to any of the parties given by the various embassies in Stockholm and Pauline and I landed the job of carrying the Union Jack and waving it at these parties. We were also given the official car which was a very good thing because there was a good deal of drink taken.

On one occasion we saw my friends the two gentlemen from Trinidad and Tobago so I took Pauline across to speak to them. At that time she was very hot on the environment, had just started the Keep Grampian Beautiful campaign and she told them about the mess of litter in Mexico. The Trinidad and Tobago men agreed that in their country there was a good deal of untidiness. At that point we spied the Chinese Ambassador a very tall man surrounded by four very small assistants and I said to Pauline, "Come on and we'll go and speak to the Chinese. I'd love to get an invitation to go to China." So we went across but before I could get my word in Pauline, having still the untidy Mexicans and Trinadadians in her mind, chimed up, "Tell me, Mr Ambassador, are the Chinese naturally very dirty people." Poor Pauline then spent some time stammering and trying to explain what she had meant but I'm afraid my chance of a trip to China had gone. We had a very short meeting with the Chinese Ambassador.

We had a very interesting time otherwise. Sweden is a very beautiful country and I really enjoyed the tours they took us on. We visited a lake round which there had been two papermills and a chemical factory which had been pouring their waste into the lake. There is a test called the silver disk test. You lower a silver disk into the water and measure how far down into the water you can see it. Before the clean-up the disk could be seen down to a depth of about three feet but now it could be seen quite clearly on the bottom of the Lake at depths of twenty or thirty feet. That had taken ten years but it showed what could be done.

The North of Scotland College of Agriculture, apart from teaching agriculture to diploma and degree level, had the very important job of advising farmers. One of the most useful advisory units was concerned with farm buildings and was run by David Souter who had done a lot of work on pig buildings among other things. My brother John who had studied farm buildings in America, persuaded David Souter to form the Farm Buildings Association in 1956. John became the Association's first chairman and it soon had members from a very large area. It did a lot of good arranging trips to other parts of the country to see innovations in farm building. Those allowed farmers to see the newest and best in farm buildings but Souter was keen to see more research into the problems.

I supported that idea and eventually we got an independent research unit set up at Craibstone to cater for all three Colleges and the advisors. The unit was quite separate but continued with its advisory role in the North College area. I was pleased to be the first chairman and to see its growth and its usefulness recognised   David Souter had a good team with Seton Baxter, Jim Bruce and Alan Robertson as the main workers. When Souter retired Jim Bruce became head, Baxter having left to go to the Sutherland School of Architecture. I left when I was no longer on the Board of Governors of the College but I was proud of my connection with the Farm Buildings Unit whose success was mainly due to David Souter's enthusiasm. My main contribution had been in persuading the powers that be (of whom I had been a part) to separate the advisory from the research functions of the unit.

I was also involved in the Bosanquet report in which we argued that there should be more graduates among practical farmers. I took a degree in agriculture myself and it was no use at all because by the time I was farming everything I had learned was out of date. But it did teach you the language from which you could discover the best from the new. It taught you to think.

I served on the BBC's Agricultural Advisory Committee. We were there to advise on how to put over agriculture on the radio and television and that was valuable because there were very few people in the BBC who knew anything about farming.

I also served on the government's advisory committee on the North Sea when the oil started. The Secretary of State was Willie Ross and he thought he should have some people who were involved, but not of the oil industry, to advise him about the effects on the people and local industry. That was all very interesting. It was on that committee that I met James Harper Gow who was chairman of Salvesen's and later knighted for his public work. I have remained friendly with him and we started well because we usually agreed on the committee. I thought a lot of Willie Ross. He and I got a fellowship of the Educational Institute of Scotland together and they don't usually give that honour to people who aren't educationalists as such. I persuaded Willie to say thank-you for both of us and he made a very funny speech on our behalf. He wasn't always funny and I remember the last time I met him it was at Sir William Young's funeral and I asked him how he was enjoying his retirement in the House of Lords. He said, "Well at least I've discovered that there is life after death."

Willie Ross didn't often chair our committee but when he did he made a first rate job. On another occasion he put me very nicely in my place. The local authority were proposing to put the Peterhead sewage practically untreated into the sea and the people of Boddam didn't care much for that as they expected it to wash up in their little harbour. Against my better judgement, I agreed to try to persuade the Secretary of State to let us spend a bit more money on at least half treating the sewage before it went out to sea. So I led a delegation to put that case to Mr Ross when he came to Peterhead. I made what I thought was an excellent case for spending another half a million or so. He just looked up at me and said "You don't really believe what you've been saying do you."

I said, "No." and that was the end of the application.

I was a director of the first Petroleum Club. And I was made a non-executive director of British Telecom Scotland when that company split away from the old Post Office. That was fascinating. We met in Edinburgh mostly. What I knew when I joined would have gone on the back of a small postage stamp. But I was there for ten years and I believe that, if you are going to make a contribution, you have to know what you are talking about. I set about learning and I did learn a good deal about telecommunications. Sir Robin Duthie was on as well. He was chairman at the time of Black's Leisure Group. We had MacDonald the chief executive of Menzies the booksellers and it was a good committee. The Telecom people thought we were alright and even did some of the things we recommended.

I had been made an ordinary member of the Order of St John in 1973 but had only served on Lord Aberdeen's committee to raise funds for the new wing to the St. John Hospital in Aberdeen but otherwise had been an inactive member. Sometime later my old friend Sir Andrew Murray who had helped me with my election campaign in 1958 rang me up. He was Chancellor of the Order in Edinburgh and he said he was in trouble because he couldn't get a local chairman to follow Lord Aberdeen who had died. Colonel Bruce had actually followed Lord Aberdeen but he had only lasted six months so the job was vacant again. I met Sir Andrew in Edinburgh and told him that he had a lot of splendid people on the North East Committee and that I hadn't really taken much interest. What I told him to do was to go up and listen to the committee and that he should probably appoint Tom Robson the accountant. "I'll just do that."

He rang up a couple of weeks later and said, "Well, I did what you told me. I went up and listened to them and then I told them I'd appointed you as chairman." That was in 1977.

"But Andrew you can't do that. I haven't even been on their committee. It will upset them."

"No. no. They're all delighted," he said. Well, it's a very autocratic order and you don't say no to Sir Andrew Murray who had helped you in your political life so I agreed. By the time of the first meeting I had read all the minutes for the last twenty years and was reasonably prepared.

Our main job was to run the hospital and that was not going well. I discovered that the main trouble was that the matron had got too old and the sister who had covered for her for many years had died. My first meeting was a very cool affair. I apologised for being in the chair but that they had me for better or for worse.

I told them that they were losing money and that it was mainly because they were making a bad job of filling the beds and that the matron would have to be retired. "Oh but you can't do that. She's been the mainstay of the place for so many years."

"Well but you can't go on losing twenty thousand pounds a year."

"But who's going to tell the matron?"

"Well that's maybe why Sir Andrew appointed me instead of one of you. Send for the matron." And you never saw a committee disappear so quickly. One after the other made excuses and left me to it. I was sitting alone at the top of the table awaiting the matron when Tom Robson rather shame-facedly put his head round the door and asked if he should stay. "It's entirely up to you, Mr. Robson," said I, and he stayed.

So I explained the situation to the matron and after a few tears, but not too many, it appeared that the job had been done and Robson was just congratulating me on having handled it so well when the door burst open and in strode one of the sisters. "You just don't know what you're doing. In your very first meeting you can't sack the matron who has been doing so much for this hospital for so long. And I'll tell you what. The day she leaves I'll leave too and so will all the rest of the staff."

I pointed to a chair, "Sit down please. Now, who pays your salary, the matron or this committee who have been trying to keep this hospital going? If it goes on the way it has been going you'll have to leave anyway because there won't be a hospital any more. Don't wait till the matron leaves. Just leave now if you like. I'll give you ten minutes to think about it." She came back in five minutes and said she would stay. And she's still there.

The hospital prospered from then on and has since had a major expansion. I have been proud of my connection with the Order and that was intensified when, in 1988, Pauline was honoured when she became a Commander of the Order.

Somewhat out of character, I also became a director of Scottish Ballet. I had always been a bit suspicious of ballet and thought there was a something effeminate about men prancing about in tight clothes, but Robin Duff of Meldrum House, when he was chairman, asked me to be a director. He put a lot of time and his own money into Scottish Ballet and I think he thought I could be helpful because of all my business contacts. I had long been a friend of Robin's as well as working with him on the county council. So I agreed to become a director.

Having joined the board I had to find out what ballet was all about. I went to several performances and became quite converted. My association with Scottish Ballet was open to misinterpretation though. Some of Pauline's American friends had heard that I was now a member of Scottish Ballet and wrote to Pauline of their astonishment saying that they could hardly imagine me in a leotard let alone prancing about on stage. They reported themselves greatly relieved to hear that I was only a committee member and was not treading the boards. Norman Macfarlane, later Lord Macfarlane, was also on the committee. However I didn't really think I was doing any good on the committee so I resigned and was replaced by Roy Thomson of Cults who eventually replaced Robin Duff as chairman.

As a governor of the College of Agriculture I was also on the board of the Rowett Research Institute which was started between the wars by John Boyd-Orr. He later became Lord Boyd-Orr in recognition of the work he did in designing the wartime diets which meant the average Briton ate better during the war than ever before despite the war effort. He was a wizard at getting money out of people including John Duthie Webster for the Duthie stock farm and out of Charlie Alexander for an extension to the Reid Library. He also got money out of Lord Strathcona for the Strathcona Club which is used for visiting staff and so on. When his Lordship opened the club he said that he was very proud to have it called after him but that it should really have been called the Chateau d'Orr because it had cost so much.

The Insitute has had three successors to Boyd-Orr. The good work was carried on by David Cuthbertson (Ian's father) and then by Ken Blaxter who further enhanced the Institute's name. Phillip James has now put the Rowett onto a different tack. They are emphasising human nutrition now rather than animal nutrition. I therefore thought I was doing just the right thing and doing it rather well when, at a Founder's Day dinner in 1983 I made an impassioned plea for the feeding of the hungry of the world. Everyone was very enthusiastic about my speech until my son Maitland came up and said, "Great speech Dad, but completely impractical."

Perhaps I was impractical too as the first chairman of Aberdeen Cable Television. Though it is doing well now under Martin Gilbert and Graham Duncan. I was disappointed with my own performance but glad to see it recover; we lost money. I was also a governor of the Robert Gordon's Institute of Technology, a director of Morgan Grenfell (Scotland) and a member of the original Matter of Opinion team on the old Home Service.

But there was one of my jobs that was particularly to my liking. I was appointed to the Clayson Committee whose job it was to recommend what changes if any should be made in the drink laws of Scotland.

CHAPTER TWENTY

The Demon Drink

REALLY ALEC Bell's remark about the Mackies coming up to blaw like whales was the best that was ever made about me. For, though I would dispute that I only came to blaw it is true that, all my life, I have been on committees and making speeches.

I used to say that if I'd had a pound for every sale of work I had opened I'd be a rich man. I had one joke which seemed to go down very well on such occasions. I would get the usual exaggerated introduction and then would tell the story of the American with the great big twenty foot long car, holidaying in Italy who came to a narrow humped backed bridge across which a little Italian farmer was attempting to drive a little Italian calf. Finally the American lost his patience and gave a loud blast on his horn whereupon the poor calf jumped over the parapet of the bridge and was drowned. The Italian farmer came up to the American tourist, put his head into the big car and said, "Too bigga da hoot for too smalla da calf."

If I had already told that story in that village I used to open with the story of the farmer who had married a young wife when he was no longer young. A friend had called to see him and asked him how married life was suiting him. "Oh, it was aa right but it was just that she was aye needin money. She asked for a poun on Monday, she asked for a poun on Tuesday

247

and on Friday she asked for twa poun."

"Goodness me," said the friend, "and what do you think she does with it?"

"Oh, I dinna ken for she niver gets it."

Then you would proceed to ask the audience not to be like that farmer but to spend plenty of money at the sale of work and that seemed to work fine.

I started public speaking very young. I was asked by the chairman of the Conservative party of Methlick to open a sale of work at Newton farm. Because the sale was in aid of something for children it was thought appropriate that a young man of ten years open it. I had just newly gone to Methlick school and I was very excited about my first speech. I can't remember what I said though I had been well briefed but, according to everybody, I was very good. Maybe that gave me a swelled head but I've been speaking at various things ever since. I guess I didn't speak in public again until I went to the University when I became secretary and later chairman of the Agricultural Society and I had to do a little speaking there. We were always hard up but, delving back into the ancient history, I discovered that there had been a grant given to start the Society and that that had disappeared. After a little investigation I discovered that the professor still had it but hadn't done anything with it. So I managed to extract this money from the professor. It had been placed in a deposit account and had earned some interest. So I think I was the best secretary and treasurer that the Agricultural Society ever had because from having no money we then had a little money. What did we do at the Agricultural Society? Oh, the same as other University societies. We just arranged the next meeting. That was a reply that my father gave when he was for a long time in a thing called the Hill Sheep Commission. They travelled around the country looking at hill farms and what not. On one occasion, when he came home after being away for a couple of days in the Highlands, he was asked by the family what they had done and he said, "Well, we arranged the date of the next meeting."

I think quite often all I did at committee meetings was to arrange the date of the next meeting. We are said to be a nation of shopkeepers but I think we are a nation of committees. Certainly I have spent my life being a member of a great many of them. On the whole I think we made a contribution to the work and life of the community one way or another.

For one such job I thought I was particularly well chosen. I spent two years on what became known as the Clayson Committee on the Drink Laws of Scotland which reported in 1973. That was a most interesting committee led by an excellent chairman, Dr Clayson for some two years. The Committee was set up because we had some very curious laws about bona fide travellers and very restricted hours of opening of pubs and so on and it was thought that the whole thing should be liberalised. Our job was to look at the question of how far that should go and to recommend what action the Secretary of State would then take. We met on many occasions in different places and one of the enjoyable bits was of course to visit pubs and see what was what. And during the course of a couple of years we became very impressed with the one obvious difficulty that pubs had of restricting drink to anybody under the age of eighteen. We had great sympathy with the barman in a crowded bar being fined or perhaps losing his job for selling drink to somebody under eighteen because somebody over eighteen could go to the bar and buy it. That was an obvious thing that had to be tackled. The opening hours were also very stupid. The committee had a chief constable on it and they're very involved with the granting of licences as well as seeing that the laws are kept. We had a lawyer, QC Ming Campbell, who is now an MP for the Liberal Democrats. We had a doctor and a psychiatrist. I'm not sure that I thought any more of psychiatrists after the end of the two years than I did when we began. But on the whole it was a nicely balanced committee and I used to say, "as the one who knows about drinking," I had a contribution to make.

We had a social worker from the Highlands who was very concerned about the fact that drinking was a bit of a problem in the Highlands even though opening hours weren't much of a problem there. Like the old story of when someone asks the hotelier when the pub closes and is told, "Oh, round about October," it being a summer holiday resort. We had a lot of fact finding excursions which I enjoyed greatly but of course there was a lot of hard work as well. We had a whole week working on the report in a hotel in the Borders. When someone remembered that the Melrose seven-a-side rugby tournament was on I got the job of telling Dr Clayson that he had a revolt on his hands. We were all going to the sevens. He thought for hardly a moment and said, "I'll come too."

At any rate we produced what I thought was an excellent report and in the fashion of such reports we would present it to the Secretary of State who had commissioned us. This was done at St Andrews House and Gordon Campbell, now Lord Campbell of Croy, was the Secretary of State at the time. It wasn't just the presentation it was also a press conference about the report so we gave them the main features of the report and then it was open to questions from the press. One of the press men asked the Secretary of State what he was going to do now, "Well, first of all I'm going to consult all the appropriate people."

That caused me to burst out before the Chairman could say anything, "Good God! What do you think we've being doing for the last two years but consulting all the appropriate people?"

So the Secretary of State had rapidly to rethink, "Oh, no. I realise that", he said, "and I will consider the report and take action."

The main features of the report were that the opening hours should be extended to 11.00 pm, that late licences should be easier to get, and that licensed premises could be open all day if the owner wanted. By and large I think the parts of the report which were accepted have done some good because it has done away with the rush to get in the last drink at 9.30 pm... you can now ease yourself off. It has also, I think, given the police some problems with some clubs which are getting more late licences. But on the whole I think it was a good report. The one thing I was disappointed about was that they did not accept our recommendation that they should give some of the universities the job of monitoring the effects of the changes scientifically instead of just relying on general impressions. Some people think our report has made the situation worse but I think it was a very good report and has made drinking a more acceptable and more social exercise. But we really don't know because there's no scientific work been done to monitor the changes properly.

Of course I've done quite a lot of drinking in my time, enough perhaps to be an expert, but I am aware that not everyone's experience of strong drink is as happy as mine. However I told the committee that as a drinker I felt I could speak with some authority. I was also a lucky chap being born with a constitution that could take a fair amount of drink and I can honestly say that there are very few occasions on which I have had a hangover. I once did though - we were over on a Milk Board trip to Ireland and the Irish do ply you with a bit of drink and I must have had a tremendous amount this particular evening, not, I think, that it was too noticeable at the time but the next morning I really had a bit of a headache. I must have looked unwell because my Irish hosts took me into a pub and ordered a pint of Guinness stout.

"It's the best thing to clear your head Mike." That was one of the very few times that I ever drank stout. But I must say that it did me a lot of good, so I'm all in favour of a little controlled drinking but not too little and not too controlled.

My main love of drink has been for the whiskies and unfortunately for my pocket I have for many years preferred the malt whiskies. At one time in the days before I spoiled my palate with too much smoking I was able to distinguish between some of the blends and quite a few of the malt whiskies. I don't know that I can still do it but I do still distinguish between the East coast whiskies and the West coast whiskies which tend to be very smoky and peaty and of course I could tell the difference between the blends and the malts which I much prefer. But on occasions where there is no malt whisky on offer I don't turn up my nose at the blends. I don't really like the peaty whiskies at least until I'm on to the second bottle. If I was forced to name my favourite whisky I would admit reluctantly that sometimes I favour The Glenlivet and sometimes Macallan's Glenlivet. As we sit here in the autumn of 1991 I am in favour of the Macallan's but they're nearly all good as long as they've been in the cask for at least ten years. It's a mistake to think that they will improve every year although extra time does help the heavier malts. Of course after a whisky is bottled it doesn't improve nor does it deteriorate It is interesting that it has now become the 'in thing' to drink malt whisky in America and my American friends blame me because many years ago I told an American importer that he would need to stock malt whiskies. He started with Glenfiddich and the last time I was in his shop he had at least a dozen malts.

The wines I'm not knowledgeable about at all except that I do know a few of the reds and one or two white wines. But when I go into a restaurant and I am presented with a wine list I usually ask advice from the head waiter if he knows anything about it. But if it's a good hotel I ask for the house wines because they know more about wines than I do and they wouldn't put up a bad wine as a house wine and it saves a lot of money.

On one occasion I took a party of eight to a little restaurant in Soho which I was introduced to by my brother John. It was a Spanish pub and was at one time run by a bullfighter... all the pictures in the bar were about bullfighting. We sat down at two tables for four and I ordered a bottle of Nuits St George for the four at my table. According to my brother John, George Brown, when he was at the Foreign Office, used to say, "Just bring us two bottles of the Nweets."

My old friend and fellow director, Hamish Watt from Keith, was at the other table. Now Hamish came on many of our overseas trips and was renowned for ferreting out the best places at which to eat. On one occasion when we ran dry in New Delhi he even managed to get us a bottle of whisky out of the British Consulate. However, Hamish thought he knew about wine and he said, "I think we'll have a bottle of white wine," and ordered a bottle of Chateaux Neuf du Pape. Now, though knowing little about wine, I knew that ninety per-cent of the Chateaux Neufs were red and I had already won two little bets with Hamish that day so I said, "Hamish, to give you a chance of your money back I'll bet you three pounds that when your wine is poured it will be red."

"Oh, I know Chateaux Neuf du Pape fine, I had a bottle just a little while ago and it was white."

"Well," said I, "is the bet on?"

"Oh, yes. It's on."

So you can imagine poor Hamish's face when the bottle was poured and it was red. It was a pretty safe bet for me. I'm not a gambling man but a nine to one chance seemed good odds and I am prepared to bet. My normal bet all my life has been a penny which annoys Pauline very much because having been brought up in Texas she likes to bet a million. I prefer a penny because at least with that I can pay.

I remember the stories my father used to tell about the drinking that went on when he was a young man. They were big drinkers. On one occasion he and the young neighbour from Smithston, next to Milton of Noth, were at a hare shoot. They all met in the house and were having coffee prior to driving the hares up over the hill. My grandfather sent the two young men away up first to the top of the hill to get into position. However the coffee and the dram extended to coffee and two drams. The two boys got up to the top of the hill and it was a cold blustery day, so my father withdrew a flask from his pocket and said, "We'd better have a dram."

So the two of them had a dram and then Turnbull from Smithston pulled out his flask and they had another dram. And then it was my father's turn again but young Smithston said, "Oh we'd better nae be caught drunk."

To that my father replied, "Better caught drunk that a frozen corpse." So they finished both flasks.

I very seldom saw my father take a drink except at a party. A bottle of whisky during the hard times would have lasted a long, long time. On the other hand, the only bottle of whisky that ever lasted a long time in my house was a bottle of Canadian Club that my cousin gave me in Montreal. I took it home with me but I had difficulty getting round to drinking it because it compared so unfavourably with the Scotch whisky beside which it was kept.

The only person who got a dram in my father's house other than at a party was the grieve when he came in to discuss the work. He would sometimes get a dram then.

Oddly enough my father did become used to the drinking habits of his family and we were all not inconsiderable drinkers in our times. We were all six of us fond of a droppie but probably my brother George and I were the most dedicated. George started fairly early at the university and I remember him astonishing me at the great Curler's Ball at Haddo House. Our father and mother were there and I, newly married, was there with Isobel. When I spotted George we moved up to the bar and within earshot of my father who was sipping very gently at a very small whisky, "What'll you have George?" I said.

"A large whisky, Mike," came the reply and in my father's hearing. I thought at the age of seventeen he might have been better not to advertise that he was on the large whiskies. My father would not have approved but he was a very tolerant man and nothing was said so George went on to have many drams with the best of them.

I don't suppose George would have ordered the drink quite so loudly if it was my mother who was in earshot as she was less tolerant than the old man. I think that that was because in her family there had been a history of serious drinking. Her father was John Yull the auctioneer and after a hard days' auctioneering he enjoyed a dram before he came home and after he came home. On top of that her brother Jimmy went totally to the drink, disappeared and wasn't heard of for twelve or thirteen years. Then her favourite brother, John, went to America and by pure chance discovered Jimmy among the down-and -outs in San Francisco. He sobered him up and for the first time, and just before his mother died, a letter came from the now reformed Jimmy so that she died happy knowing that her son wasn't lost after all.

None of my mother's brothers stayed at home. George went to Australia and I can remember every year a letter coming saying that they couldn't afford to come home this year but that they would be coming next year in the summer time. But George was never able to come home. His son came though, at the expense of the Australian government, when he came over to fight in the war. He was in the Australian airforce and came to North Ythsie for his leaves as he couldn't go home to Australia. He saw snow there for the first time.

At any rate mother disliked drink because of her family's history but she was not averse to a glass of sherry and wasn't too authoritarian about it. But, in any case, if she had tried to stop any of us it wouldn't have worked. She used to say, "A glass of sherry is enough for me," but she did like a glass of cider and if you gave her a glass of the good strong Devonshire cider it used to go to her legs and she would go a bitty stotty though, of course, she would never admit it.

CHAPTER TWENTY-ONE

NESDA

ONE OF the things I was very proud of was the work that NESDA did (the North East of Scotland Development Authority). It was formed before the Grampian Region was cobbled together out of Aberdeenshire, Banffshire, Kincardine and the City of Aberdeen. The City joined reluctantly as they wanted their own relevant authority. Their representative on NESDA at the time was R A Robertson, a very awkward gentleman he was who used to complain almost all the time. On one occasion, after I had led the first delegation to the Houston Oil Show, he annoyed me particularly. It was a very successful do, we took over seventy people there and they all made a lot of contacts before the end of the visit. Everybody kept coming and saying how well they had got on and how friendly the Americans had been so I said to our chief executive, John Hutton, "We need to give some hospitality back to these people." So we asked all our participants to ask their American contacts for cocktails in the Sheraton Hotel. Some three hundred people turned up and they drank an awful lot of drink of one kind and another. Of course we had no authority to do this, so I paid for it. When we got back to Scotland, John Russell, the County Clerk, kindly said, "You really can't pay all that yourself Mike." It had come to over five hundred pounds which was a lot of money in 1970. But I told him that, as we had no expense account and no authorisation to spend the money, I thought I would have to pay for it.

"I'll tell you what, John" I said, "Charge a hundred and fifty for expenses and that will do me."

This came up at a meeting of NESDA in Stonehaven and R A Robertson leapt to his feet and said, "Who authorised spending of a hundred and fifty pounds?"

I remember being quite annoyed and saying, "Well, as a matter of fact, it cost me five hundred pounds of my own money and this is just a little of it back but, if there's any nonsense, I will start claiming the full five hundred." There were no further protests.

Incidentally, I was later chairman of the Peterhead Harbour Board and to my surprise and horror at the time the Secretary of State appointed R A Robertson to the Board. I feared another time with an awkward member. In fact he couldn't have been more helpful and took some sub-committees for me and we became quite pally. It had only been because Aberdeen City didn't like NESDA that he was awkward on NESDA.

In the development work we were quite lucky to have had James Craig as the county clerk who managed to buy land at the Bridge of Don. It stood empty for a long time and there was always criticism to the effect that there was nobody going to expand out of Aberdeen. But there was great excitement when the first client, Gray Watt did want some land. That was the sole factory for a long time and then A & R Gray took another parcel of land. Then of course the oil thing began in Aberdeen and since then there hasn't been nearly enough land suitable for industrial development. The new County Clerk John Russell had already started negotiations to buy land from Tom Adam of Denmore. I was quite friendly with him and managed to persuade him to sell a bit but to consult his tax people about how much he should sell. So we bought land from him and a good thing too because after our expedition to Houston there were more and more firms coming to Aberdeen all needing land. Some of them took just an acre to begin with. I used to advise them that they should take a decent bit because in no time they would be needing two acres and three acres and two of them, I remember, doing exactly that. The first was Baker Oil Tools who have expanded enormously and VETCO was another. I could claim some credit for getting them as we entertained their directors and the chairman. I poured a great deal of my vintage port (of which I was very proud) down their throats while persuading them them to come to Aberdeen instead of Dundee which they were also considering.

Of course Aberdeen won the battle because we already had an airport. For that the whole area is indebted to Gandar Dower who by chance landed in Aberdeen in the 1930s and bought the field he landed in and started the first Aberdeen Airport and a service to London. He was a curious gentleman who was determined that he would succeed. He told me later that the reason he was so determined was that his father who had been a business man wanted him to be a business man too but he wanted to be an actor (he could recite great screeds of Shakespeare and what not) but he eventually became interested in aviation and came to Aberdeen with his friend Captain Fresson, who started the Highland Line with flights to and from Inverness. Gandar Dower then concentrated on the airport and the route to London. He thought he should have had a public honour for this and he badgered everybody under the sun to get himself an honour and, later in his life, he paid for a dinner in his own honour in the Skean Dhu Hotel at Dyce to which I was invited. I was to speak for the people of Aberdeenshire in gratitude for the fact that we had got a nice airport. I was happy to do that but I made the mistake of saying that I couldn't understand why he had not been publicly honoured for this work. Afterwards he caught me and said he'd like to speak to me and thereafter he badgered and badgered me to get him an honour of some kind because he would just like his father, who was sure Gandar had been a failure, to see on his gravestone Gandar Dower OBE or whatever. I did my best for him but he didn't have much hope because anyone who tries to get an honour for himself is almost sure to be forgotten for ever and ever amen. But he did deserve it and it was a pity. However he was very proud when we got his portrait painted and it is hanging in one of the rooms in Dyce Airport.

Peter Cook and Ronny Dean of Davidson and Garden had the bright idea that there should be a new town at Westhills to cope with the development we thought would come. A lot of scorn was poured on the idea but I always thought it was the right idea and always supported it. I can claim some credit for getting some money spent on the water supply and drainage all the way to the new Dyce sewage treatment works which made the development of Westhills possible. Now of course the whole area is full and they're looking for more land. Peter Cook, who was chairman of our roads committee, deserves some credit for that because, before the Westhills land had been bought, he bought a bit of land alongside it. There was an immediate demand for the houses, which showed the developers, who by this time were led by Sidney Denham an insurance tycoon. Ronnie Dean had failed to get the finance, but Denham succeeded and it was really a success story. Now they are trying to do the same thing at Kingswells. I think that is a pity because that would fill up a bit of green space between the city and Westhills - but that is no longer my worry.

We were very lucky with the first chief executive of NESDA. I worked very happily with John Hutton who is now one of Her Majesty's reporters when there's an enquiry into public applications. He was a most excellent executive. He worked quietly but remembered everybody's name, remembered what they did and he was an enormous bonus and certainly a bonus to the chairman. His assistant was Malcolm Bruce who was becoming more and more interested in politics until I had to say to him on one occasion, "Malcolm, you'll have to make up your mind because the committee don't like somebody being involved with one political party." So he made up his mind and now he's an MP. He was a very good assistant but some of our members, particularly the Tories, didn't think it was right for a public employee to be so involved in party politics.

CHAPTER TWENTY-TWO

Aberdeen and District Milk Marketing Board

ONE OF the most interesting jobs I have done and I did it for a long time, was to be on the Milk Board. I joined my father on the Board in 1949 and resigned as chairman in 1982. People used to ask why it was that England could manage with one Milk Board and yet Scotland needed three. It was a matter of history because the different areas were ready to exploit the Milk Marketing Acts at different times and Aberdeen, which already had what was called the Milk Agency was ready before the rest of Scotland. When James Singer resigned in 1964, I became chairman and I must say it was a most enjoyable experience. Not long after my appointment the chief executive, John Wilson, who had been there since the start, retired and we engaged Michael Boyle. It was the start of a most happy association. He had worked for both the other Boards so we got a man with invaluable experience.

Michael Boyle was a first rate administrator and when we went on trips all the arrangements were meticulously made and fortunately as we travelled the world together we became great friends. As well as the Board business there were the Federation meetings which involved the representatives of the five British Boards and there was an international body which met around the world. It met in Australia, Japan, India and Canada in my time. I always insisted that if members had to go to meetings overseas their wives should go too. It does save the wife wondering whether the husband is misbehaving when he is away and it made for a much more enjoyable tour when the wives were there at night and could come on the sight-seeing tours with us.

The English Board were lucky to have as their chairman, during all my time, Sir Richard Trehane who was also the chairman of the international body. He had a vision of what should be done in marketing and led them ably for many years. The Scottish Board were no less fortunate in having Willie, later Sir William, Young at the helm. He represented the producers' case very ably to the Department of Agriculture though latterly we thought he lost his grip a little bit. The North Board had Michael, later Sir Michael Joughin, and he and I used to gang up on Willie and keep him right. Those were the days of the annual price review and meetings with the Department were very important. I think they listened and were on the farmers' side, but, of course, they had to satisfy the Treasury.

Every four years Aberdeen had to entertain the other four Board members and Pauline took in hand to organise parties. On one occasion we had a Texan barbecue at Westertown and we asked the butcher, James Presley to provide fifty T Bone steaks three quarters of an inch thick. I don't think he had had an order like that before but he produced the most beautiful beef. Each member was supposed to cook his own, including Sir Richard Trehane who had never done such a thing before. Each was provided with an apron with his name on it. They all made a stab at it but many soon handed over to my son Maitland or my friend Bill Henderson who was there to help the helpless. Jim Jackson, the vice chairman of the English board was a great trencherman. He not only ate a big steak and all the trimmings but went back for the last steak which was being kept for Tom Folley, Michael Boyle's assisant, who was waiting politely (but rashly) for all the guests to be served.

Four years later we asked those who had been to the first party to bring their aprons which most of them had kept and they were presented with a chef's hat with their names on them. Pauline had standing frames to hold yards of ale and we had a competition between the champions of the five boards to see who could drink the yard of ale in the quickest time with the least spillage. Poor Jim Jackson caused a good deal of hilarity because having had plenty to drink he proceeded to spill most of it. George Chambers of the Northern Ireland Board did it very speedily and didn't spill a drop. He was very proud of his prize of a yard glass which hung over his desk in Belfast for many years. James Singer the former chairman enjoyed the fun and games though quite old by then. I got Maitland Junior to take him home when he was getting tired. James thought this was one of the staff, with him being dressed in his apron and chef's hat, and gave my son half a crown of a tip.

But it wasn't all fun. Prior to the milk boards, retailers and manufacturers used to buy direct from the farmers. Generally there was little competition and they ganged up on farmers to offer them very poor prices. Those who were far away were particularly badly hit. The Milk Marketing Acts gave the boards a monopoly and all the milk went to the boards at a uniform price except for a small discount to those who were very remote. There was then great competition between the boards to see who could offer their farmers the best price. That was largely a question of who could sell the biggest proportion of their milk to the retail trade because that which went for butter or milk powder got much lower prices. That gave the Aberdeen Board an advantage because we were good at selling liquid milk and we were able to top the league by paying the farmers most.

During my time we moved from the old fashioned creamery at Kittybrewster to a modern creamery at Lilybank. About half of our milk went to the liquid market and most of the other half went to make butter so we had to do something with the skimmed milk. We made a major investment in spray driers and were very proud of the powder we could now make and were putting the flags up because we had got what looked like a lucrative export order for the powder to a firm in Singapore. Unfortunately, something went wrong and there were black specks in the powder. Trevor Owen the factory manager went out to see it but there was no denying it and the whole lot was condemned. We had to take the whole lot home for re-processing. So in my last year we had our first loss. It was a great disappointment.

The whole milk marketing scene is under review at the moment and while it is no longer my worry I do hope they don't let it slip back into the old days when the retail purchasers could dictate terms.

Willie Young argued for many years that there should be just one board for Scotland but I think he was wrong because we all had slightly different problems. The North board had remoteness particularly with Orkney and we had the advantage of the high proportion of our milk going to the liquid market. I opposed all plans to merge the Scottish boards or the five UK boards... if we had merged there would have been no standard of comparison and no competition.

I used to enjoy the Federation meetings, particularly when it was the turn of the Northern Ireland Board to entertain us and I became very friendly with their people. On one of those visits we were in Newry which is just on the border and Michael Boyle and I managed to persuade John Lynn our host to invite a few members from the trade to cross the Border from the Republic and join us for dinner. Sadly only one turned up. The only one with the courage was Martin Mullaly who was a great character. He later took Michael Boyle and myself on a tour of some plants in Southern Ireland and to dinner at a very nice little village. In the course of the meal we managed to persuade him to play a bit of a trick on John Inglis of the Scottish Board who he was to be entertaining soon after. When John reached the biscuits and cheese he asked if the butter was Kerrygold. But Martin had the waiter primed to answer "Oh, no. We have nothing but Twin Spires here, sir." That being the Aberdeen Board's butter and a bitter rival of his Scottish Pride John Inglis was fairly shocked.

Martin was a real man of courage. When he was sixteen he joined the Republicans in their fight for independence from the British. He was caught in 1916 and had his big toe taken off so that they would recognise him if he were ever in trouble again. He was caught again in 1922 and was almost shot. He was still in favour of a United Ireland but one which would rejoin the British Commonwealth. I learned in Ireland that we were lucky to be free of their religious troubles in the Aberdeen Board. I asked John Lynn how many Catholics were on his office staff and I wasn't talking about cleaners. "Well now Mike," I was told, "We don't differentiate and we don't really know."

I asked for the general manager, David Armstrong. He gave me the same answer. "Well, go and find out," said I. He came back and said they had one Catholic. A year later I asked the same question and the answer was that the one Catholic's job had disappeared... but another had been taken on, on the security staff. It seemed a curious choice. I found the enormous expense of the troubles very depressing. When John Lynn drove me to his office, I was astonished when the security men stopped us at the gate. They got us out of the car and searched it. I said, "Heavens. Why would the chairman need to be searched?"

John Lynn explained, "Who is to know if they have my wife and my grandchildren kidnapped. If I don't do as they want they will damage them in various ways." If that's what the IRA do there is no excuse for them. But I'm not sure that the Protestants are without sin in all this. It seems to me that there will come a time when the parents will rebel at their sons being sent to Ulster to be killed, while not succeeding in keeping real peace. I believe the parents are going to demand a solution. What would happen if they told both sides the troops would be out by a certain date? I suspect it would focus the minds on a political solution.

But back to the milk boards which have done a tremendous job in furthering artificial insemination. It has improved dairy breeding greatly and has helped get first rate beef off the dairies by pioneering new beef crosses. Now with Multiple Ovulation and Embryo Transplant the rate of genetic improvement is accelerating and the boards should be proud of their achievements. My father did some canvassing for artificial insemination in the early days but was turned down at one farm. The wife gave as her reason, "I widna like it masel." Fortunately hers was a minority view and the A I has been a huge success.

CHAPTER TWENTY-THREE

Guardian of Bennachie

I SUPPOSE that having been Lord Lieutenant of my county of Aberdeen must really rank as the honour of which I am most proud. And yet there is an honour even nearer to my heart. It is a title which I still hold and which I have no intention ever to give up. That is the title of Guardian of Bennachie.

Bennachie is a landmark in my part of the North East. In fact I must be able either to see the Prop of Ythsie or Bennachie if I am to feel that I am home.

Apart from the fact that it could be seen from any part of what was my world in my formative years, my affection for this unremarkable little hill (it is only 1,783 feet high) dates back to holidays with my brothers and sisters. We were sent each year to Westertown for a week with Mr Cumming my father's great manager and my guide and philosopher when I was learning about farm management in the early days. It might seem like a terrible sentence to have up to four of the boss's children for a week but if the Cummings thought that they certainly didn't show it. They made the holiday one of great adventure and treasured memories for us.

There were expeditions, two in the front and two in the back of Mr Cumming's Bayliss-Thomas car to the Keith Show, for example. That must have been a great day though the main thing I remember was being unimpressed by the horse racing which I didn't understand. But the main and unforgettable day of the holiday was when we would climb Bennachie.

We took a haversackful of food for our picnic prepared by Mrs Cumming and off we set. John would lead, I would be second and Jean third followed by Mary and Mr Cumming bringing up the rear and making sure no one straggled. I remember the breathless excitement each year as we scrambled the last thirty feet or so up the rocks to the top. Then there at our feet was the whole of my world and much more. As we ate our picnic, Mr Cumming would point out where we had come from, Westertown, North Ythsie and anywhere else in Formartine which we wanted to have pointed out. Then it would be over to the cold side of the hill to see distant lands like the Vale of Alford.

When we got back to Westertown we had our supper and then a ceilidh. Some of the men came in until there were maybe twenty folk in the old farm kitchen. Mr Cumming played the melodeon and we all sang the old songs. It was a warm end to a great day and certainly the highlight of our annual holiday.

Throughout my long life I have climbed Bennachie many times and even managed to drag Pauline to the top so that she could survey Aberdeenshire in its entirety.

Small wonder, then, that I was pleased to join the Baillies of Bennachie when they were set up in 1973. That was the brainchild of Dr Danny Gordon for many years the general practitioner at Ellon He had become distressed by an increase in the amount of broken glass and litter that was being left on the hill by the increasing hoards of climbers. With five friends he called a public meeting in Inverurie. The name Baillie was compounded of the two meanings of that word. The town baillie calling for order in his town and the cattleman who was also called a baillie giving his cattle tender loving care. There were and are four objectives 1) to preserve amenity and fight litter and vandalism. 2) To preserve rights of way and footpaths. 3) To study the geology, and biology of the mountain and preserve its flowers and animals. And 4) To collect and preserve the bibliography of the mountain. The idea was to look after and promote all aspects of Formartine's only Grampian mountain. They would get a carpark built, maintain the paths and encourage tidiness. Then they would publish books about the history of Mons Graupius where the Romans camped two thousand years ago, and the songs of the hill behind which the immortal 'Gadie Rins'.

To become a Baillie of Bennachie was to cost each member just one pound. No wonder then, that there are now four thousand Baillies, for the subscription is still a pound and that covers the Baillies for life.

The Baillies have been a wonderful success and their books sell all over the world. I was therefore very pleased, in 1975 when I was Lord Lieutenant, to be offered the titular leadership of the Baillies with the title of Guardian of Bennachie. This is not an arduous job. The Guardian's duties are simply to make a short speech at the annual Baillie's Picnic in the Back o' Bennachie Forestry Commission land when we huddle in the rain eating our sandwiches in celebration of the old hill. I also have to shake hands with the Baillies when they arrive at the picnic and each year about three hundred of them do come from all over the world. It is a great day and a great example of the way we should care for our heritage. I offered to retire when I was seventy-five but I am happy to say that my resignation was refused for I am very proud to be the Guardian of Bennachie.

It is the one job I will never give up for I have it for life.

CHAPTER TWENTY-FOUR

And So...

I HAVE been a Lucky Chap to have had this life. But it wasn't all pure luck. I was lucky that I had the services of doctors whose skill have been such a help to me in evading the Great Reaper. I told you of my uncertain start and how I was pulled into the world to the hazard, as my father thought, of my ears. Then I had chronic headaches for many years until Dr Fraser prescribed and cured me once and for all. By-passing the doctor, I went back to that chemist six years later and Mr Michie astonished me by remembering, not just my name, but the number of my prescription. He told me, "I remember thinking how unusual for one so young to have liver trouble."

When I was at the University I had a very sore throat and so I had my tonsils and adenoids out. That was done at the same time as my youngest sister Catherine who was only eight. She didn't have much bother but that operation seems to get worse as you get older and it was very uncomfortable for a couple of weeks. Still it was a lot better than the sore throats. I also lost an appendix somewhere along the way.

My good friend from the University, Bill Michie, who became one of the best surgeons in Aberdeen, discovered I had a paralysed bowel, opened me up, had a look and decided that it would cure itself and sewed me up again. He was right, it got better and on the two occasions on which it has happened again they just cured me with ten days of a drip feed. So I was a Lucky Chap again. I was less lucky when I had my gall bladder trouble. That was very uncomfortable and Bill was going to take it out but suffered a slipped disc the day before the op. Luckily there was a good alternative on hand. Mr Mavor took it out and that was an immediate success.

When I was seventy-six I had a hip replacement done as my hip had become very sore and stiff with arthritis. That was such a great success that I decided to have the other one sorted too. Unfortunately they said they couldn't do that as I had a leaky heart valve and that that would have to be done first. So I went to Ross Hall Hospital in Glasgow where Mr Davidson split me open and installed the valve from an American pig in the place of my leaky one. He had thought that he would have to replace some choked veins round my heart with transplants from my legs but decided that what I had would see my time out. Davidson told me that it was just as well they had operated as my valve was "just a lump of calcium" and that it would not have lasted much longer. Again I have been a lucky chap, for the pig valve has been a great success. I much enjoyed my neighbour Alison Skene's remark when she heard about that operation, "Now you'll be a bit of an American and a bit of a boar," she said.

Since then I have had the other hip done. That was rather fun because Pauline had one done at the same time and we were able to get adjoining rooms in the St John's Hospital. The day we had our operations we were offered a drink in the evening as is usual in the St John's Hospitals. However Pauline was astonished to be asked if she would like to have her drink with me in my room. "But," she said, "I haven't even been up yet." It was no problem. They just wheeled her bed through to my room where I was enjoying a bottle of Glenmorangie and she had a drink from her bottle of Bell's. That operation has been a great success for us both. I can walk quite smartly but not too far before I get a sore back. If I take two walking sticks I can still tackle longer walks but I don't like to be seen with *two* sticks.

So I have had a wonderful life and without too much more help from the surgeons I hope for a lot more to come.

I have been brought up and lived in the Church of Scotland, I still go fairly regularly to church, and, as a Christian, I do believe in an after-life and have no fear of death. However my enjoyment of this life is such that I am in no hurry to see what form His truth takes. And my faith is not so complete that I don't fear that I will miss things in this life. These are such exciting times I sometimes rage at the thought that I might die and miss them. What will come out of the collapse of communism? Where will the space travel which I saw start all those years ago in Cape Canaverell lead? How big will the European Community become and will it be a United States of Europe one day?

One of our great comforts is that every Saturday morning Michael Rogers comes to give us a massage. It is a measure of my interest in what's going on that he brings me a copy of *The European* as a luck-penny and I read that with the greatest of pleasure. I don't think there are many other readers of *The European* in Banchory.

So here we are, surrounded by the beautiful antiques which Pauline has collected over the years, in our spacious bungalow on the edge of the golf course. Between us we have have eight children and twenty-one grandchildren, so life would never be dull or lonely even if it were not for all the many friends, accumulated in this long life, who come to visit us and who invite us out.

I have indeed been a Lucky Chap and I intend to be so for some time yet.